P9-DTN-184

Selected one of the BEST REAL ESTATE BOOKS by the late Robert Bruss, nationally syndicated real estate columnist.

IRWIN 2002 Award

Industry Recognition of Writers in the News award for the most inspirational campaign of 2002 from The Book Publicists of Southern California.

NABE 2002 Award

North American Bookdealers Exchange, Oregon. Pinnacle Achievement Award for the Business category.

www.schumacherenterprises.com
e-mail: mschuma233@aol.com

PRAISE FOR
BUY AND HOLD FOREVER

"THIS BOOK RATES HIGHEST HONORS… Schumacher practiced what he preached by amassing a real estate fortune worth at least $20 million using the techniques explained in this OUTSTANDING book."

—Los Angeles Times

"David Schumacher's strategies are brilliant and work in today's market. Steve Dexter is just the man to continue David's legacy of conservative, consistent investing in an always-changing market."

—John Schaub
Florida real estate investor and author of
Building Wealth One House at a Time: Making It Big on Little Deals

"The title says it all. Timeless advice on how to become financially free in an unfree world. Mandatory reading if you're serious about changing your financial life forever."

—Mike Cantu
Real estate investor and educator based in Riverside, California

"Schumacher was the man people in the real estate industry turn to when they want answers. He was the broker's broker and the investor's investor. This is THE ONE AND ONLY BOOK THE SAVVY REAL ESTATE INVESTOR NEEDS. It's required reading in all my college-level classes."

—Wesley Barney
Real estate investor, columnist, college lecturer, author

"When the national media raves about David Schumacher—including the top real estate magazines in America and even the *Los Angeles Times*—what else is there to say?… *Buy and Hold Forever* is the ultimate how-to book for the seasoned investor or those just starting out. It's packed with advice on choosing property, recognizing real estate trends and even dealing with tenants. Dave was THE REAL ESTATE INDUSTRY'S GRANDMASTER. He might just be the best ever. I keep his books within easy reach on my shelf."

—Larry Leichman
Author, *90% Off Real Estate*

BUY AND HOLD FOREVER

BUY AND HOLD FOREVER

How to Build Wealth for the 21st Century

David Schumacher, Ph.D.
and Steve Dexter

Book design by Arbor Books
www.arborbooks.com

Printed in the United States of America

Buy and Hold Forever: How to Build Wealth for the 21st Century
David Schumacher, Ph.D. and Steve Dexter

1. Title 2. Author 3. Real estate investment

Library of Congress Catalog Card Number: 2009911358

ISBN 10: 0-9701162-6-8
ISBN 13: 978-0-9701162-6-0

David dedicated this book to
his loving and devoted wife
Margaret Christine Schumacher,
for her tireless effort
and support of all his projects
during their 29 years of
wedded bliss.

Together they made a formidable team.

Dr. Schumacher's success in real estate was way beyond his wildest dreams. In 1999, David and his wife Margaret were able to donate $1 million to the city of Hermosa Beach, California for the renovation of the Schumacher Pier Plaza in memory of his identical twin brother, Paul William Schumacher, who passed away February 16, 1971.

March 19, 2007: $1 million to Mission Hospital, Mission Viejo, California for the construction of The Schumacher Healing Garden, in loving memory of David, who passed away there peacefully on July 26, 2006. The Healing Garden is part of the hospital's new Patient Care Tower and Chapel, opened in November 2009. At completion, this facility was the most technologically advanced imaging center in the USA. David would have been proud to be part of the impact that this facility provides to *his* community.

September 8, 2007: The Schumacher Concert Series was established at The Covington Episcopal Retirement Community, in Aliso Viejo, California, where David spent the final two years of his life. David hoped his love of music would continue to enhance the lives of all the residents.

October 2009: A matching gift donation towards the construction of the Secret Garden at The Covington, comprised of a waterfall, a koi pond and a stream surrounded by trees, plants and flowers in a beautiful, tranquil setting. The waterfall is named "Sir John's Falls" in loving memory of

David's father-in-law, John Dilkes, who resided almost five years at The Covington luxury retirement community along with David and Margaret.

In 2009 funds were donated to construct a 7,500-square-foot orphanage in Nairobi, Kenya. A project conceived by one of David's relatives, Jim Baldwin, founder of Smile Seekers, Inc. of Riverside, California. The orphanage is named Smile Seeker House, a home for 50 children. David's participation with Smile Seekers dates back to its inception in 1999 when children from dysfunctional families gather together every Sunday, dressed as clowns, and visited seniors in many Riverside retirement homes.

Philanthropy became an important part of Dr. Schumacher's life. After his real estate success he was able to give back to the community. He firmly believed that what goes around comes around. Margaret is continuing this concept.

Dr. David Schumacher wrote *Buy and Hold* so that he could pass on his knowledge to others in the hope that, they too, would be successful. This is an excellent, invaluable real estate guidebook that can be referred to over and over again whether you are a novice or real estate expert.

One of Dr. Schumacher's final wishes was to be able to work with his friend Steve Dexter on an updated version of *Buy and Hold*. His failing health did not permit this.

But Steve Dexter is carrying on his fine work.

Acknowledgments

Words from Dr. David Schumacher

David Schumacher, author, is especially grateful to Larry Leichman and Joel Hochman, and to their staff at Arbor Books, for their continued interest in publishing this book.

Special recognition goes to the late Dr. A.D. Kessler, former owner and director of *Creative Real Estate Magazine,* along with his assistant, Jaclyn S. MacNary, publication and chief editor of the same magazine.

I am deeply grateful to Dr. Erik Page Bucy, who was co-author of my original *Buy and Hold Real Estate Strategy* book for his continued interest and support. Dr. Bucy, a professor in the Department of Telecommunications at Indiana University, Bloomington, is the author of four books and numerous articles. His service has been invaluable in the preparation of this book.

Thanks to Susan Vilican, our property manager for her devoted service with the real estate properties in the South Bay area of Los Angeles County. She has a unique ability to select excellent tenants and she keeps updated on all the latest community activity and information.

Thanks to Bob Tetrault and Ariane Gatlin of Professional Home Property Management, Inc., Santa Ana Heights, California, who do an outstanding job of managing our Orange County properties.

I shall always be grateful to my family: my father, Maxmillian Schumacher, my dear mother, Minnie Louise Schumacher, and my twin brother, Paul Schumacher, who are my eternal guiding spirits. They always had great faith in my abilities throughout their lives.

Thank you to the National Association of Realtors and the California Association of Realtors for their contributions in gathering data for this project. I am continually grateful to the following societies from which I have obtained professional designations:

National Association of Realtors (NAR); Certified Commercial Investment Member (CCIM); Society of Real Estate Appraisers (ASA); National Association of Independent Fee Appraisers (IFAS); Certified Business Counselors (CBC); and Certified Review Appraisers (CRA).

Finally, I am grateful to my dear friends, William Adams, Steve Dexter, Michael Kilroy, Donald Haggerty, William Gorman, Bruce Norris, Pat Hansen, Jack Fullerton, Moe Saleem Rawda and William Bozarth, for their generosity in sharing their ideas and concepts and for their loyal support in my endeavors.

Steve Dexter's Current Biography

Steve is an invited expert commentator for CNN/Money, CBS Radio, Fox TV and numerous other newspapers and media outlets.

- He is author of the book *Real Estate Debt Can Make You Rich* published by McGraw-Hill. The book was rated one of the top five real estate books of the year by Bob Bruss, a nationally syndicated columnist for the Washington Post Media Group.
- Steve's last book was *Prospering in the Rising Wave of Bank Foreclosures.*
- He has been a distinguished speaker at the Harvard Business School, Harvard Law School and Harvard University Graduate School of Design. He has mentored many of their students about entrepreneurship and real estate investing. He also has spoken at Northwestern University's Kellogg School of Business Management located in Chicago.
- He is a member of and speaker for NAREE (National Association of Real Estate Editors), a professional group of authors and major newspaper journalists who write about the national real estate market.
- He writes articles for several national real estate journals.

- Since 1990, Steve has worked as a consultant, advising people how to structure their loans and/or purchase properties.
- He has been the president of National Capital Funding since 1995.
- He teaches courses in investing and real estate finance at colleges across Southern California. He writes a free bimonthly e-newsletter, *Economic News You Can Use.*
- He has personally funded over $500 million in real estate loans.
- He coaches budding real estate agents and mortgage brokers.
- He is an active real estate investor and owns 27 investment houses in Southern California and around the country. Steve Dexter continues to offer mentoring to hundreds of investors across the nation.

Preface to Current Edition

When *Buy and Hold* was first published in 1992, I did not know of Dr. Schumacher or his book. I was living in Southern California, looking for people who knew something about real estate investing, and I was told I must go and hear Dr. Schumacher. Finally I did and his teachings about analyzing quality neighborhoods, his helping me get my first book published and his friendship have enriched my wife, Susan, and me beyond our wildest dreams.

The book was widely respected when it first came out, and I have since learned that Dr. Schumacher was regarded as the "pope of real estate investing" by other highly successful investors who have been in the business a long time. Dr. Schumacher's long-term philosophy has resonated with many wealthy individuals of wonderful character and helpful hearts. All who have read this book and applied just part of his teachings have benefited greatly. You will, too.

This book covers almost everything you need to know about building great real estate wealth. Buying property is not just for short-term money gain; building real estate wealth is about acquiring properties that will be valuable for a long time. I've experienced his mantra that if you buy and hold quality housing in a prosperous area, how can you lose? The more you anticipate what people will want and need and where they'll be years or decades from now, the better you will do. This book taught me how to forecast my property's market value five, ten or twenty years from now and how to anticipate regional trends that affect where I buy.

After meeting him in 1998, I was impressed when Dr. Schumacher seared upon me the importance of investing in quality neighborhoods. There are concrete ways to measure quality that are outlined in this book. His buying and holding real estate forever has excited me to buy many single-family houses in areas of high demand, has permeated my teachings of real estate finance at several colleges including Harvard Business School, and has greatly been in the background of the writing of my first two books, *Real Estate Debt Can Make You Rich* and *Beat the Banks—How to Prosper in the Rising Wave of Bank Foreclosures*.

Dr. Schumacher is sadly no longer with us, having died at the age of 86 with his loving wife, Margaret, at his side. Margaret wanted to have his great legacy continue and contacted me about updating the book. I feel honored to do my best while commenting on the dramatic changes in the market and what to do next.

Updating a classic book is a monumental task. The basic philosophy of the writer cannot be changed. Upon first glance, I thought, how can I improve upon perfection? It must always be Dr. David Schumacher's book, not mine. I approach his work with the eye of a master restorer who looks at a classical painting that is being refurbished. I carefully studied the text to bring his wisdom into the twenty-first century. I will illuminate the dramatic changes in the market to show how his principles are more useful now than ever. Hopefully, adding my insights and experiences as we go along will benefit you.

All who read, understand and apply Dr. Schumacher's principles will be better prepared to attain great wealth that can ripple across generations. Be ready, therefore, to make major changes in your approach to life.

Simply rereading his book with a focused eye toward improving it has helped me immeasurably.

This book is for you. By taking just a few of these ideas and applying a little bit of the energy behind them, your view of real estate, yourself and life itself will forever be changed.

—Steve Dexter

Contents

1

Introduction

How would you like to buy a piece of real estate, say a single-family residence, and own it 30 years later, free and clear of all encumbrances, at a value of about 30 times what you paid for it? Does this sound fantastic? Well, it happened to me. In 1960 I bought a single-family residence with no money down. It had a total purchase price of $12,000. Today the property is worth $360,000. Other than fixing up and maintaining the property in a proper manner, I didn't put any money into it. From 1960 to 1964, I bought seven properties along these lines, with not more than $3,000 down on any one property. At that time, the prices ranged from $32,000 to $85,000. Today, these same properties are worth in excess of $1 million each.

A CHANGING MARKET

The buy-and-hold philosophy is invaluable because it works well in all markets. I am proof of that because I bought most of my houses in double AA neighborhoods. Because they are located close to the centers where my tenants work and close to the major highways on which they drive, my houses rent quickly and for more money—even in a down market.

"If you buy well-located real estate in high-demand neighborhoods, you eliminate the most risk in all of real estate because, in good times and bad, there will always be somebody who wants to rent or buy your house."

—Steve Dexter

I have been teaching this credo in my college classes for years and it infiltrates my whole investment philosophy. I turned down many deals that, while seemingly well priced, were not located well. Others bought in those areas where I feared to tread and held houses without knowing local renter preferences. When you invest without knowing what you are doing, you are not investing; you are speculating, which is much riskier. When prices are rising and everybody seems to be making money, it is easy not to notice the mistakes you are making because a rising market bails out all fools, including the speculators.

Without the knowledge that you will learn in this book, you may get into trouble, too.

Partly because of the speculators, the real estate market in most areas of the United States is undergoing unprecedented changes. These include:

1. The largest house price decline since the Great Depression.
2. The largest number of empty houses on the market in history, mostly due to speculators buying houses that did not rent well.
3. Record high foreclosure rates causing the largest number of bank foreclosures…ever.

Most of the houses I bought over the years and hold in areas of high demand have not declined in value as much as surrounding areas, and they still continue to rent well. By following Dr. Schumacher's principles, I beat the regional averages.

And even more importantly, my properties stay full and rent for market price, or close to it. Longer-term wealth building takes more time, but the path is well marked by the pioneers who have walked it before us. Like Dr. David Schumacher has.

FIND THE LOCATION

My concept, the buy-and-hold strategy, first involves finding a desirable area where you think potential economic growth will occur. The beach area, where I bought my properties in the 1960s, was in a dilapidated state. The community was run down and the city was financially stressed. The resulting problems created an undesirable environment. Today, the situation has reversed completely. The community has improved tremendously, rents have gone up dramatically, real estate prices have skyrocketed, and today it is a very desirable area.

Now, why did this improvement occur between 1960 and now? It happened because the city experienced economic growth, due in large part to the industries and businesses that came into the area, including aircraft manufacturing plants and information processing companies. Infrastructure improvements, such as expansion of Los Angeles International Airport, also benefited the area. At the same time, as industry grew and infrastructure improved, the growth of new housing was minuscule. Almost everything in the area was built up, yet housing prices and family income levels were fairly low. But by looking at the neighborhood, you could see that income levels would rise due to the creation of new engineering and professional jobs that would raise individual salaries and cause family income levels to rise as well. This situation created the possibility of real estate values rising along with family income.

As the carpet of spreading population is laid across the American continent, we find even more investment opportunities reflecting recent demographic shifts. People are moving to cities of high economic growth that were mere blips on the radar screen twenty to thirty years ago. Population has flowed from the Snow Belt to the Sun Belt, from the industrially ailing East and Midwest to the economically vibrant West and South. The actual picture of recent growth, as measured by the 2000 census and the census estimates for 2006, is more complicated.

There has been a shift into America's heartland. These interior boomtowns (none touches the Atlantic or Pacific coasts) have grown 18% in six years. They've had considerable immigrant inflow, 4%, but with the exceptions of Dallas and Houston, this has been dwarfed by a much larger domestic inflow—three million to 1.5 million overall.

More Americans are moving from coastal areas to escape the higher taxes and increased costs of living. The interior boomtowns generated 38% of the nation's population growth in 2000 through 2006.

Domestic inflow has been a whopping:

- 19% in Las Vegas
- 15% in the Inland Empire (California's Riverside and San Bernardino counties, where much of the outflow from Los Angeles has gone)
- 13% in Orlando
- 12% in Charlotte
- 12% in Phoenix
- 10% in Tampa
- 9% percent in Jacksonville

Domestic inflow was over 200,000 in the Inland Empire, Phoenix, Atlanta, Las Vegas and Orlando. These are economic dynamos that are driving much of America's growth

These interior boomtowns, which the census says have experienced above-average income growth, will be vibrant areas in the twenty-first century. I will examine more cities that highlight Dr. Schumacher's investment philosophy in later chapters.

COMPARABLE SALES

Because no two real estate parcels are exactly alike, it is difficult to determine what real estate is truly worth; although there are comparable sales, there are no identical sales that can prove true value. Consider the example of bread (the kind you eat). In a city the size of Los Angeles, over one million loaves of bread are baked each night. Suppose each loaf of bread is sold the next day for $1.50. The sale of one million loaves of bread establishes the price at $1.50 a loaf. Now, you wouldn't walk into a bakery and offer the counter person $1.25 for a loaf of bread because the established price is $1.50 and there are a million sales to prove it. Real estate is just the opposite. With real estate, there are no exact sales to prove what the property is truly worth.

As mentioned, the single most important factor in the buy-and-hold real estate strategy is finding the right location where it is possible to conservatively predict potential growth. There are thousands upon thousands of communities in the United States where such growth will continue to occur. As America moves into the future, the economy will continue to change and grow and the prosperity will create new opportunities in industry and science. Although it may not seem so now, the real estate market will provide unprecedented opportunities for the knowledgeable real estate investor.

ECONOMIC GROWTH

How to determine whether economic growth will occur in a given community is a major theme of this book. The buy-and-hold real estate strategy explains how to position yourself in the path of this growth, where you know that a major infrastructure expansion or renovation is going to happen. For example, in areas with potential industrial expansion, with opportunities in research and development, where people are making good wages and have the potential of increasing their income levels, the effects on real estate values can be tremendous. If you buy real estate in the path of growth and hold on to it for a period of time, you will prosper. On the other hand, buying a property with the goal of flipping it over after a year or two reduces your chances of experiencing any appreciation at all.

Just because you find a growing community with new people moving into the area does not mean that wealth will necessarily be present. Look at the tremendous populations of India or Pakistan, or many of the countries of Africa where wealth does not exist for the average person. In order for real estate values to increase, industry and new jobs must accompany a growth in population.

There are many factors that go into finding a good location and then holding onto a piece of property for a long period of time. It is not a simple matter and requires considerable discipline and judgment. Above all, it is important to have an objective for your investing. Mastering the buy-and-hold real estate strategy involves understanding how this works.

ANALYZE THE AREA

Having a long-term objective does not equate with finding a bargain property around the corner, fixing it up, flipping it over, and buying another piece of real estate. The buy-and-hold concept is more structured than a "buy and sell" approach. Before investing, it is important to first analyze the community for signs of potential growth. If you are interested in living in an area where you can make some money, it is imperative to consider how much money is being spent on improvements. This is a critical element of the buy-and-hold real estate strategy.

BUY AT LEAST ONE PIECE
OF REAL ESTATE A YEAR

In the early 1960s I moved into the Southern California community of Hermosa Beach. I lived there for a year and studied every real estate sale that occurred. I visited city hall, the county court house, and county recorder's office regularly to keep abreast of what was happening in the community. I then plotted all this data I was gathering on a giant map of the area. After a year had passed I felt that I was familiar enough with the local trends to start investing in real estate. For several years running I proceeded to buy one property per year. At the end of a 30-year period, my net worth had increased astronomically—not only because I made smart investments (by analyzing the property I bought and estimating the potential growth of the community), but also because I held onto those investments. My projections of the area's growth potential, which I periodically updated and modified, gave me the confidence to continue investing over the decades.

If you do your homework and find property in an area that you know has potential growth, you do not have to buy real estate at bargain prices (say 30% to 40% below market value) or even distressed properties to make this concept work. Rather, locate the best property in the community you can afford and pay the fair market value of the property if necessary. While it is always preferable to buy real estate below market value, over the long run paying fair market value isn't going to make any difference: 30 years from now the property will be worth many times what you paid for it, making the original purchase price irrelevant.

Of course, you always want to pay the lowest price you can when you buy, but many people try to steal properties. They think they always have to buy properties way below market value. Some of the best investors I know who buy and sell a lot of property tell me that the houses they flip tend to be in distressed neighborhoods, and the houses are often of low quality.

If you buy and hold well-located houses in high-demand neighborhoods, I believe you eliminate the most risk in all of real estate. In good times and bad, there will always be somebody who wants to buy your house or rent from you. I have paid retail prices to get into the neighborhoods I want.

Acquiring real estate on proper terms is the third step to making a good long-term investment following the buy-and-hold real estate strategy. Knowledge in this sense is more important than money. Being an educated investor with a modest amount of investment capital is far more preferable to having a lot of money and little knowledge of what to do with that money. The buy-and-hold real estate strategy emphasizes the importance of understanding the concepts you are working with to enable you to perform accurate analyses of the types of real estate you are interested in.

CONCEPT OF VALUE

Understanding the concept of value is central to the buy-and-hold real estate strategy. Value is both created and destroyed by the actions and attitudes of people. Because value is affected by how people view the overall real estate market, as well as individual properties, a thorough going estimate of potential growth takes the likely attitudes of people into account, whether they are buyers, sellers, real estate professionals, city officials, or economic policy makers.

Despite fluctuations in short-term appreciation, the market value of desirable real estate will invariably rise over time. It might not be evident over a specific period due to recessionary trends or inadequate activity in a given community, but because each piece of property is heterogeneous and unique, real estate is the type of asset that is advantageously affected by inflation, even when inflation is low. As discussed in the book, real estate, because of its use value as residential, rental income or storage, etc. is probably a better investment than the stock market.

Six salient factors will prove real estate to be a superior investment far into the twenty-first century:

1. Inflation—rents go up, building materials cost more and the price of gas makes commuting to faraway areas more expensive.
2. Economic exuberance—more jobs being created pushes up demand for area housing.
3. Geographical limitations—oceans, mountains, rivers, lakes, etc. constrain limitations on local growth, which puts pressure on existing housing. Southern California's coastal strip of land bordered by the Pacific Ocean and the Santa Monica Mountains is a prime example. Another one is the peninsula of San Francisco. That land abutment has made that city's real estate some of the most expensive in the country. Everybody wants to be there.
4. Political limitations on growth—as soon as an area gets to be more crowded, streets become congested and local services become overburdened. Area governments start passing ordinances to make it harder to build new housing or add square footage to existing structures.
5. America's population will double—another 300 million new residents are expected to exist by 2060. Areas that exhibit economic dynamism will do particularly well.
6. Seventy-two million more echo boomers—this generation, born between 1976 and 1994, are just now starting to come online by buying cars, renting apartments and houses, and then purchasing their first houses.

The buy-and-hold strategy will work with vacant land, commercial properties, residences, industrial properties, special purpose parcels—virtually any type of real estate investment. The principles found in this book will enable you to benefit from the long-term investment advantages of smart real estate decisions.

2

Determine the Type of Real Estate to Best Fit Your Needs

Once you have decided to invest in real estate, it is important to determine the type of property that best suits your personality, skills, temperament, time availability, and practical needs. You wouldn't expect a 65-year-old widow with a dependent sister to own and manage a fraternity house anymore than you would expect a 30-year-old first-time investor to own a retirement home.

In considering the different types of real estate investments available, it is essential to find the right match between the type of property you are interested in and the individual needs that you have as a person. Real estate is classified into two basic categories: income or investment property, and non-income-producing property. The return on capital invested in investment real estate stems from net income produced, whereas the return on non-income-producing property is measured primarily in private or public use value.

Types of Income Property

- Vacant land
- Single-family homes
- Condominiums and townhouses
- Duplexes, triplexes, and fourplexes
- Apartment buildings

- Office buildings
- Shopping centers ("strip" and "anchored")
- Commercial and industrial properties

Non-Income-Producing Property

- Personal residences
- Churches
- Schools
- Parks
- City halls
- Courthouses
- Other government buildings

As a potential investor, you should look for property you are genuinely interested in and enthusiastic about. Give consideration to the long-term investment concept rather than a quick buy and sell for a meager profit. What you want to do is find a property that not only suits you, but also has growth potential. I would never buy a piece of property I wasn't interested in. When you first start out, it is best to buy something that you are familiar with so that you can analyze the growth potential of the community and neighborhood.

When I first decided to buy real estate and grow rich, I geared myself towards apartment buildings in Hermosa Beach, California, an ideally located, quaint (though at that time, dilapidated) residential community in the South Bay area of Los Angeles County. When I started, I was single and liked the idea of having a home on the oceanfront—a recreational facility and residence all in one. My first purchase was a six-unit apartment building right on the oceanfront on a strip of land called "The Strand," which looks out onto the beach and the blue Pacific. (Hermosa, appropriately enough, is Spanish for beautiful.)

The property was close enough to downtown that I could commute to work. This particular building was ideal for my needs because it has so many different floor plans—three one-bedroom apartments, one three-bedroom apartment, one two-bedroom apartment, and one small single unit. During my first few years of ownership, I couldn't afford to occupy the nicest apartment, so I lived in the smallest unit and rented out the best apartments, which brought in much-needed rental income.

Dr. Schumacher's brilliant observations of value being nothing more than the "anticipation of future benefits" hit me hard. A lot of deals are proffered to me and seldom do people talk about the growth potential of the area. I always ask them, "What will that property be worth, five, ten or twenty years from now?" And I get blank stares back at me most of the time.

One house I bought is in North Fontana in San Bernardino County, California. That area of town is set to explode in population because of the brand-new extension of the 210 freeway, which connects Pasadena with the Inland Empire city of San Bernardino. Now the commute for my Fontana residents who work in Los Angeles is cut in half.

I am excited for my residents to have quicker access to the entire Los Angeles job market. Twenty years from now the Southern California metroplex will have expanded tremendously, and so will the value of my houses.

Changes in the infrastructure of any area, like newly constructed freeways, bridges, community centers, libraries and schools, will increase the livability of the area far into the future.

Neighborhoods that people like to live in are great buy-and-hold areas. When you find out that there are plans to improve a specific area, you will do well to follow the money.

RESIDENTIAL VS. COMMERCIAL PROPERTY

You should never invest in something you don't know anything about. I am a great believer in becoming informed. However, I also feel that most first-time investors are far more naturally suited to invest in residential real estate than commercial property because they live in a house, they associate with their neighbors, and they are more inclined to know how to treat residential tenants than commercial tenants. If you work for Coldwell Banker's commercial division, you might be inclined to invest in commercial property. The majority of investors aren't, however. Consequently, if you happen to win the lottery tomorrow, I would advise investing in what you feel most comfortable with, which in most cases would be residential property.

Vacant Land

There are many different kinds of vacant land acquisitions that are good investments. There are also many vacant land purchases that are purely speculative, some of them bordering on gambles. Vacant land by itself produces no income until it is improved and put to a profitable use; the possible exceptions being vacant parcels that are used for parking, storage, or landfills. In general, any profit derived from vacant land usually comes from the increased value of the land over a period of time. The following work increases the value of raw, unimproved land, creating land that is improved:

- Landscaping and grading
- Installation of utilities
- Construction of roads, curbs, and gutters
- Construction of buildings

When you own a parcel of vacant land, it is very important to determine its highest and best use—the most profitable use—so that the land can produce the greatest return over a period of time.

Many years ago, Ringling Brothers, Barnum & Bailey Circus used to come to downtown Los Angeles and erect their huge circus tent on a vacant lot close to Washington Boulevard and Hill Street. The circus usually occupied the land parcel for about two weeks out of the year.

Obviously, the circus was the highest and best use of that lot during the two-week period it was in use. However, the land would sit vacant the other 50 weeks of the year.

Duration of use is very important to consider when contemplating a vacant land purchase. Sometimes, the most profitable return from the vacant land parcel is not measurable in monetary terms, but rather in community services, such as schools, parks playgrounds, or libraries. Vacant land parcels that lend themselves to monetary returns should be carefully analyzed to determine the most profitable use over the longest period of time.

Oftentimes, it is very difficult to determine what the highest and best use of a vacant land parcel should be until the surrounding area is developed or shows signs of positive development. If you have a land parcel in a populated area, especially if it is in the path of future growth, the property can increase in market value as the community improves.

An expensive parcel of vacant land requires substantial holding power on the owner's behalf until it can be developed and be put to a profitable use. Caution is the watchword for the first-time investor considering vacant land for a long-term investment. It is generally unwise to purchase vacant land for an investment unless you can see an immediate use for the property.

RESIDENTIAL PROPERTY

Single-Family Residences

Single-family residential property is great if you have the right tenant. If you don't have the right tenant, it can be brutal. Successfully finding the right tenant to live in a house is the best thing that can happen. I have some tenants in a house I own in Los Angeles who think and act as if they own the place. And they don't want me bothering them. I also have a house in Hollywood. The tenants there recently wrote me a note saying they spent about $400 fixing up the yard and wanted to know what I thought about it. I said, "Wonderful. Send me the bill." And that was that. They always pay their rent on time and never complain about anything. It works out just super.

> Great success is to be had in managing single-family-house tenants. I was pleasantly dumfounded when a resident I hated to lose re-concreted a driveway, built a new wood fence and refurbished an old wood floor for me. If you screen for the right residents to live in your properties, this can happen most of the time.

A good strategy to employ when buying residential property is to look for an older house in an area of high density that is, or eventually might be, zoned for multiple residential use. Oftentimes, it is possible to purchase the entire property—land and improvements—for about what the land alone is worth. If the property is in a prime location and increases in value over time, you can pay off the mortgage and end up with a desirable development site for an apartment house.

A *friend of mine once purchased two adjacent single-family homes on a parcel of land that measured 100 by 200 feet. Zoned for multiple residential uses, the land would permit the development of 30 apartment units. The property was purchased in 1960 for $60,000 with $7,000 down. After three years, the rent from the two houses was bringing in enough income to make the payments. With a land parcel already paying for itself, my friend had no trouble getting a construction loan and was able to build his 30-unit apartment building. The neighborhood has improved in 30 years' time and today that property is worth about $6 million. Not bad for $7,000 down!*

I have invested exclusively in single-family houses. I always thought that people need houses to live in, and they tend to treat them as their own homes. Managing these homes has been easy for me to the point that they almost run themselves.

After 20 years of being a mortgage broker and lending on all sorts of structures, I know lenders love single-family residences (SFRs)—they're the least-risky pieces of real estate on which they can loan. Better rates and terms are offered on SFRs. The more a house conforms to the other houses in the neighborhood, the better. I am fond of buying older, three-bedroom two-bath houses in established pride-of-ownership neighborhoods because if lenders like them so much, who am I to argue?

A person living in a SFR is in the highest-demand, most-marketable piece of real estate today—the holy grail. It is the easiest to sell if the lender has to take it back. By far, single-family detached houses have the largest number and variety of loan programs available today. SFRs are usually in stable neighborhoods and tend to hold their value well in down markets.

Condominiums and Townhouses

When you own a condominium or townhouse, you must belong to a homeowner association and pay monthly dues. There is a set of guidelines from the association you must abide by known as CC&Rs (covenants, conditions, and restrictions). These rules govern the use of the property. The homeowner association of a condominium complex, for instance, could limit the number of visitors who can stay with a homeowner or tenant at any given time. Some property owners find CC&Rs restrictive. As a landlord, I tend to look on them favorably because they ensure that tenants respect the rights of others and adhere to a set of uniform standards.

Homeowner associations charge a monthly fee. It goes toward maintaining the grounds, pool, common elements, the building exterior, security, and waste removal. For me, this works out just fine. I own 30 condominiums in three separate projects that are virtually hassle-free. Whenever there is a vacancy, the on-site manager is responsible for filling it, so I don't have to worry about renting the places. All I have to do is pay $400 each time I have a vacancy. Altogether, I pay $6,625 in homeowner fees per month. But my condominiums are all more or less self-sufficient. It's a headache-free situation, really. And that's well worth the expenditure.

For my wife and me, these condominiums are like having a vacation resort. We have one unit that we keep vacant for ourselves. The complex is close to a major commercial retail center, so numerous restaurants, department stores, professional offices, and movie theaters are all within walking distance. In addition, we belong to the local performing arts center.

As with my apartments on the beach, these units have recreational and investment value. One day, they're going to make us millions of dollars. Not only that, these little condominiums, which each have 500 square feet of floor area, have the lowest rents in the neighborhood.

One drawback to owning a condominium is that if your complex becomes embroiled in a lawsuit and your fellow property owners in the association vote to raise homeowner dues on account of legal fees or additional maintenance expenses, there isn't much you can do except comply and pay the additional fees.

Besides homeowner associations being sued because of construction-defect lawsuits and mismanagement of their budgets (the most common reasons), I would add that condos can be excellent investments if you buy them cheaply enough. And, you can find more of them on sale in times of market distress because:

1. They closely resemble apartments with storage-space limitations and parking problems, particularly midrise and high-rise projects.

2. Some of them are not particularly kid friendly.
3. Homeowners' associations can go broke raising monthly assessments, causing increased financial strain on the borrower. It's very common to have condo associations go bankrupt—more owners go into foreclosure—during economic downturns if they can't raise enough money.
4. Association dues increase because they don't keep a cap on expenses.
5. The project's overall maintenance is mismanaged.
6. They are older buildings in continual disrepair.

Lower-priced condos are very beneficial to the housing market because that is where most homeowners start. It is entry-level housing for first timers.

Seniors love condos because there is no outside maintenance, so they can "lock and leave" their units to travel or go see their grandkids. The best projects are well located near urban amenities. Condo projects in the urban cores are a coming trend.

We have a condo located on the water next to a boat marina. Because of its waterfront location next to a boat dock, our unit stays rented and is very resilient to price fluctuations.

Duplexes, Triplexes, and Fourplexes

Duplexes are a good first-time investment because you have the option of inhabiting one unit and renting out the other(s), which helps make the payments and pay the taxes. A four-family flat, or fourplex, does even better and generally takes no more effort to take care of than a duplex. If you live in one unit and take care of the other three, you're already on the property to deal with whatever problems and situations arise.

A duplex, triplex, or even fourplex is usually a mom-and-pop operation. The owners may need the rent to help make the payment on the loan and pay the taxes. Maybe they figure that someday, as they get along in years, their mother or father might live in one of the units so they can keep an eye on them.

For a number of reasons, many people don't like the idea of living in an apartment before being a homeowner. But certainly to get started, if you can buy a two- or four-unit building and live in it for a while until you can raise the rents, then refinance it, you'll be able to buy a single-family residence. Then you would have a good start on the road toward building an estate.

Owning real estate is a long-term investment. When I first started investing in income property, I had to hold on to the property for about seven years before the cash flow would go from negative to positive. I bought most of my properties with very little down, so my mortgage payments were comparatively high. If you find a good piece of real estate, you'll be able to do wonders with it. But the key to the whole thing is to find the right property that, through your research and analysis, will increase in value.

A doctor friend of mine once wanted to buy a dilapidated 40-unit building in downtown Los Angeles. It upset me because here was a respected physician who helped people get well, and yet he was thinking about acquiring this run-down property. It was available at a cheap price, but that purchase would have forced him to become a slumlord. The property didn't fit his need. After thinking about it, he decided to buy a place on Burton Way in Beverly Hills, and he eventually made a killing without having to compromise his position.

Apartment Buildings

It is not easy for first-time buyers to start off with apartment buildings, unless they have inherited the property or a lot of money from a rich uncle. This said, an apartment building is one of the best investments there is. A friend of mine who had accumulated a substantial amount of equity in four single-family residences and two duplexes recently decided to trade his equity for a 38-unit apartment building in the San Gabriel Valley, which he bought for $2.5 million.

Since the mortgage on the apartment is high compared to the income, he has a negative cash flow of about $2,000 a month. But he has faith in the area and believes that in a few years he will experience a positive cash flow. In 30 years, he will own an asset worth at least $6 million and have no outstanding mortgage on the property. There aren't many investments that offer this certainty, and size, of return.

To own and manage a large apartment complex with a negative cash flow requires a certain amount of income and discipline. But the rewards can be fantastic. If you are thinking about buying an apartment building, it is important to decide what you like and what kind of people you can work with. Then, locate a property in a good location that fits the quirks in your personality.

Before making an offer to purchase an apartment building, be sure that the size and configuration of the rental units conform with the demand factor for similar apartments in the neighborhood. Study the building's occupancy in relation to community facilities. For instance, a three-bedroom apartment building that attracts families might work fantastically near a high school, whereas studio apartments for single professionals would probably be a poor investment choice if they were situated next to an elementary school.

Study vacancy rates, planned construction projects, and the developments in the surrounding area that act as a source of employment for potential tenants. Such developments may include hospitals, shopping malls, colleges, financial centers, business parks, and the like. With a specific property in mind, it is useful to look at the neighborhood and the subject building as a potential tenant would. The following is a checklist of items to consider when assessing the property:

- Is the outside appearance as attractive, or more attractive, than competitive buildings?
- What is the condition of the balconies, porches, sidewalks, common areas and landscaping?
- Are there any roof leaks or signs of water damage? Are the gutters and downspouts adequate?
- Does the apartment complex have adequate parking?
- What advantages, such as proximity to traffic arteries, public transportation, shopping centers, churches, and schools, does the location offer?
- Are there any detrimental influences, such as adjacent noisy streets, railroad tracks, or obnoxious odors or excessive noise from industrial plants?
- How do the size and configuration of individual apartment units compare with the competition?

- How do the rents compare?
- Does the subject building offer the same amenities, such as parking, swimming pool, recreation center, or workout facilities, as the competition?
- Are there any structural defects or visible building flaws in the foundation, roofing, or framing?
- Are the walls and floors soundproof, so that noise from one apartment will not disturb other tenants?
- Are the apartments clean and well maintained?

The importance of knowing the physical characteristics of the apartment property before making a firm commitment to purchase cannot be overemphasized. Be sure that all mechanical appliances in individual apartment units are in good working order, including refrigerators, ranges, dishwashers, garbage disposals, exhaust fans, individual air conditioners, heaters, and laundry facilities. Building-wide, inspect the electrical service, as well as plumbing and heating in sufficient detail to determine if there are any major, foreseeable problems. In addition, it might be necessary to obtain a termite or other infestation report. Finally, to determine whether the building is settling, you might want to place a marble on the floor and see where it rolls. (For a detailed discussion of an apartment appraisal, see Appendix B.)

COMMERCIAL

Office Buildings

Office buildings are a difficult first investment. Adequate income is the key. If you decide to buy an office building, be sure to make a thorough tenant-demand analysis of the subject property. Briefly, a demand analysis would include a forecast or estimate of the need and desire for office space in the community over a long period of time and what the future competition from other similar existing and proposed projects might do to the office building market. If there is nothing in the immediate area renting for $1 to $50 per square foot of floor area per month, it would be virtually impossible to get any more for your space unless you have a better quality building.

It is not advisable to buy an office building unless you really know what you are doing or have an immediate need for it. The current glut of vacant office space in most major metropolitan areas makes investing in this type of real estate quite hazardous.

About 18 years ago, I made an appraisal of the Wilshire Medical Building at the corner of Wilshire Boulevard and Bonnie Brae Street in downtown Los Angeles. When I finished with my appraisal, I met with a group of doctors who owned the medical building as well as a large lot in the rear of the complex. I told them at the time that they ought to build a hospital on the lot because if they didn't, they would have a difficult time keeping the medical building leased. Other developers would come into the area and build office buildings adjacent to the medical buildings, driving the medical tenants out.

The best arrangement for a commercial property is an owner-user. For any commercial property, whether it's a restaurant, business, supermarket, hardware store, or clothing store, the ultimate tenant is an owner-user. If you own a medical office building, it is best to have doctor participation. To keep commercial tenants in the building over a period of time requires that they get a piece of the action. If you are interested in buying an office building, you might want to syndicate it through a partnership, corporation, or trust with a group of professionals who will occupy the space.

I used to represent a company that has seven office and industrial buildings. The company leases these buildings from the employees, who own the properties in a profit-sharing trust. This trust is set up through the Securities and Exchange Commission. The company leases these buildings on a short-term basis, and every three years they have to be appraised to figure out how much the employees have make to increase their pension fund benefits.

If you are planning to purchase an office building for an investment, be sure to obtain expert, unbiased advice before you commit yourself to anything.

Specialty Investments: Mini-Warehouses

Similar to other types of commercial real estate investments, a specialty investment such as a mini-warehouse requires specialized knowledge. The key to a thriving mini-warehouse business is a good location. If you owned a mini-warehouse in a high-density resort community or bustling metropolis, you'd be successful because there is such a high concentration of people who have wealth and all sorts of junk they don't need or want. A storage facility would attract ample customers. Even so, it's more of a speculative investment, really.

Recently, a friend of mine who owned a mini-warehouse went broke. He's one of the smartest guys I've ever met. He understands the tax laws and the economic forces of finance and has given many lectures on these subjects. But he had to file for bankruptcy protection recently because the mini-warehouse he owned and operated was so poorly managed. He didn't know how to generate enough interest and enthusiasm to fill up the building. He basically didn't know how to market his product properly.

With expensive commercial investment, there is a lot of money going out each month, so you've got to be sure that it comes back in. That might not sound difficult, but sometimes it takes tremendous effort and expenditures to first find suitable tenants and then to get everything that is coming to you, even when you have signed leases.

Shopping Centers

There are two basic types of shopping centers: "strip" and "anchored." A strip shopping center, or mini-mall, consists of a collection of independently operated or franchised retail stores with a common parking area but no "anchor" or main tenant that dominates the complex. An "anchored" shopping center, on the other hand, is characterized by a substantial commercial tenant, such as a major drug or discount store, supermarket, or department store that serves as a primary tenant to anchor the project.

Strip Shopping Centers: Mini-malls

Mini-malls can make secure investments if you have good long-term leases with reliable tenants and you understand the retail business. With some understanding of the commercial real estate business, you can probably make it work. But all kinds of outside factors can change the value of the property. The traffic pattern can change because of a decision by the state transportation department; the local planning commission can recommend a zoning change; a key store in your complex can declare bankruptcy and go out of business. You're vulnerable to all of these factors, plus the rulings and decisions of local, state and regional agencies.

Moreover, some cities are difficult to do business in. They'll impose taxes and assessments. They won't allow you to put up a sign, to set up a display in front of your store, or to erect any kind of awning that upsets the character of the street. They'll ticket anyone who is two seconds over the parking limit. Whether by design or happenstance, some cities do everything they can do to harass customers and keep them away.

I've seen this happen in many cities. On the one hand, the city council says it likes business, but on the other it seems to do everything it can to undermine economic activity. The city won't provide adequate parking; the parking police will ticket too much; a laborious permit process makes new construction virtually impossible. By doing such things, the city destroys the business incentive and, along with it, the value of commercial property. Instead of leasing their commercial space at market value, property owners are generally obliged to accept reduced rents on account of severe restrictions imposed by the city government.

If you are going to invest in commercial real estate, you have to know how to get around these kinds of problems. A person who is not oriented to fight city hall has no business owning property affected in this manner.

Anchored Shopping Centers

A good anchored shopping center will do tremendously with a strong anchor tenant because it will yield a percentage of the gross income from the retail activity. We once owned a building occupied by a furniture store in the San Fernando Valley. Our monthly income averaged about $1,200. From the lease, we received 6% of the gross income with a minimum of $1,000 a month. During good months, when the store did $100,000 a month, we were entitled to $6,000, owing to our 6% fee.

If you have a calculating mind, an anchored shopping center can become a source of great revenue. But, as with a mini-mall, there are many things you have to look out for. When you own a shopping center, your main concern is competition—the type of stores next door, down the street, in the neighborhood and surrounding area. In addition, new innovations, new commercial developments, and new ownership of existing centers can all take a bite out of your business, especially when money, in the form of construction loans, is available for development. It takes a person with great foresight to accurately assess the risk involved, find the right complex to invest in, and succeed.

It's far riskier and takes more ingenuity and more knowledge to own a shopping center than to own, say, an apartment building. Even in an economic downturn, people need a place to live, so the residential market remains relatively stable despite periodic dips.

First-time investors are not likely to buy commercial properties unless they have uses for them. Commercial real estate involves a completely different set of factors to consider than residential property. Quality of tenants, amount of income derived, and possibility of increased income are important factors to analyze, along with the duration of income. Long-term commercial leases are good to have in a recessionary market because they ensure a steady income stream. However, under inflationary conditions, short-term leases may be more desirable because of rapid increases in leasing rates during the upward cycle.

Industrial Buildings

Generally, industrial property doesn't fluctuate in value like residential real estate does. Most industrial buildings are single-purpose buildings built for one specific use. If the economy changes, that can create problems. Smokestack industries are being hit from all sides. Oil refineries, chemical plants, and other hazardous industrial plants are restricted in many areas because of smog and other environmental conditions. In addition, the whole manufacturing process is constantly changing in response to new technology.

The best time to invest in industrial property is when long-term demand is the greatest. Our world is changing dramatically from a technological standpoint. And sometimes, industrial real estate doesn't keep pace with these changes. A building can become functionally and economically obsolete before it begins to deteriorate physically on account of factors ranging from new processing techniques to lack of demand for the product.

For every 400 people who could buy an apartment building, there are probably 10 who should buy an office building. And for every 10 people who should buy an office building, there is probably one who could buy an industrial building and understand what to do with it. Whether you are experienced or just starting out, an industrial building is not an easy investment.

Since I have many houses, it is incumbent on me not to spend too much time on any one house. I liken it to having a horizontal apartment complex with my units spread across different areas of town. The tenants manage the property for me. I get help from local handymen and next-door neighbors who help me keep an eye on the properties.

THE TIME FACTOR

When choosing the type of property that is right for you, the amount of time you have to maintain it becomes an important consideration. An older building, for instance, typically requires more upkeep and maintenance work than a newer building. A triplex or fourplex may require direct oversight and many owners often live on-site. But with a large apartment building or commercial complex, a property management company can be hired to take full charge of finding good tenants, collecting rents, and providing proper maintenance and repairs.

LOCATION

Residential

With both residential and commercial real estate, location is critical. But with a commercial property, you can have a good location today, and it could become a lousy location two years from now because of adverse influences created by governmental actions.

Municipal and county governments can change the traffic pattern to widen the street in front of your business, taking part or all the land in front of your property for public use as a right-of-way. They can also impose restrictions on the property that make ingress and egress difficult. When one-way streets are created, they sometimes cause tremendous problems for commercial property owners. Most cites also have the authority to limit the size and style of business signage. I could think of a whole host of actions they could take that would have a negative impact on commercial property.

A different set of rules seems to apply to residential real estate because people live in these properties; when residents band together as a unified group, they can strongly influence elected officials. Many public servants in city hall have a different perspective. They are representing the people who put them in office. And so if the sentiment in the community is anti-growth or anti-business, the city council is likely to vote in favor of restricting commercial activity.

Oftentimes, the local electorate will be up in arms if you change a concept that has to do with housing. The council chamber will be filled. But if you have a change of concept that has to do with commercial property, usually very few people show up for the public hearing.

If you own a single-family residence and you have a low mortgage that is almost paid for, you are not likely to lose it. Although most zoning laws are local, our representatives in Congress wouldn't do anything to dramatically affect American homeowners because all of them have large constituencies of homeowners. (Interestingly, the National Association of Realtors has the largest lobby in Washington, D.C.) The same is true of local elected officials.

As mentioned, the location of residential income property is crucial. In certain locales, beachfront and resort property are considered to be solid investments. However, many beach and resort communities have had very difficult times. The specific location you choose to invest in cannot be considered too carefully. Recreational properties located in areas that have year-round tenancies attract a certain type of renter, one who is prone to a carefree life-style, frequent parties, and loud noise. Many investors may find that type of tenant undesirable.

I do better with people on the beach than most other landlords I know, because I've been on the beach for so long. I know what to look for. I know how beach people are. I know what some of their traits are, their likes and dislikes. A lot of people aren't willing to become property owners in a beach community because of all the characters and problems you have to deal with. Admittedly, I've had to put up with quite a bit. For me, it's well worth it. But a great many landlords can't put up with loud noise, swearing, beer drinking, and the like.

In 1957, a few years before I bought the beachfront apartment I live in, there was a riot in front of the property that caused a lot of damage to the building. When I moved in, I vowed never to get mad at the people on the beach because if something were to happen, they were going to be the ones to protect my property. A few years ago on the Fourth of July, I was at another beachfront property of mine where a second riot started. Some guys created a big rumpus and started throwing rocks and anything else they could get their hands on. Because I got along so well with my tenants, they stood guard to protect my building when the mayhem started. I bend over backwards for the guys and gals who play volleyball in front of my places, and in return they've paid me back in ways I never would have imagined.

I'll do anything I can for someone who rents from me, as long as they're paying their rent on time and not disturbing anyone else. But a lot of property owners won't do that. They get easily disturbed.

A friend of mine owns a six-unit building down from me on The Strand. For the life of me, I can't figure out why he owns the place. He can't keep it occupied. He doesn't know what to do. He doesn't know how to treat people who live by the beach. He goes over there every other day and pesters the tenants and won't leave them alone or give them any privacy. If they make a little bit of noise, he gets mad. If people talk back to him, he doesn't know how to handle it and gets upset. If his tenants pound a nail in the wall or accidentally break a window, he threatens them and raises a ruckus. It's not in him to accept these things. But why worry about a $50 window? He gets $1,500 a month from that one apartment. Why should he care? It's all relative.

I've owned and been renting property for 40 years, and I've never had any serious trouble with a tenant. You just have to know how to treat people. A lot of it depends on your attitude and your approach. If one of my tenants breaks a window, I'll make him replace it. But it doesn't bother me.

Very seldom do you find a tenant who will take care of the property like the owner will. One of the questions you have to ask yourself when you purchase an investment property is whether you can emotionally handle it if someone doesn't take care of the place the way you would. It is important to treat your investment as a business and not take it personally if someone trashes the place. It may not make you happy, but don't become ill over it because it probably will happen more than once.

Different localities engender different mentalities. As well as I understand and get along with people at the beach, I once bought a single-family residence in Hesperia—a rural town about 80 miles from Los Angeles. I never had so many problems in all my life. We couldn't communicate with the people there at all. We finally had to get rid of it.

Besides solving communication problems, living near your income property can also serve a valuable utilitarian purpose. When I started teaching real estate appraisal courses at Los Angeles City College in the 1950s, I acquired a four-unit building in Hollywood. I bought the property for two specific reasons. First, I needed a place to stay that was close to work and the campus. It was ideally located. Secondly, I used it as the subject of a hands-on exercise for my students, an assignment to physically go through the steps and prepare an appraisal of the property at its current market value. So this purchase satisfied two specific, practical needs I had at the time.

Commercial

In addition to location, the positioning of commercial property is extremely important. A bakery next door to a church is not as good for the bakery as a location next to a post office, because a church is typically used only one day a week, whereas a post office is open six days a week. In the downtown business district of a community, where building codes may not be as rigid as suburban areas, whoever owns the property decides what he thinks would be a good development. Oftentimes, this results in a hodgepodge. Because of this situation, many opportunities are created.

By contrast, a shopping center under the same management and ownership that is governed by a master plan may strive to put stores and activities that benefit each other side-by-side. You might find a flower shop next to a jewelry store because it helps the jewelry store. Or the management might put all the shoe stores together so customers won't have to walk from one end of the complex to the other to find another shoe store when their mind is on shoes. All the clothing stores, candy stores, or restaurants are together. Everything is strategically placed, giving individual business owners less control over what they can do. The degree to which this occurs would be a point to analyze and study when investing in commercial property.

FINANCING

If you only have a business to use as collateral, you aren't as likely to have the security that banks require for a loan than if you own a piece of real property free and clear. If you have a business and a residence as your basic assets, the institutional lender is very likely to give you a substantial loan with good terms.

Today, you could get a loan on the residence for around 6% interest or less and a loan on the business for 12% or higher. But, whereas you can get a 30-year loan on a house, you can probably only get a one- or two-year loan on the business.

As far as financing of residential property is concerned, if you own from one to four units, it's relatively easy to get a loan. Generally, residential buildings with more than four units are considered apartments, so they fall into a different category. An institutional lender would require a substantial down payment. Lenders are more critical and more concerned about the net income derived from an apartment building. They would investigate the transaction more from an income standpoint.

LANDLORD RESPONSIBILITIES

Another important consideration in determining the best type of investment to fit your needs is whether you are comfortable with the role of landlord and all the attendant responsibilities of dealing with other people. Technically, a landlord is someone who surrenders the right to use his or her property for a duration of time in exchange for an agreed sum. People who are bashful about imposing on others will have a difficult time imposing on their tenants or asking for the rent.

Before investing in a property, you should ask yourself several questions. Can you get along with other people? Do you know how to go out and collect the rent? When do you get mad? When do you not get mad? How are you going to find somebody to clean and rent your apartments if you work all day? Are you competent enough in accounting to keep your own books? Can you do your own handiwork? There's a host of things to consider before you leap.

Residential vs. Commercial Property

If you own a commercial property and you're leasing to a guy who runs a store, you're dealing with him on a business basis, and you can be hard-nosed. But when you rent a residential property or apartment unit, your tenants live there. It's their home. If you're dealing with a guy who has a wife and two kids, there can be a lot of emotion involved. It's harder to throw them out, or even make decisions that will affect them adversely.

Before buying, the most important thing is to become as informed as possible in the type of real estate you're going to be investing in, whether it's a single-family residence, condominium, duplex or triplex, apartment buildings, or a commercial or industrial property. How do you acquire and then manage the investment? And how do other people who are successful operate their investments?

Learn everything you can. Read books on the subject. Go to night school. And realize that when you own a piece of real estate, you have the opportunity to become independent. It's not like going to a job where the boss can tell you one day, "Well, we don't need you anymore. Good-bye." With real estate, you have something that can make you self-sufficient. You therefore owe it to yourself to learn as much about the type of property you are interested in as possible.

Most of all, learn from other people's mistakes because countless others have tried before you. There are those who have failed miserably, and there are those who have succeeded beyond their wildest dreams. You can determine which kind of investor you will be.

HOW TO BECOME A MILLIONAIRE

The case of Sam Smith, a mechanical engineer with a degree from Harvard, is instructive here. For 15 years Sam was employed by a Fortune 500 Company, in middle management. In 1990, Sam's future looked very bright. He was climbing up the corporate ladder at a remarkable pace, his wife and two children were living in high style and Sam wanted to be a faithful employee until retirement. In 1993, the company had a different idea.

The economic upheaval occurring in the national economy had a tremendous adverse impact on Sam's company, which in turn put about 30% of the workforce out of jobs. This has happened to hundreds of thousands of devoted employees who felt that they would have secure jobs until retirement. Sam received a very substantial severance payment. It amounted to about $80,000. Sam was in a real dilemma. He was able to find a job, but it was at only 50% of what he was earning at the Fortune 500 company.

Sam's life savings was tied up in stock which he had purchased from his former company under a retirement plan. The value of the stock took a nosedive when the company went into decline. In order to retain a lifestyle which will satisfy Sam, he must invest his $80,000 in a secure investment that will yield capital appreciation plus income.

After Sam's serious loss in the stock market, he doesn't want to buy more stocks, especially if he has no control or idea of what the top management of a company or the economy might do to improve or destroy the common stock value.

Someone pointed out to Sam that if he bought an income-producing piece of real estate in a location that has a good potential economic growth with capital appreciation, an increase in value could occur within a 25-year period.

The type of real estate that would fit into this pattern would be: houses, an apartment complex, an office building, a commercial building or shopping center, a good industrial property, etc. If Sam buys an income property he would be acquiring a "hands on" asset which he can physically pick out and which meets his needs, desire and objectives. The opportunity of high-leverage funding and long-term appreciation can succeed if the investment Sam purchases is in the right location. The success or failure of Sam's investment is under his control.

In my opinion, a desirable plan for Sam would be to invest his $80,000 in an apartment property located in an area that has good growth potential. The apartment property is recommended because most people are more familiar with dealing with housing than commercial or industrial property problems.

Let's say Sam purchases an apartment property for $400,000 and a down payment of $80,000. The first mortgage is $320,000, payment is $2,262 per month for 25 years at 7% interest. If the proper location is selected for growth potential, in 25 years the apartment property should be free and clear and the asset worth at least $2,500,000. The net income from the apartments should provide for a good retirement. Sam will have become a millionaire.

3

Real Estate: An Investment, a Speculation, or a Gamble?

Investors with venture capital have several options to choose from—namely, money-oriented investments, such as long- and short-term savings plans, stocks, bonds, mutual funds—and real estate. Fortunes have been made by speculating in real estate and playing the housing market like the stock market. But in my opinion the wisest investment strategy incorporates a view that neither relies on frenzied Wall Street buying-and-selling practices, nor leaves the fate of your investment to the vagaries of chance: Real estate investments located in desirable areas are bound to improve dramatically over time.

California is a great example of the long-term potential of an area. It is hard to go wrong there. According to the California Association of Realtors, the median house price for a single-family house in 1970 was $32,000. Home values tripled by the end of that decade. They went on to double in the 1980s and doubled again in the 1990s.

Nevertheless, it is useful to compare the advantages of a long-term real estate investment program to the volatility and uncertainty of financial investments. There are three basic levels of risk with regard to capital investment: (1) safe return, (2) speculation, or (3) gamble. A safe return is something you can count on, while speculation depends on the whims of the market, and a gamble is left to chance. What determines whether an investment creates a safe return, a speculation, or a gamble is the amount of risk you are willing to take. In monetary terms, a risk rate is equivalent to an interest rate. Do you want to take a gamble and go to Las Vegas and place all your chips on the black? Do you want to speculate in the commodities market? Or would you rather buy real estate in a desirable location as a long-term investment and get a safe return?

Much attention has been paid in the business press lately about how little of their money Americans save on a per capita basis compared to other industrialized nations. But did you know that saving may actually be hazardous to your wealth? Savings plans don't begin to take advantage of the inflationary trend of our capitalistic economy. Say you were able to save $3,000 annually, earning 6% compound interest. After 20 years, your account, which would accumulate to $110,000, would only be worth about $37,000 in today's dollars. Hardly enough to retire on.

INVESTMENT OPTIONS

The cash-rich investor has a variety of good investment options to choose from, including U. S. Treasury securities (bills, notes, and bonds), certificates of deposit, blue chip stocks and bonds, and high-rated mutual funds, which are among the safest investments available. However, most of these investments do not have the added advantage of capital appreciation, which well-located real estate does have.

For a time in the early 1940s, I worked in the family store selling bakery goods. A regular customer of ours would delight in telling me how great he thought his insurance annuity was. This guy, who had a wife and three kids, said that he was paying $33 a month to an insurance company for 20 years. After that time, he was going to receive something like $300 a month for the rest of his life. I thought to myself, By golly, he's got it all wrong. Here's a father who can't even buy donuts and ice cream for his kids and he's putting money into something he has no control over. He had no idea what executives running that company would do or what decisions they would make with his and everyone else's hard-earned money.

*E*xecutive Life Insurance Company in California provides
*a good example. Before it was seized by state regulators
who shopped around for a new buyer, some 350,000 policyholders stood to lose a hefty portion of their money.*

Assume that when you were 21 years old, you started paying $50 a month to
Executive Life and that today you're 65 years old and scheduled to receive
an annuity from the now highly leveraged insurer. All your money is out
the window if the company goes broke. I have never felt that acquiring an
annuity was in anyone's best interest financially.

Now, suppose that instead of putting your money into a company that
spends millions of dollars in salaries for overpaid executives, accountants,
and attorneys (who spend a portion of their time figuring out the most
effective ways to beat their policyholders out of a few dollars), you had
taken that $50 a month and put it into an investment that you had control
over, such as real estate. It's better to have your own asset and let it appreciate than to allow other people and institutions to determine your financial
future.

> During the investment meltdown of 2008, AIG insurance was slated
> to be rescued by the US government. My next-door neighbor had
> just received his annuity check—the major chunk of his retirement
> income—from AIG and was praying and hoping it would go through.
> I remember the look of panic on his face. I never want to be in that
> situation.

When most Americans get to be 65 years old, they have little or no security. They usually have to depend on Social Security, a retirement account,
or some kind of pension fund they receive for having worked all of their
adult life. But, increasingly, pension funds are being milked and are really
in bad shape because of leveraging and other types of financing schemes.
The holders of these accounts, the pensioners themselves, may end up
with practically nothing. In this situation, you can find yourself in extreme
hardship through no fault of your own by being the indirect victim of mismanagement. If you are not able to control your finances, you are not able
to control your destiny.

But if you have your finger on the money that you are planning to retire on, you have the opportunity to build an estate and gain control over your financial future. I would much rather own an apartment building worth $1.5 million than a life insurance policy that I've paid on for 30 years that will only yield $800 a month when I retire and pay $50,000 if I die.

*A*s *an appraiser, I first got the idea of buying and holding real estate when I looked at a chart and realized that it would cost more to construct a new building the next day than it would that day. Currently, a good quality apartment building in the Los Angeles area can be built at around $100 per square foot of livable floor area. Ten years from now, it might cost $150 per square foot to build the same apartment building. Even if costs don't rise that fast, you certainly know that it isn't going to be any cheaper to build in the future. Moreover, as the cost of construction rises, it tends to make older buildings more valuable.*

Any investment entails at least a modest amount of risk. Without a doubt, US Treasury bonds are the safest investment available. Another safe investment is a long-term leased fee interest in a land parcel with leasehold improvement (building) worth considerably more than the land. I also believe that the right piece of real estate is every bit as good as a US government bond.

Good property located in growth areas should be regarded as a safe return investment, as opposed to a speculation or gamble. The long-range forecasting techniques discussed later in this book will enable investors to determine areas with the greatest growth potential. Providing you do your research, the right real estate investment will take care of you for life.

SPECULATIONS

Speculative purchases are sometimes a matter of mental attitude as much as anything because value, like beauty, is in the eye of the beholder. One investor may look at a piece of property as a purchase for speculation while another may view the same property as a long-term investment. Both people could be correct in their analyses, as the property could be speculative during the short term and a highly profitable investment in the long term.

In general, slum housing in difficult neighborhoods is considered highly speculative because it is subject to civil unrest and is hard to operate. Rent collection and maintenance are difficult because the conditions in which you are buying are rough. Expenses are likely to be quite costly. These properties therefore demand a higher rate of return on capital investment to justify the necessary expenditures. Consequently, they tend to be regarded as speculative.

It is important to analyze the community in which you are interested in buying to see that you don't make a poor investment. For instance, you don't want to purchase property directly adjacent to a community redevelopment project that will take eons to rebuild and force you to take a long-term negative cash flow. Granted, the property will eventually appreciate in value. But the question is, how long can you hold out?

Sometimes, it is impractical to acquire property on a street where the city has planned a widening project. Nor do you want to get into a situation where the highway authority plans to shave 30 feet from your front yard in order to create a major thoroughfare that prevents you from getting in and out of your driveway.

A real estate speculation doesn't necessarily entail a quick turnaround; it could be long term, too. A gamble in real estate could also be long term. For instance, today you can go out to the California desert or to some other places where desert subdivisions have collapsed because of their building and ownership costs, and buy up an old subdivision. Then you could sit on it for decades until growth catches up and somebody comes along who is willing to market it.

I have a friend who started buying vacant land in Kern County, California. He would go to these tax sales and, not having even inspected the property, put up a few thousand dollars to buy land and oil leases. Eventually, he ended up with about 65 parcels spread throughout four counties. Over time, land became valuable and a water district was formed that irrigated the land, and the land dramatically increased in value. It worked out really well for him. He could speculate by investing in land without having to worry about tenants, maintenance, or other concerns.

FIXER-UPPERS

A lot of people are in the business of buying older houses, fixing them up, and then selling them for a profit. Many of my friends and associates have bought fixer-uppers and have done beautiful jobs rehabilitating them. When the newly refurbished property goes up in value, the investor sells it and moves into a better house. That's not what I would do, but a lot of people are successful at it.

Say a person buys a house for $300,000 and puts $50,000 into fixing it up. Then the market falls off and the property can't even be sold for $300,000, let alone the additional $50,000 cash the owner has invested. In this situation, his only recourse may be to hold on to his investment over a longer period of time by renting the property to offset his loan payments and remodeling expenses. Obviously, timing the purchase and acquiring property in a foreseeable up market is critical when speculating like this. Buying houses, fixing them up, and reselling them can be very lucrative if you are careful in your timing and selection of the right properties.

Speculating in real estate, in my opinion, is riddled with drawbacks. Even though it may result in a net profit, selling property exposes you to a tax on capital gains. Most people sell their real estate prematurely when they see a relatively small profit. Selling property in a neighborhood with appreciating land values prevents many income property owners from ever achieving a positive cash flow. It also limits the amount of equity they could have accumulated and borrowed against to make other investments. Buying and holding real estate for just a brief period, then selling, is clearly a short-sighted approach to what is better regarded as a decades-long process of wealth accumulation by making a purchase that considers and allows long-term appreciation in value.

Presently the federal capital gains tax rate is at 15%, which is lower than the tax bracket for ordinary income, but that rate will not last long. That does not include the state capital gains treatment. In every state it is different but in California, capital gains are taxed as ordinary income.

The opposition to cutting capital gains taxes is usually rooted in the belief that the tax cuts benefit only the wealthy. However, this is only partly true. While most wealthy people own stocks and other capital, there are plenty of struggling businesses and middle-class families

> depending on capital just as much. In reality, the cutting of capital gains taxes has proven to benefit the economy when tried in the past on multiple occasions.
>
> Historically, when capital gains taxes were raised it tended to harm the US economy more than help it.
>
> As government deficits grow, look for that favorable tax treatment to come under renewed assault.

There are several inherent advantages to keeping the desirable real estate you acquire. Aside from qualitative attributes, there are four basic measurable benefits derived from ownership of income property, abbreviated by the acronym SEAT:

- *Spendable Income:* With income property, you can realize a positive cash flow.
- *Equity Buildup:* Building equity allows you to borrow against your property to make other investments.
- *Appreciation:* Holding on to real estate enables property owners to realize substantial appreciation in value.
- *Tax Benefits:* Property owners reap tax benefits by depreciating on improvements and personal property.

People who finance second mortgages receive monthly payments from the borrower. Second mortgages can be a fabulous source of income, but they are also somewhat speculative. In a down market, for instance, if the second mortgage comes due and the borrower doesn't pay, the property may have to be foreclosed on. Conversely, if the first mortgage holder forecloses on his note, the holder of the second has the option of taking over the property by making the payments. If you know what you are doing, the market for second mortgages and trust deeds can be fabulous because you should be able to make 12% to 15% on your money. But it's not for the investor who is just starting out. Various forms of "creative financing" arrangements are discussed in chapter 13.

The purchases or acquisition of second mortgages or second trust deeds is also speculative because they are junior liens to the first mortgage. In other words, they are in a secondary position in the mortgage line. If the borrower under the first mortgage defaults on his payments, the holder of the second mortgage isn't paid until the foreclosing holder of the first mortgage receives the full amount of unpaid principal plus legal expenses. Ultimately, it is very difficult to plan a long-term real estate investment strategy around speculation.

MEANS OF FORCED SAVINGS

One of the primary benefits of investing in real estate is that making payments on property is a means of forced savings. Each month the owner of a piece of property must make a mortgage payment that, in essence, represents a deposit. Every time you make a payment you reduce the principal sum due on the mortgage, thereby increasing the equity. In essence, you're forcing yourself to save because the equity accumulates each month. It's a structured activity.

When I was teaching real estate courses at UCLA Extension and Los Angeles City College, I used to invite a stockbroker as a guest speaker to tell the class how fabulous it is to own stocks and bonds because they can be sold in two minutes. Then, after he would leave, I would emphasize to the students how it is even more fabulous to own real estate precisely because you cannot sell it in two minutes. You can't sell real estate to solve your immediate financial problems because real estate is not easy to sell. You have to find another way to solve your problems. Some financial advisers think that is a disadvantage, but I think it is a terrific advantage because it compels you to think things over before you make the decision.

Suppose you have a diversified investment portfolio and owned both stocks and real estate. Suddenly, a crisis strikes and you need $50,000. The first thing you would sell is the stock. If you didn't have any stock, you would figure out another way to solve your dilemma. You might borrow some money on your real estate or you might figure out another way to obtain a loan, but you aren't going to get rid of your real estate because it usually takes a period of time—weeks, months, or even years—to sell.

So you think of other ways to solve the problem. To me, that is a tremendous, built-in advantage of investing in real estate. It forces you to hold on to the property and, rather than receive a small profit, give it time to appreciate. Maybe your dire financial situation or problem will pass. Once you get over that hurdle, you'll still be left with the property. If you hold it and keep it for the long pull, you'll be much better off.

The number of high-paid athletes and celebrities who make great sums of money and maintain their wealth through the ownership of real estate is very limited. Many people who come into a lot of money do not have the ability to hold on to their riches. It is a foreign situation to them. Take Huntington Hartford, the heir to the Great Atlantic & Pacific Tea Company fortune.

In 1957 Hartford received a $90 million inheritance—over $692 million in 2009 dollars if you adjust for inflation. In the early 1960s, Hartford started spending money like it was going out of style. He invested in an art gallery, a magazine, and an artists' colony—one ill-advised scheme after another. He never failed to lose money. In a single-handed attempt to revive the West Coast theater scene, he bought a performance house in Hollywood and renamed it the Huntington Hartford Theater.

Hartford, last I heard, lives in a little cold-water flat on New York's East Side and receives a relatively small stipend from a trust fund. If he had considered a good real estate strategy, he could have had 10 times as much to squander!

Owning real estate also enables you to refinance the mortgage for up to the market value of the real property and, if possible, to take out a second, third, or fourth mortgage loan against the property. The new loan money can be used to buy other real estate, improve your current property, or do with what you want.

The following table shows that if you have a $200,000 investment with a 10% return, you're entitled to a 10% return forever. But since properly selected real estate has the added advantage of appreciation, you may be able to get well in excess of a 10% return. As Will Rogers once replied to a potential investor who asked what he should invest in, "Land, because they ain't making any more of it." On the other hand, there's no limited supply of savings accounts.

A Comparison of Investment Returns:

Savings Accounts
$200,000 deposited in a savings account in a bank.

Real Estate
$200,000 invested in a commercial property. The premises are leased to a Triple A tenant.

Assume for this illustration:

10% interest per year is paid on the amount deposited.

10% interest (risk rate) is commensurate with the risk involved in ownership.

In both cases, this would yield $20,000 per year return on each investment.

Key Differences:

As long as the $200,000 deposit remains and as long as the institution pays 10% interest, the investor will receive $20,000 per annum. If these conditions are met, the $20,000 per year can be received forever.

The $20,000 per year represents a return on the investment in real estate comparable to the return on the savings account. The real estate investment also is entitled to a recapture of capital attributed to the building so that at the expiration of the life of the building, the investor will have sufficient money to replace the building.

OUTSTRIPPING INFLATION

Besides being a reliable investment, real estate properly selected, will outpace inflation better then any other investment. As previously mentioned, land values can rise much faster than inflationary trends because of local factors of supply and demand. Rather than yielding only a small interest payment or dividend, real estate in prime locations can appreciate at 20% a year or more. What savings plan can offer that rate of return? The principal sum in a bank account is not affected by inflation. It's a fixed amount of money accorded a moderate rate of interest. Real estate, on the other hand, is sensitive to the economy and can skyrocket accordingly, thereby acting as a hedge against inflation—provided that you are in the right location.

I would add that rents will rise as the cost of living increases. Real estate is a great inflation hedge. When you lock in the interest rate on your loan, you are basically fixing the cost of your money forever. Paying off today's debt with tomorrow's cheaper dollars is an excellent inflation hedge.

HETEROGENEOUS NATURE

I've acquired much of my real estate with little or nothing down. I once bought an apartment building with three mortgages against it and put 15% down. At the same time, I was buying a house, and the broker agreed to use his cash commission from the apartment building as the total down payment on the house. He took a third mortgage on the apartment building so I could buy the house with nothing down. Essentially, I bought it with his cash and the broker was happy to make the deal! Various forms of "creative financing" arrangements are discussed in chapter 13.

There are so many ways you can go in real estate, which is why I consider it a heterogenous investment. Consider financing. A standard down payment with a conventional loan is generally considered to be 20% of the purchase price. However, with a VA loan guaranteed by the Veterans Administration to eligible veterans and spouses, no down payment is required. With a Federal Housing Administration, (FHA) loan, only 3% down is required to a specified limit when the residence is owner-occupied.

I worked on a deal recently where I put 15% down on a condominium in Orange County, California. The bottom had dropped out of the market and the prices had fallen precipitously. The seller couldn't find a buyer, so I assumed the first mortgage and paid him a 15% down payment. As mentioned, banks usually want 20% down to make a loan. With non-owner-occupied property, however, if you can get the seller to carry a 10% second mortgage and you have 10% cash, oftentimes you will be able to comply with the banks' requirements with less than 20% out of pocket.

With real estate, you have the advantage of finding a buyer who has a particular set of circumstances that will fit your needs. You may be able to sell a property to one person for more, or buy from someone else for less.

For example, I would expect to get more out of owning the place next door to where I live than somebody else would because it gives me control over the tenant mix and the noise. In addition, it enables me to collect the rent easily. It's ideal for my situation, so maybe I would be willing to pay more if the property came up for sale, especially if the current tenants were constantly disturbing the peace.

A few years ago, I bought a condominium from a savings bank that had REO (real estate owned) properties. This was a studio apartment within walking distance of an elaborate shopping center with every type of store and service imaginable. The condominium unit, which looked out onto the swimming pool, was located next door to a guy who loved to blare his stereo. One day I asked him if he would kindly turn the stereo down and he said, "No." So I went to my real estate broker and bought the unit.

Then, the tenant on the corner had a big dog that barked a lot, so I bought that unit, too. A few months later, the unit right above us came up for sale. Even though the sellers were asking 10% more than I thought it was worth, I decided to buy that one too because I didn't want somebody above me stomping around, making a lot of noise. That's the American way to do it, isn't it?

DEGREE OF CONTROL

As a heterogeneous investment, real estate allows you to be creative. If you own a piece of real estate, you have control over how you're going to fix it up, how it is going to look, and, within certain regulatory guidelines, who you are going to rent it to. One of the things I used to tell my students was that if you want to make money in real estate, buy a piece of property and figure out a higher and better use for it. When you arrive at a solution and apply it, you're bound to do better. Through creative rehabilitation of real estate, you can create opportunities.

Say you have a four-unit apartment building in which all the units have two bedrooms and two baths. If your city would permit you to convert the four units into eight single apartments, you might be able to generate as much as 30% more rent. That would be a more profitable use for the property.

Or, if you owned a single-family residence in an area that was zoned for commercial uses, perhaps you could convert it into a restaurant. It might be fabulous. During the energy crisis of the 1970s, a lot of gas stations that were put out of business were converted into flower shops, nurseries, and convenience stores—essentially, higher and better uses.

Regardless of the real estate investment, there is no exact formula to tell you what the ultimate outcome will be. But with a good property located in a growth area, you can fore-see its potential future value. Moreover, you can improve or alter the use to generate additional income.

I once owned a five-unit building on Camerford Avenue in Hollywood. It was located just around the corner from Paramount Studios and a few blocks up from the Wilshire Country Club. Despite these auspicious landmarks, the place was a real dog and needed fixing up. The property was flanked by an alley in the rear, and trees and shrubs were overgrown on the lot. But between the back of the building and the alleyway, there was a backyard about 30 feet deep. Soon after I bought the property, I discovered that whenever I went to collect the rent, I was not able to find a parking place. People who worked at the studio would take up all the street spaces, and there was no on-site parking for the tenants.

The old street parking arrangement simply could not accommodate the current population density. Realizing this, I immediately hired some workers to tear out the growth in the rear portion of the lot, thereby clearing room for five parking spaces—one for each tenant. By creating this new parking, I was able to raise the rents dramatically. The people who owned the building before me could have made the effort to provide parking for the tenants, but they prob-ably didn't think about it. I paid $3,000 to have the shrubs removed and the area paved with asphalt. But I got my money back in 12 months.

With real estate, there is the added opportunity to be inventive, to express some of your own thinking to improve your position. You don't have this option with stocks, bonds, savings plans, or any other types of investments I know of because you don't have control over them. But with real estate, an innovative idea can be a real boon. Let your ingenuity unfurl and creativ-ity soar, and the sky's the limit! This points to another great advantage to investing in real estate—it's not structured. Being successful in real estate requires experience, knowledge, education, and the guts to get out and do it. But there's no precise formula. Every piece of property is unique and requires a slightly different approach.

Stocks and bonds, which don't have this flexibility, cost the same regardless of who buys them. Moreover, the stock market is hypersensitive to world events and the national mood and will fluctuate wildly based on rumor, whereas the value of real estate is determined by local economic conditions that in areas like Los Angeles and Seattle are stable and consistently outperform the national average.

In the stock market, everything is standardized. You can't get someone to pay more for a given stock than what it's selling for. Stocks are also highly volatile. No one can predict the direction of the stock market. You can read a company's annual report and its latest financial statement, but you have no control over how that corporation is being run.

Information on the judgment and ability of the people who run the company you buy stock in is not readily available. Consider what happened with the collapse of the Enron energy company, which was once the world's largest wholesale energy merchant and its stock a Wall Street favorite. A series of bad decisions and accounting cover-ups by the company's management team and auditors left the firm bankrupt and put thousands of employees out of work. The company was accused of electricity price manipulation in California and executives of the company's accounting firm, Arthur Andersen, were indicted for obstruction of justice. In the wake of this corporate scandal, former Enron Vice Chairman John Clifford Baxter committed suicide and President Bush called for stiff new penalties for corporate criminals as well as a crackdown on boardroom scandals, and Senate Majority Leader Tom Daschle announced an "investor's bill of rights" plan.

A crisis of this magnitude demonstrates just how little the average investor knows about the internal operations of major corporations, even those that have a prominent media profile. When you invest in real estate, you can keep a much closer watch and maintain tighter control over your investment.

PRIDE OF OWNERSHIP

Qualitatively, real estate offers what property owners call pride of ownership. Property, besides having the potential for being converted to a higher and better use, can also be modified to the owner's personal liking. With real estate, you can build a monument to your own ego, acquire a lavish estate, or simply settle for having the nicest house on the block! Real estate is therefore an asset that can meet a specific personal need.

Real property, whether a residence, apartment complex, or a commercial or industrial building, is a tangible investment that you can touch, feel, walk around in—one that you can physically appreciate, in other words. Real estate, unlike stocks, bonds, and savings plans, can have sentimental value. Real estate is the only investment you can live and work in. Real estate has myriad values, only one of which is "use value" (see chapter 10).

RISK

What is the difference between a safe return investment, a speculation and a gamble? The amount of risk you are willing to take to get a return on capital. Often it is difficult to tell exactly when an investment ceases and a speculation begins, or when the speculation turns into a gamble.

Examples of safe investments include US government savings bonds, Treasury bills, and certificates of deposits of up to $250,000 insured by the United States government (Federal Deposit Insurance Corporation, or FDIC) till December 2011. High-grade utility and municipal bonds and high-grade corporate bonds also fall into the investment category.

Comparable ownership in certain types of real estate is every bit as safe as US Government savings bonds. Safe real estate investments include long term ground leases with well located buildings where the ratio of improvement (i.e., building) value to land value is four to one or higher. To illustrate, let's say that you own a land parcel which has a present fair-market value of $1 million and you have leased it to a developer for 99 years—but you have not subordinated the land to a construction loan. Subordination means moving to a lower priority, as a lien would if it changes from a first mortgage to a second mortgage.

If the developer constructs a $4 million building on the leased land (four to one ratio), the owner of the land (or lessor) would have an asset considered to be as safe as a government bond. If the ground rent is not paid, the $4 million building reverts to the landowner.

The annual yield or return on safe investments is generally very low compared to speculative opportunities. The rates of return on government bonds set by the Federal Reserve are based on market conditions. However, a secure real estate investment like the one described here can have many advantages that are not available to bond holders.

As a former real estate appraiser, I had the opportunity to appraise many commercial properties in Hollywood and downtown Los Angeles.

I often marveled at the one-of-a-kind clauses negotiated into long-term ground leases. Frequently, they benefited the present landowners at the expense of relatives who would inherit the assets.

One leased-fee interest I valued was an original 99-year lease on a 13-story department store building with 54 years remaining. The attorney who originally prepared the lease negotiated an extremely high net rental income for the first 50 years and inserted a clause that called for a significant decrease in rent over each remaining seven-year period. Today the ground rent on the subject property is by far the lowest rental per square foot of land area in downtown Los Angeles.

The original thought was that at the end of the lease term, the building would revert to the landowners, at which time the rental income from the whole property would become the landowners'. The original owners were more concerned about receiving the maximum rental they could during the first 50 years of the lease, rather than what they would leave to their heirs.

Today, many entrepreneurs consider a good real estate investment to be the purchase of a property that has potential appreciation, with a 6% to 8% net return on the cash invested. Central to the concept of risk, generally, is that the more return on the investment, the greater the risk. The more desirable the location of the property, the lower the risk return will be.

If the risk rate gets into the 15% range (the percent return on investment), the property is probably in the speculation category. Such properties include apartments, strip commercial centers and special purpose properties where collecting rental income is difficult. The purchase of vacant land in undeveloped areas can also be highly speculative. In my opinion, buying real estate with little or no money down is speculating, especially if you purchase property with a short-term mortgage with a required balloon payment for which you have no realistic way of paying off the lien before the due date.

During the real estate boom of 2001 through 2006, many investors went on buying sprees. They were betting on the future direction of interest rates and property appreciation without even knowing it. Loan companies were offering loan programs with short-term rates that were fixed for two, three and five years because they were told they could always refinance or sell before the loans adjusted to a higher rate. Many of these investment loans only required 5% down payments.

> I know because I was there, making loans and advising them not to over-encumber themselves. One client I had took his business elsewhere when I told him he should not take a two-year rate at 3.5 % but get his loan fixed at 5% for 30 years. The payment was about $140 higher but that meant a negative cash flow on his property.
>
> Years later he called me, wanting to refinance, but I could not help him because the loan guidelines had changed and interest rates were way higher. He lost that house as well as many others he bought out of state.

Gambling is by far the riskiest means of money handling. You can place your capital on the black and in a couple of seconds you have either doubled it or lost it all. Relating gambling to real estate purchases seems remote. However, I can remember a friend buying two vacant lots facing the ocean on the island of New Caledonia and another acquaintance buying a lot in Florida, all of which turned out to be under water.

In both instances the property was not inspected before purchase. In my opinion both of these transactions were real estate gambles. Every real estate acquisition should have rewards commensurate with the amount of risk you are willing to take.

INVESTING IN IRAS VS. REAL ESTATE

Not long ago, a banker told me that if I were to invest about $140 a month into an IRA account, at the end of 25 years after all payments were made and nothing was taken out of the account, the total sum would be about $500,000. That would be a half million dollars in 25 years. Certainly that is a sizable sum of money. But if you figure inflation over the 25-year period, the $500,000 will probably buy you less than what $100,000 would buy you today.

Real Estate

Suppose, instead, you were to purchase a piece of real estate. I will use an example of a property that I bought in 1965 to illustrate this point. I paid

$1,000 down on the property. The total purchase price was $12,000, and payments were $95 per month on a private mortgage for 25 years, at 6% interest, until paid.

Today, my property is worth $900,000. The property also has tax shelter because it is income producing. When I bought it for $12,000 I allocated $11,000 to the building and $1,000 to the land. The building has given me many years of depreciation at $550 per year, which offset the income as taxable. It was a good tax shelter.

Now, when you have an IRA account you don't have any of these advantages. You don't have the advantage of being able to use the property, rent it or to change the use of the property. Real estate works out completely differently from the IRA account.

Many people say, "Well, if I had the IRA account and I did this for the 25 year period, I probably wouldn't spend the money." But suppose during the first 15 years of the IRA account, you had a financial crisis. You would be tempted to take the money out of the IRA even if you had to pay a penalty. Real estate is much harder to liquidate.

Benefits of Real Estate

One of the great advantages of owning real estate is that it is hard to sell. It may take a long time to do it. You have to have the right conditions and sometimes the right financing necessary in order to make a sale. So when people are desperate for money they usually look for another source to solve their money problems.

Of course, the main benefit to owning property is that if you buy in an area with growth potential, your property should go up in value. If you go out and research an area, analyze a community thoroughly and become familiar with a neighborhood and make good solid projections, you can find fantastic buys. This is what I have been doing for a long period of time and it has worked very well.

Stocks vs. Real Estate

Most people think that investing in the stock market is a good idea because "you can sell stocks within a day, but it takes a long time to sell real estate. You can have a property on the market for six months or longer." There is no way to gauge whether tomorrow morning the stock market is going to drop 200 or 300 points. But you do know that when you buy real estate the market doesn't drop dramatically over a day or two. It takes a while to see significant change in real estate prices.

One of the great advantages of owning real estate is that it *is* so hard to sell. It may take a long time to do it. You have to have the right conditions and sometimes right financing necessary in order to make a sale. So when people are desperate for money, they usually look for another source to solve their money problems.

Of course, the main benefit to owning property is that if you buy in an area with growth potential, your property should go up in value. If you go out and research an area, analyze a community thoroughly, and become familiar with a neighborhood and make good solid projections, you can find fantastic buys. This is what I have been doing for almost 50 years and it has worked very well.

Compared to stocks and bonds, property has a use value that financial investments can never have. I believe that after 25 years, real estate is far more valuable because you can live in the property, accommodate family and friends, or reap the benefit of income off the property. Cash investments offer none of these advantages.

Drawbacks

I realize that if you sold the property after 25 years you will have to pay a capital gains tax. Consider over all how I only put $1,000 down and then never again having had to take out of pocket costs to maintain the property as the $150 monthly rent provided sufficient cash flow to cover maintenance expenses, real property taxes and insurance, etc. As the property became more valuable, the rental income increased from $150 to $2,500 a month.

We had to manage the property, but this seemed worthwhile because of the improvement in the neighborhood over time. The community helped to make this property a valuable and unique purchase, which helped to keep it rented for a long time.

Real Estate Can Parallel the Stock Market

In 1929 Joseph Kennedy, father of John F. Kennedy, was heavily invested in the stock market. Joe Kennedy was familiar with what was going on in the world at that time. He foresaw the coming depression of the 1930s. He sold many of his holdings short, thereby making millions and millions of dollars while most people in the market went broke. The stock market took an extremely heavy loss, yet for real estate the average loss was about 30% of its original high value over a period of about five to six years. When you consider that buildings depreciate through physical, functional and economic obsolescence, the loss in real estate value was not so severe.

In January 2000 the stock market set a record high, with the Dow Jones Industrial index reaching 11,722, because prosperity in the nation had experienced steady growth due to a positive economic forecast, job creation, low interest rates, low unemployment and other positive indicators. Then, in a major market correction owing in large part to the dot-com implosion, but other factors as well, the stock market dropped sharply over several months. Nationally, we've been in a bear market ever since. Real estate value is vulnerable to the actions, attitudes and thinking of people, but only in *specific geographic areas*. One area of the country could be very good for real estate investing at a given time while another area could be very bad.

But, providing you're on the right side of the transaction, money can be made even in an environment of declining real estate values. For example: In 1989, a house sold for $800,000. The seller then leased the house from the new owners for $3,000 per month. After three years the seller was ready to move out of the house. In 1992 real estate prices took a severe drop, and when the buyers came to California they found that the market value of the real estate had dropped so dramatically, that they abandoned the property and it went into foreclosure and was ultimately sold to the original owner for $350,000. That is $450,000 less than what he sold it for. So in effect the original owner who sold the property for $800,000 bought it back for $350,000. That would be a comparable situation in the real estate market to Joseph Kennedy's performance in the stock market.

Selling short in real estate is a different process than in the stock market, but the concept is still the same. The most important thing is timing. If you buy the property at the right time then you can be almost assured that you are going to make a substantial profit when you sell. If you buy the property at the wrong time, it could be a disaster. It doesn't matter whether it's the stock market, real estate or any other type of investment. If you severely overpay, you could get hurt.

One Astronomical Investment

The Fidelity office building in downtown Los Angeles, on the corner of Sixth and Spring Streets, was sold in 1928 for a reputed $3.5 million. It was completely occupied, with offices on the upper floors and a bank on the ground floor. The building was in good condition and in the financial district of downtown Los Angeles.

Around 1932 the building was almost completely empty because so many businesses had gone broke. The owners who purchased the building for $3.5 million could not make the payments on their loans; therefore the building went into foreclosure.

Around 1945, immediately after the war, the building was purchased for about $1.2 million. Within the next few years, the building was fully occupied with higher rents than in 1928. The economy did a good job in increasing the total income due to the dramatic need for office space immediately after World War II.

Any office space in downtown was renting at a premium. So the people who bought the property in 1928 couldn't hold on to it after the depression and the new owners came in at a much lower purchase price and made an astronomical investment because they had the opportunity to rent the office space that was available due to the tremendous post-war demand.

My Recommendation

In my opinion, a young person should invest in an IRA for five to ten years. Then consider transferring the IRA funds into a down payment in real estate, which has capital appreciation capabilities over a long period of time to further enhance wealth for their retirement years. Do your homework. The best thing to do is to study the market thoroughly before you invest. Be sure you are buying the right property at the right price and at the right time.

$1,000 PER MONTH FOREVER

How Much Is This Worth?

If someone said to you, "How much money would you pay today to receive $1000 per month forever?" This is not for years or for life, but into eternity. I asked this question to many of my students and received interesting answers. Many students think that it is impossible to put a price on the opportunity. One thought that $1 million might do it. Another person said, "Well, forever, you would run out of money."

If you think about it, it's not very difficult to realize that the interest derived from a sound investment could meet the requirement. The statement that the $1,000 per month will be received forever simply means that if you have a capital investment which returns a secured income and the investment is not eroded by time, the interest return will last forever.

Suppose you invested $240,000 in a US Treasury bond that pays 5% interest per year. As long as the $240,000 remains in the safest investment there is and as long as the investment yields 5% interest, you'd earn $12,000 per year, or $1,000 per month. If everything remains constant, $240,000 will be required to yield $1,000 per month forever. Obviously the security of the investment and the interest yield on the investment are the key features governing the final result.

Why is this concept important for the real estate investor to understand? When you buy investment property the same thing happens. Let's say you made a real estate investment, acquiring a commercial property for $240,000. The $150,000 of the purchase price is allocated to the land, while the building has a value of $90,000 and an economic life of 30 years.

Let us further assume that the net income from the subject property, at the time of acquisition, is $15,000 per year. After accounting for depreciation, as described below, the real estate investment is yielding the same $12,000 annual return as the US Treasury bond. However, the real estate investment enjoys an added increment of value that the bond investment doesn't have. The subject land investment will theoretically produce an interest yield in perpetuity (forever).

In our example, $90,000 of the total $240,000 purchase price is attributed to the building and a 30-year remaining useful life is assigned. The additional $3,000 per year (the difference between the net income of the real estate and the bond interest) is net income required to compensate for the loss in the wasting asset (the building). $3000 per year for 30 years equals $90,000. Theoretically, this $3,000 per year is placed in a sinking fund or other interest bearing account, allowing the real estate investment to have adequate funds to replace the wasting asset (building) so that after 30 years the investment can continue on forever. In actual practice, oftentimes the real estate becomes *more* valuable over the theoretical life span of the building, provided the original real estate purchase is in a location that reflects economic growth.

In a capitalistic economy, inflation is inevitable. Yes, we can have disastrous economic turndowns or depressions, such as the 1932 era, as well as the recessionary period of the early 1990s and the dot-com bust of the present time. But while the economy experiences trials and tribulations, we can always be assured that inflation will prevail.

Real estate is a hedge against inflation. Certificates of deposit, savings bonds and other financial instruments are fixed asset accounts and are generally not affected by inflation, except to the extent inflation affects the interest rates applicable to such instruments. Real estate can be highly leveraged and the monthly payments of principal and interest pay down the loan with inflated dollars.

Consider the following example: In 1967, I purchased a four-unit property for $65,000. I made a $5,000 down payment and the seller carried back a first trust deed of $60,000, with payments of $300 per month, at 6% interest, with payments of interest only for the first 10 years. After the first 10 years, the trust deed began to amortize, with payments of $350 per month, at 6% interest until paid. There was no specified due date on the trust deed note. In 1997, the income from this property was $5,275 per month, and my payments were still $350 per month on the trust deed note. When I bought the property in 1967 the seller was very motivated to create a transaction, and I can remember how difficult it was to raise the $5,000 for the down payment, but look at the income flow now.

This is an excellent example of the contrast between the sellers investment on a fixed asset (the first trust deed) yielding $350 per month in principal and interest and my real estate investment, which was dramatically affected by inflation and other factors, which yield $5,275 per month without touching or eroding the principal investment (the property itself).

4

Setting a Realistic Objective

In *Alice's Adventures in Wonderland,* the Cheshire Cat says to Alice, "If it doesn't matter where you are going, then it doesn't matter which way you turn." Investing in real estate can be like a trip through the looking glass if you are not sure what you hope to accomplish. When it comes to buying, it is important to have an objective, even one that may eventually change over time. Everyone changes his or her mind at some point. That's not the important thing. The important thing is to have focus. The worst thing in the world is to go off on a hundred different tangents.

> *People who have concrete goals, even ones that are difficult to achieve, find they can keep their mind better focused on what they set out to accomplish. These are the people who, more often than not, turn out to be the great achievers.*

Before I became vice president and director of training and research for an international appraisal firm, I ran the Los Angeles office and held the position of district manager in charge of hiring. Now and again, somebody would come in and want a job as an appraiser. I would interview them and ask what type of appraisal work they could do. If an applicant would say, "I can do anything," I'd show him or her the door. Those are the kind of people you don't want. You want someone who has expertise in a particular field and who has decided what he or she wants to do.

Those who have a direction or goal and know what they want to accomplish are very fortunate, particularly if they know it early on. Lots of people in their twenties and thirties have no more idea what they want to do in life than the man in the moon. Ask them what they can do, and, like the would-be appraisers I used to turn away, they'll say, "anything." Those are the kind of people who have difficulty being successful.

When you go to college, I think it's important to know what you intend to learn and what you hope to get out of it. Likewise, when you buy a piece of real estate, it's important to look at it as a vehicle to accomplish some objective. Do you want to make a million dollars? Do you want to buy property for the long-term to ensure your security when you get old? Do you want to buy five properties in 10 years? Whatever your objective is, you should look forward to it.

Many buyers don't have a long-term objective when they acquire a residence, other than to live there and raise a family, which is an objective, of course. But if you broaden your definition of what real estate can do for you and buy with a definite goal in mind, you're going to be far better off than just buying on a whim because you will have a plan of action. If you can buy an income property in which you could house your business or otherwise use to enhance your situation, that would be a superb position to be in. The property will be twice as valuable in a sense.

Another reason for an objective is that it places your investment choices and decisions in long-range view. Investing isn't an end in itself. With a solid goal before you, it is easier to hold on to a piece of real estate over the long pull and actually realize the property's contemplated future potential than if you had no objective in mind and were enticed to sell the first time it rose in value. In addition to making a profit, practical real estate objectives could include:

- Using real estate as a tax shelter.
- Building an estate to leave for your children or heirs.
- Generating additional income through rental properties.
- Accruing a source of retirement income.
- Sending your kids through school.
- Accumulating equity to start a business.
- Acquiring property for philanthropic purposes with the goal of eventually donating your estate to a church, college, or charity.

- Having something to keep yourself occupied in retirement.

- Keeping your money safe from the ravaging and corrosive effects of inflation.
- Property rents and real estate asset values tend to rise with cost of living.

Regardless of your age and station in life, when first starting a real estate investment program, it is important to assess your needs and desires and to lay out a blueprint of how you want to accomplish your ultimate goal. A 65-year-old retiree with a substantial life savings and a lot of free time will have an entirely different objective than someone who is 25, single, and making $40,000 a year. If you develop a framework to act out of and adhere to it, the odds are in your favor that you will succeed.

If you acquire a good piece of real estate and build up substantial equity, you will be able to do many things. But, the reward in real estate is commensurate with the risk you're willing to take. You have to take a chance, but you have to take one that's in your favor. The thing you should never do is overextend yourself.

It shouldn't be a question of, "Well, let me think about it, and maybe I'll do it and maybe I won't." Once you begin your investment program, you can't be noncommittal or depend on someone to make your decisions for you.

Unfounded fears breed procrastination. After ten years of teaching seminars to students at all skill levels, I have heard all the excuses for why people don't act. As a matter of fact, I've said some of these things to myself:

1. Real estate will never come back.
2. I don't know how to get started.
3. I am going to lose all my money.
4. Interest rates are too high.
5. Prices are too high and are going down further.
6. It is hard to get a loan.

7.   I can't afford those payments.
8.   Too much negative cash flow.
9.   That property is too beat up.
10. I will never be able to rent it out.
11. I should have bought ten years ago.

The saying "courage is not the absence of fear, it is the ability to carry on in spite of it" is the truth. I just followed enough of Dr. Schumacher's teachings so I did not make too many mistakes.

A former student of mine, a moderately successful real estate broker, started his investment program with more dedication than money. With a small savings, he was able to purchase a house and, by buying in the right location, was able to trade up after a few years for a duplex. One by one, he acquired six properties. Recently, he consolidated all of his holdings into a brand-new 59-unit apartment building. He was able to make the down payment, decided to buy it, and focused on getting it rented. His objective is crystal clear. All he has to do is keep that building rented for the next 30 years and he'll be a multimillionaire, because he will be close to paying the mortgage off and the building will have appreciated to about $15 million by that time.

INCOME PROPERTY AS A TAX SHELTER

A shelter is created by a transaction that reduces tax liability by providing tax deductions or credits. Income property is one of the best ways to shelter your wealth. Many real estate investments can be set up to provide all of the income derived from a building tax-free and allow you to reduce other taxable income by showing a paper loss. This paper loss can be the result of allowable depreciation from the building.

If you sell investment real estate for cash or term financing, you are required to pay capital gains tax on your profit. Profit is defined as your property's tax basis at the time of sale subtracted from the adjusted sale price. The adjusted sale price is the total sale price of the property less certain allowable costs of sale. If gains are treated as capital gains, and not ordinary income, lower tax rates and certain exemptions may apply.

If you have saved your money over the years and built up a nest egg, you can make a real estate investment and expand the investment into a like-kind income property of equal or greater value by doing a 1031 tax-deferred exchange. The exchange becomes an extension of the original investment and, as long as you are trading up and don't take any cash out of the transaction; you can defer any tax on capital gains. If you have inherited a large amount of money and don't know what to do with it, real estate can provide a good tax shelter if you are property-oriented.

If you bought a commercial building that has a substantial long-term lease, you would have a tax shelter in the form of allowable depreciation on the improvements. If the property was in a growth area where the value would continue to rise, the purchase of an industrial building might be a good investment, provided you had or could find substantial tenants. The quality of tenants is extremely important. Triple A tenants, those with unquestioned financial strength, are the best.

BUILD AN ESTATE

When I started investing in real estate, I resolved that I wanted to make a million dollars by the time I was 50. It might have taken me a year or two longer, but I've since reached my mark and then some. And once you make your first million, it's easier to make your next million. My net worth now is several million, after 30 years investing in real estate.

I remember as a boy thinking about whether I'd ever be "rich." My mother used to tell me you have to think high to rise. She used to talk about a distant relative of ours who vowed not to get married until his net worth was $250,000. When he reached the $250,000 mark, he decided he wasn't going to get married until he made $500,000. Some people never think they're successful no matter how much they make.

> *The sooner you realize that there is no easy way to get rich, the better off you're going to be. If you are going to make money as a writer, you have to work tirelessly. If you are going to make money in your own business, you have to be committed. If you want to make it as an appraiser, you have to work at it. Similarly, if you want to make money buying and holding real estate, you have to realize that it takes knowledge, dedication, and hard work.*

There is no easy way to make money, and real estate is no exception. But the difference between real estate and other endeavors is that you can identify a long-range objective and know where you are headed. You can't live beyond your means and do this, however.

Nothing is greased on all sides. The advantage to investing in real estate is that you can continue to work full-time and invest in property on the side. Once you have your money in the right place, it grows for you. It's going in the right direction. I don't know of any get-rich-quick schemes that work, unless you figure out a way to win the lottery.

Trying to get rich quick in the commodities market brought me to this realization. I tried three different times over a period of four years before I realized that commodities were not for me. I even took night school courses studying the commodities market with brokers who were really well versed in it. I hired them as consultants to advise me on what to do. But I lost all my money in spite of that.

During this time, I had a job working as an appraiser. One day I decided that maybe I'd be better off putting my hard-earned money in real estate, a field I knew something about, rather than going for broke in the commodities market, which mystifies me to this day. So instead of going to night school to learn about commodities, I decided to redirect my efforts toward investing in real estate. My first deal worked out so well, I decided to continue buying.

Building an estate to leave for your children or heirs can be very advantageous for your family and a good way to get your kids started in life. Investing in real estate enables you to put property in a trust so that the children will have benefits when they reach a certain age.

JOINT TENANCY, COMMUNITY PROPERTY, AND TENANCY IN COMMON

When a piece of real property is purchased by two or more people, it is necessary to have a proper ownership deed to meet the needs and requirements of those participating in the transaction. Depending on the laws of the state you live in, there are three different ways to take title (legal possession) to a property—in joint tenancy, as community property, or as tenancy in common.

Joint tenancy is ownership by two or more people with the right of survivorship, or the right to acquire the interest of a deceased joint owner.

Upon the death of a joint tenant, the interest in a property does not go to the heirs but to the remaining joint tenant. When real estate in this situation passes into new ownership, it is assigned a stepped-up basis to reflect present market value. Depreciation on the improvements for tax purposes can then start over, providing the property is income producing.

For example, say a hot property in a booming area was purchased for $100,000. The owners, in this instance a retired husband and wife, hold on to it for 10 years, during which time the value swells to $500,000. Since they own the property as joint tenants with the right of survivorship, the husband has a $250,000 interest. When either spouse dies, the entire property will pass to the other without probate, as survivorship prevents heirs of the deceased from making claims against the property.

Assume the husband passes away. Under joint tenancy, the wife automatically inherits the husband's interest in the property. Although the property's former basis for tax purposes was $100,000 (with $50,000 allocated for each spouse), the wife's new basis now increases to $300,000—her $250,000 interest in the current market value of the property plus half of the old basis. For tax purposes, the wife can start taking depreciation on that stepped-up market value, the new $300,000 basis.

A different set of circumstances occurs when real estate is held as community property, which is defined as real and personal property accumulated through the joint efforts of a husband and wife after marriage, and owned by them in equal shares. This method of ownership exists in Arizona, California, Idaho, Louisiana, Nevada, New Mexico, Texas, Washington, and Wisconsin.

When a California couple decides to get a divorce, half of all the property acquired by joint effort during the marriage goes to the wife and half to the husband, regardless of which spouse earned a greater income or invested more money in acquisitions during the marriage. One of the advantages of living in a community property state is that when one spouse passes away, the surviving spouse receives a stepped-up basis on income property, which allows a greater tax write-off through depreciation.

In community property, the stepped-up basis is equal to the increased value of the whole property. If, for example, a house was acquired for $100,000 and the property is now worth $500,000, the stepped-up basis would be $500,000.

When a person who owns real estate as community property or in a tenancy-in-common arrangement passes away, the estate has to go through a probate process to establish the validity of the will. An estate consists of the total assets of the decedent. Probate is handled by a court administrator to ensure that all those involved in the will are treated fairly. When the residue of an estate is passed on to an heir or heirs, the estate must first pay inheritance tax. The court can then distribute the assets or sell the real estate. Probate takes one year, two years, sometimes longer.

Tenancy in common is ownership of real property by two or more people who hold an undivided interest without the right of survivorship. After the death of one of the owners, the deceased's share in the property is passed on to the party or parties designated in the will. Under this arrangement, all of the investors have to sign the deed in order for the entire property to be conveyed, but each tenant may convey his or her share independently. Real estate syndication groups, a method of selling property whereby a sponsor sells interests to investors, may take the form of a tenancy in common.

Placing your real estate into a living trust, family trust, or similar instrument alleviates the need for probate because the property is named specifically for the people in the trust. If you place your assets into a trust, you, as the trustee, hold the property for the benefit of another, the beneficiary named in the trust.

REAL ESTATE AS A SOURCE OF INCOME

Another goal that investing in real estate could accomplish is generating additional income through rental properties. Many people put their money in the bank and draw on Treasury bills or certificates of deposit. Whenever I received any excess income, I put it back into real estate. Every investor has different ideas and different needs. One person might buy a vintage automobile; another may start a new business. After losing all my money investing in the commodities market, I always thought the safest way to make money, and the safest place to put my extra income, was in real estate.

It is difficult to predict the amount of net income that can be generated from a multiple-unit income property. Generally speaking, the larger the building, the more cash flow it will produce if properly financed and managed. But, all factors being equal, the larger the complex, the more business-oriented you must be to turn it into a paying entity. Duplexes and small unit properties can be more casually managed by people who have other occupations and lack property management experience with larger unit buildings.

Obviously, financing is a key factor in determining cash flow—the money left over after subtracting all property-related expenditures from rental income. In addition to monthly mortgage payments, property-related expenses might include renovation costs, vacancy and credit losses, maintenance costs, taxes and insurance, and utility bills. If the property is free and clear of debt, it should produce an immediate positive cash flow.

If you own a heavily mortgaged income property in an area with growth potential, it could take seven to ten years—or more—for the rental income to be enough to carry the mortgage payments and pay all of the property-related expenses to allow you to realize a positive cash flow.

I would add that many people just getting into real estate think they can get positive cash flow right away. This is a BIG MISTAKE. It's not so easy most of the time, especially for newbies. If you are going to take on heavy leverage with very little of your own money in the deal, you are going to have negative cash flow if you have bought your properties in economically dynamic areas. High-job-growth areas mean high demand and usually push prices up much more rapidly than rents. Rental appreciation takes longer than price appreciation.

Dr. Schumacher urges patience and time to let your properties season and grow. However, I have had properties cash flow from day one. Here are four ways to help you find those positive cash-flow deals:

1. Buy the property well below market value. Less debt means lower payments.
2. Have a larger down payment.
3. Have the seller help you buy the house by having you put some of the equity on the sidelines through creative seller financing. Lower payments will help you until the rents catch up. More about this in later chapters.
4. Have a partner infuse cash into the deal for a share of the equity appreciation.

---

*M*any people have the idea of making a million dollars in their lifetimes. A young guy I once knew wanted to make a million dollars by the time he reached the ripe age of 40. Since California did not have a state lottery at the time, the only way he could see making his fortune was by *investing in real estate. So he figured out a way to acquire a fourplex with a low down payment and obtained a 15-year mortgage on it. He knew that if he paid off the mortgage, at the end of 15 years he would have a million dollars in real estate, which is every bit as good as cash.*

Sure enough, by the time he was 40, he had the thing paid off and owned an asset worth a million dollars. Had he not been structured in his activities, his story might have had a much different ending. But because he had a definite goal and knew to stay true to this course, he became very disciplined and figured out a way to do it. The best decision he made was to select a property in a growth area where a 15-year appreciation factor could be forecast with a degree of certainty.

L et me tell you about one of my college students. She used to attend the Church of Religious Science in Los Angeles and believed in the power of positive thinking. She once told me she was interested in making a lot of money, so she took a series of evening classes in positive thinking where the instructor taught her how to keep her mind active and focused on her objective at all times. To help visualize her goal, she bought a coin book that had a picture of a $10,000 bill printed on the cover. She then made photocopies of the simulated bill and pasted them all around her apartment. She had them in her living room, her bathroom mirror, all over the place. She also had her car painted gold and gold-colored carpet laid in the living room.

She did all this to condition herself to think only in terms of making money. Now, at the time I knew her, she had very little savings. But with this money, she went out to the desert and bought a large parcel of land with a partner, a very shrewd fellow. They broke up the property and started selling it off in small parcels. They did this until they had enough money to put a down payment on a dilapidated apartment building back in Los Angeles.

After sitting on their first apartment building and getting it to produce a positive cash flow, they started buying rundown 30- to 40-unit buildings in problem areas, old brick structures that the city was about to condemn. Because these brick buildings did not meet stringent earthquake requirements, they were able to purchase some of them for nothing down because the owners were concerned about their personal liability should a severe tremor occur.

Although these two started investing in real estate without much capital, they were conditioned to visualize a golden objective, and they took a chance. Today, they must own about 10 apartment buildings on the fringe area of downtown Los Angeles and they've since made all their buildings earthquake resistant. Together, they're probably worth about $25 million. Focusing on an objective and being persistent can pay off in incalculable ways.

Advantages of Rental Income

There are four levels of income:

1. Employee. If you are an employee and receive W-2 income, you are paid hourly and trade your time for money.
2. Self-employed. You may be self-employed but still have to be present to be paid. Doctors, lawyers and plumbers fall into this category
3. Business. The next step is if you have a business that generates revenue whether you are there or not.
4. Portfolio. This highest level of income is from assets that throw off income day or night.

One of the great benefits of having rents as income is that they are *portfolio income*. Income generated from an asset is income that you do not have to work for, and it poses some great tax advantages.

Rental income is tax shielded since the IRS allows interest, taxes, depreciation and any other expense having to do with the upkeep,

---

management and acquisition of your real estate investment. And there is no FICA or Medicare tax, either.

With no Social Security (FICA) or Medicare tax deducted, portfolio income has a savings of 15.3% compared to self-employment income or 7.6% if you are an employee. Check with your tax professional to see how it applies to you.

THE GENIUS OF BEING GOAL-ORIENTED

What is your definition of a genius? Most people think a genius is a special person who can come up with ideas nobody else can. My definition of a genius is quite different. A genius to me is a person who has the ability to clearly visualize the overall objective, someone who doesn't allow himself to be distracted by all the trivia of daily life. In other words, a genius can see and understand what the future result will be and avoid being bogged down by the unimportant details. If your objective is clear to you and you don't let the little things in life interfere with the ultimate goal you're trying to accomplish, you could be a genius, too.

A friend of mine recently asked if there was anything I did when I first started investing in real estate that enabled me to survive during lean times. I told him that the most important thing that kept me going was the drive to be financially independent and not have to rely on someone else to pay my bills.

One day my brother Paul and I discovered that there are only about 200 beach-facing lots in the entire city of Hermosa Beach. We reasoned that if we enjoyed the view from The Strand, the row of houses facing the beach, there must be other people who think it is worth something, too. With only a limited number of properties and few for sale, the demand was bound to push prices up over time.

After concluding that the area was unique, I decided that if I could buy a property on the oceanfront, regardless of what I had to pay, it would be an excellent buy—as long as I could live with the terms and my monthly mortgage payments. Once the area became saturated, those who wanted to live there would have to pay more because of the scarcity and uniqueness of the housing. I never lost sight of that even when property values started to rise. I was able to keep my focus because I like the beach and was aware of the potential appreciation. I started buying more property on the beach when, a few years later, it became obvious how good the market was going to be. If you can find a property you derive enjoyment from in an area with growth potential, you can't lose. In addition to having a good investment, I now have a place to live and for visitors to stay.

If I explained this concept to an auditorium of 500 people, I'll bet you there wouldn't be five people who would follow my advice. Most investors would probably agree that this is what they should do. But very few would act. Instead, a decade from now, they will be telling all their friends, "Well, ten years ago I should have bought that piece of property over there because now look what it's worth." With an objective, you won't regret missing opportunities like that. When they present themselves, you'll recognize how they can fit into your overall program and you'll act on them.

Throughout my investment career, though it's not as long or storied as Dr. Schumacher's, I invested in areas I liked. Those neighborhoods may not have been my first choices of where to live, but I liked the people who enjoyed living there. Most of them owned their houses.

If you rent to residents who are like the neighbors, you will like the people you manage. It makes managing properties fun for me.

Sounds pretty basic, doesn't it? But it is exactly those friendly and hardworking attitudes that make those communities desirable areas wherein people want to live. I could see the growth coming from a mile away.

COLLEGE EDUCATION

In the mid-1950s, I did an appraisal for a guy who bought a commercial property in Beverly Hills with the ultimate objective of providing money for his child's college education. When this man's son was born, the child's grandmother gave the boy $4,000 to be invested in an asset to further his college education. The father decided that, rather than putting this money into a meager trust fund, where the money would accumulate interest and the child probably would end up with about $50,000 at the age of 21, he would invest in a piece of commercial real estate.

The property was a single story retail store, which the father intended to use as a retail outlet for his printing business. The purchase price of the property was $40,000. He bought the property with a 10% down payment, or $4,000, and the seller carried back a first mortgage for $36,000. The interest rate on the loan was 6%, amortized (a constant payment of principal and interest) over 20 years.

The father negotiated the transaction whereby he purchased the property in his son's name through a trust where the father possessed power of attorney. The deal was structured so that the son, having a 100% interest in the property, owned it as an individual. The father then "leased" the property from the son. The "rental payments" were calculated to be sufficient to make the loan payments, as well as pay for the property taxes, insurance, and maintenance costs.

At the end of 20 years, the mortgage was paid off. During this time, the property experienced a tenfold increase in value, to $400,000. Clearly, the son had an asset worth considerably more than if his father had invested in an annuity. Not only was this property, which is owned free and clear, able to finance a top-flight college education, it also provided him with an excellent start in life. The $4,000 his grandmother gave him turned into a prized asset. This illustrates one of the many ways an ingenious investor can accomplish a worthwhile objective by using real estate as a means to achieve a desired end.

Another use of real estate to help underwrite a college education was demonstrated to me by a client of mine who had four daughters ranging in age from four to thirteen. Their father realized how costly it was going to be to send all of his daughters to college. So when the oldest daughter was fifteen years old, he visited the local university where he felt the children might be happy studying for their degrees and purchased a two-bedroom condominium within walking distance of the campus.

Over the next three years, he rented the condominium until his first daughter was old enough to enroll in college. In the decade that followed, the condo became a second home for his daughters during their college years. They could walk to classes without needing a car. Instead of charging rent, the father insisted that each daughter work part-time while attending classes to help make the mortgage payment. Their portion was still considerably lower than what renting their own apartment would have been. This program worked out extremely well for the entire family and, after the last daughter graduated with her degree, the father put the property on the market and sold it for about seven times the original purchase price.

PHILANTHROPY

I've known people who, because they are dedicated to their churches, buy property with the goal of donating it; others accumulate large sums and give to charity, to a children's hospital, or to cancer research. I had a friend who owned a large estate in Laguna Beach, California. When he was getting along in years, he decided to donate his property to the city for artistic and cultural activities.

He purchased the property because he liked the area and realized how valuable the property would be as a public asset and donation to the city. That was his objective. It worked out well for him because he got to use the house for the duration of his lifetime, and because the city owned the property, he didn't have to pay any property taxes. I did an appraisal for him segregating the value of the estate into five separate portions, allowing my friend to donate one segment of the estate to the city each year for five years. By doing this, he stayed within IRS limits for gift tax donations. It turned out well for everyone, and the city received the property after he passed away.

Another goal might be to set up a foundation, charity, or scholarship program to give something back to the community. I figured out a way to convert one of the properties I have into a very worthwhile use. The property consists of three small apartment units attached to a spacious four-bedroom house with a large living room, a dining room, and a patio area in the front. I want to convert this property, if I can, into a seven-bedroom, single-family residence with five bathrooms and one small apartment for a caretaker.

My plan is to transform this property into a charitable retreat for underprivileged Native American children. Eventually, I want to have it endowed in such a way that the property will accommodate a full-time, live-in housekeeper. I estimate that about 10 kids and three parents can spend weekends there. A different group could go each weekend on a cost-free basis. But right now I don't think the city will approve the use change. A few vocal homeowners in the neighborhood don't like the idea because they think it might lower their property values. I don't think it will adversely affect property values or the neighborhood. Eventually, this is what I am hoping to do. So that is a very practical objective that can benefit people through real estate. You don't have to be Andrew Carnegie to set up a charitable foundation.

OWNING AND MANAGING PROPERTY AS A RETIREMENT ACTIVITY

One of the main advantages to owning real estate, in my opinion, is that it gives you something to do in your old age. I think that is very important. When my father sold his business and wanted to retire, he bought a three-unit complex on Fountain Avenue in Hollywood. He bought this particular property because he liked the people who lived there and it kept him occupied. He would sit down and talk to the tenants for hours.

When he came home, I'd say, "So Dad, you went over there to collect the rent?" And he'd say, "Yeah" and then start telling me about all the problems everybody had. I'd ask, "Did you collect the rent?" And he would say, "Oh, I knew I forgot something." That property was a terrific thing for him. It kept him busy. On the other hand, he would have had nothing to do if all his money was in stocks, except to call his broker.

The three units my father purchased were very unique. Each was a two-bedroom structure. The unit in the middle had a bright, canary yellow kitchen. It was a beautiful paint job, but when you walked into the room, the color resembled that of a kindergarten playroom. We looked at it and decided we could never rent the place with a kitchen like that. But we put a sign up anyway and a lady came by who said, "You know, I've always wanted a kitchen that was bright yellow. I'm so happy. You don't know." That was funnier than a ham sandwich without the ham.

Debt Is a Wonderful Discipline

The truth of this title depends upon how you use and accumulate debt. If someone has 20 different credit cards and runs up debt on all these cards and has difficulty paying the bills, then I would say that that debt is a burden. I would consider a person who buys a Rolls-Royce or Ferrari and has a difficult time making the payments, to be debt-burdened also. But if an individual has accumulated an astronomical amount of debt, where the debt actually helps the person make money and achieve a long-term objective, then the debt can be most important.

Now there are all kinds of people who have debts. People acquire debts by getting divorces, by having to support their children or their spouses, or by being on the receiving end of a settlement that forces them to make payments. But if the debt is beneficial to the individual who is paying it, it can be worthwhile.

As a mortgage broker who puts people in debt for a living, an author of a best-selling book on debt, and an investor who has used debt to buy millions of dollars' worth of properties, I know the discipline of debt well. When I promise to pay it all back, I will make those payments before I eat.

A mortgage—which literally means "death pledge" in Latin—is good debt because it is tax advantaged and is secured by an appreciating asset. People get in trouble when they take on too much of it without the means to pay it back.

I view real estate debt as a responsibility, not as a crushing burden, as many Americans do—such as those who live off credit cards and consumer loans. Borrowing a million dollars and having a tenant pay it back is the surest way I know to become wealthy because I know, like the title of my first book says, real estate debt can make you rich.

Staunch People in the Community

In the early 1950s a friend of mine got married and immediately started a family. He and his wife were doing quite well. Each had a job working in a restaurant. They purchased a home in the San Fernando Valley with 5% down. They could hardly make the payments, yet they went to the furniture store and told the sales assistant that they owned the house. The furniture company worked out a deal whereby the family could buy furniture to fill their entire home even though they could not afford to pay for it outright. It was amazing how they were able to accumulate this astronomical debt because they had a house. The furniture company figured they were staunch people in the community.

Have a Long-Term Goal

I believe that debt is a wonderful discipline if used properly. By that I mean that you can use debt to buy something where the objective is apparent and involves a long-term goal which you expect to accomplish.

An example of debt being a wonderful discipline would exist if you own a house that is worth $200,000 and this house has a $150,000 first trust deed on it. Now if you make the payments every month on the $150,000 trust deed, you continue to own the $200,000 house. If you don't make the payments on the $150,000, you are going to lose your house. With the $200,000 house, you are in effect being forced to make the payments and these payments are, in essence, a means of forced savings.

> Every time you make a payment on the house you are forcing yourself to save money because you are paying down the loan. You are increasing your equity and if the property is in a good location and with reasonable inflation, your net worth will increase dramatically over time.

Are You Used to Handling Debt?

If you are not used to handling debt, you have to be very careful when taking on debt. A friend of mine, many years ago, received a gift of $5,000 from a relative. She placed the money in the bank, but she was afraid that the bank would go broke. So she would go down there every day to see what was happening. It worried her and she became sick because she didn't know what was going to happen to the bank. Finally after a while she decided to withdraw all the money from the bank. She purchased a few items and then became happy spending the $5,000.

Managing Money

Lots of people do not know how to manage their money. Money is very important because the whole economy is based on it. If you don't know how to manage your own money, particularly if you go overboard in taking on debt and accumulate lots of bills and cannot pay them off, they swamp you, you become burdened and it can be disastrous. Many people are in that situation and it has the potential to destroy them. So you have to be very careful.

5

How National and Regional Trends Affect Real Estate Growth

This chapter begins our discussion of long-range forecasting methods. The first step in analyzing a given area's growth potential is to place it in the greater context of what is happening to the economy. The national economy and the actions of the federal government can have a profound effect on every usable piece of real estate in the nation. Therefore, it is useful to assess:

- Whether the gross domestic product (GDP) is in a growth mode or in a period of contraction.
- Whether the overall number of jobs is increasing or falling off and what the rate of unemployment is.
- Whether construction and home building on a nationwide basis is up or down.

By looking at these and other economic indicators, such as interest rates, you can begin to get a feel for the direction of various national trends important to the real estate market. And by studying past trends and cycles, it is possible to predict what will happen in the future. For instance, the US economy has endured 12 recessions since the end of World War II, but overall GDP (formerly GNP) has more than tripled despite these temporary setbacks. Real estate appraisers often look for this type of historical data to formulate their opinions of a property's current and future market value.

INFLATIONARY/RECESSIONARY TREND

If you acquire a good piece of real estate, such an investment will act as a hedge against inflation because it will increase in value with the inflationary trend of the overall economy. In fact, real estate values frequently increase much faster than inflation because of supply and demand.

The best time to buy a piece of property is when the economy has hit the depths of a recession and is about to start up again. If you can get in and hold out for two or three dips over a 10-year period, you'll probably be out of the woods, even if you bought for very little down and have relatively large payments. Recessions are hard on the economy, but land values in good areas can still appreciate because of inflation. After a recession, land values are almost always at a higher level. (In a depression, however, real estate prices tend to fall more rapidly than overall price levels.) As long as you can live with the terms of your financing, inflation should take care of the rest.

In a capitalistic economy, you can rest assured that inflation will exist because it makes it easier for the government to function. The government, which borrows money at the present rate through the sale of savings bonds, generally pays back its obligations over 10 years with soft, or inflated, dollars. Within this system, it always takes fewer of today's dollars to pay back yesterday's loans.

As Dr. Schumacher says, inflation rewards the debtor—the person who owes the money. But you need to live with the terms of your debt. Even sophisticated investors get hung up on this one.

One of my clients came to me wanting to refinance his properties in Sunset Beach and Huntington Beach as well as one duplex in Hermosa Beach. All of those Southern California coastal cities are in great locations, but his adjustable-rate loans were not so great. He had taken out negative amortization loans, where the payments can greatly increase if you are not careful. His payments were going to more than double in one month.

With these option ARMs, he had three choices: Make a payment that was fully indexed, one that was interest only or the minimum payment, which was artificially low. Unfortunately, for three years he chose the minimum payment, which caused his loan balance to go up by twenty percent.

> He had been trying for a year to refinance out of this loan that was going to blow up on him, but I could not help him since all that deferred interest ate up his equity. I never did hear back from him. Hopefully, his short-term focus on maximizing cash flow by taking an exotic loan will not do him in.

Real estate goes in cycles. Substantial downturns in the real estate market have happened at least a dozen times in my lifetime. But I'm not interested in the dips. It is more important to consider the long-term trend of the country. Will it continue for the next 20 or 30 years? Read the newspaper with your long-term objective in mind and don't get tripped up in all the minutiae. A genius is a person who has the ability to clearly visualize the overall objective, who isn't distracted by the trivia of daily life.

National economic trends are most pronounced when the country experiences some kind of major crisis, such as a war, recession, or depression. These developments are accompanied by dynamic forces that affect the market value of real estate. They create a change in the government's demands for resources and supplies, and they change the population's demands for goods and services. If the economy has a normal annual growth rate of 2% to 3%, that indicates an inflationary trend and a healthy growth pattern, in my opinion.

Inflation vs. Depression

A depression is hard on a lot of people, but over- or hyperinflation is a disaster for everybody. Even during the Great Depression, when there was 25% unemployment, some areas of the country still managed to do pretty well. I grew up in the 1930s, when things were at their worst, near an area in Los Angeles known as the Miracle Mile district, a stretch of Wilshire Boulevard between Fairfax and La Brea Avenues. This area was virtually immune to the nationwide economic crisis, and I witnessed this firsthand.

But, when you have inflation, it affects every person in the country because everyone's cost of living goes up while their buying power drops. Whether the economy is on an inflationary or recessionary trend, you have to be cautious and not overextend yourself. To ensure against any unforeseen adverse developments, you should have at least six months' cash reserve on hand to be able to make your mortgage payments and pay your bills. Your ability to withstand a tremendous recession is much greater if you do that.

> The water-view house we have in Laguna Beach is a wonderful example of a property holding its value in times of distress. During a market when the median house price declined 24% in Orange County, our little burg has held its own and even appreciated a bit. Some non-ocean-view houses in Laguna scarcely a mile away went down a lot, which underscores the importance of knowing your areas well.

Interest Rates

Interest rates are extremely important. The lower the rate, the more money there is available for construction and housing, and for economic activity in general, such as consumer spending. When the housing market is good, home building and buying surges, which in turn creates jobs. When houses are sold, it stimulates demand for hard goods, such as refrigerators, stoves, other appliances, furniture, carpets, drapes, and other long-term investment items. This type of spending helps boost the economy tremendously. (Soft goods, as opposed to hard goods, are items that wear out or are used up in a short period of time, such as clothing and apparel, foodstuffs, and other non-durable or perishable items.)

If you look at money as a commodity, when money is in short supply and harder to get, interest rates go up. Conversely, when there is a lot of money around and the demand or pressure is reduced, interest rates are lowered. It's a question of supply and demand. If you look at money as a non-durable good, as an essential item like bread, it becomes something you have to have. Everybody has to eat bread; otherwise, you're not going to have a balanced diet.

Now if all of a sudden, only half of the bread baked in America were to be available tomorrow, some people would invariably go hungry and their diet would suffer. In this circumstance, bread is going to become extremely valuable. Whether you like it or not, it will go up in price. In fact, the price of bread under these conditions is probably going to go out of sight. Again, it's question of supply and demand.

If, on the other hand, somebody bakes more bread than is needed there would be so much of it that you could find it lying on the street and could buy it for almost nothing. The same situation is true with money. So it is useful to think of money as bread.

When there is a slow real estate market and interest rates are low, it can be an optimum time to buy. When interest rates are high, like they were during the recession of the early 1980s, buying becomes more treacherous because of the unfavorable high-interest financing that is available. For people who are in a position to buy property, high interest rates are not necessarily a hindrance because they force sellers to be realistic. Of course, there is more activity when interest rates are low—much more. I think it's good to assess the condition of the economy but not to be too concerned about interest rates.

Real estate sales activity can't always be good. But a lull may depend on what segment of the market you are looking at. If one part of the market is bad, such as high-priced single-family homes in expensive suburban areas, another area, perhaps condominium sales in lower-priced urban locations, might be good. There is always a good segment, regardless of what interest rates are doing and regardless of the state of the economy.

Even if interest rates are high, the investor who is educated, knowledgeable, and shrewd can go out and still make money because he understands the problem and knows that certain sellers will always be motivated, regardless of the economic climate. If you have available capital and are familiar with your subject, there are very few situations where you wouldn't want to buy real estate, except if you could foresee a serious depression.

Another factor to consider is that at some time in a person's life, real estate might become a burden. Say a property owner passes away and the property goes into probate. No matter what the economy is like, the court must distribute the assets of the estate. If real estate is involved, it might be necessary to sell the property to pay inheritance taxes or satisfy other outstanding obligations.

POPULATION GROWTH

In one of my first real estate lectures in 1956, I predicted that "the trend is toward the Far East, with Los Angeles fast coming into its heyday." Just as the East Coast flourished when Europe was rich and powerful, so the

West Coast is now thriving as the economies, and population, of Pacific Rim countries intermingle with the western states. I don't claim to have a crystal ball, but my prognostication has come true. The handwriting was on the wall.

Over the past few decades, the migration of people from Asia, the South Pacific, and Mexico to the United States has never been more pronounced. A lot of Americans object to this. But I think this influx of population gives the United States a tremendous advantage. During the late 1800s and early 1900s, great numbers of European immigrants, including people from Germany, France, Italy, Great Britain, and Ireland, came to America. They were willing to come here and take a chance. They had the ideas, the stamina, and the foresight to do it. They helped make this country what it is.

The same is true today. I think people who migrate to the United States are those who are willing to take a chance, who have vision and foresight, and who are willing to work towards a new and better life than they had in their old country. And in putting their skills and ideas to work in new ways, they benefit our country. The difference now is that instead of Europe, the new immigrants are largely from Asia—namely Korea, Japan, Vietnam, Singapore, Indonesia, and the Philippines, the Middle East, India, and Mexico. Roughly half of the nation's population growth in recent years has resulted from increases in the Asian and Latino populations.

Many Americans are frightened by foreigners. People here think they are coming to take our jobs; I don't. In the 1980's, there was considerable concern about Japanese investment in the United States. Such developments led to sensationalistic trend stories where the sellers were charged, in effect, with economic treason. The headlines might as well read: "Oh My Goodness, Look What's Happening." In my opinion, foreign investment, as well as immigration, provides a tremendous infusion of new labor and capital to the economy and gives a tremendous boost.

The Immigrant Advantage

When considering the distribution of income and wealth in the US, another factor that should be taken into account is the sharp rise in the number of immigrants. The stock of international migrants (those born in other countries) in the US grew by nearly 10 million from 1995 to 2005, reaching a total of 38.5 million according to the World Bank.

In 1950, the population of the US was 150 million. Today, the latest census estimate for the nation is 301 million. People in America move around more than people in most other parts of the world.

We will be 400 million strong by 2040 and 600 million strong by 2060.

The top-ten cities a hundred years ago would have included places like Baltimore (now at 631,366, the nineteenth largest), Boston (590,763, twenty-second), Cleveland (444,313, fortieth) and St. Louis (347,181, fifty-second).

Los Angeles, the nation's second-largest city with 3,849,378 people, had a population of just over 100,000 in 1900. Dallas, Houston, San Antonio, San Diego and San Jose, California, all had fewer than 100,000.

Phoenix, which a hundred years ago was not even among the 100 most-populous cities, grew by more than 40,000 residents during the twelve months that ended July 1, 2006. It passed Philadelphia, which has lost about 70,000 residents during the 2000s, to become the fifth-biggest American city.

Far into this century, in the future, these Sun Belt areas that are absorbing the bulk of the nation's domestic immigration and attracting foreign immigrants looking for better lives will be the boomtowns. As long as the water problem is solved, these areas will more than double in population, become more urbanized as population density unfolds and become America's future beacons of economic prosperity.

As more and more people move to the United States, the population density will increase. The fact is that we live in a vast country. We have miles and miles of desert land that can be converted to productive, habitable uses as long as there is an adequate water supply. The United States still has a relative abundance of raw land and natural resources that can accommodate a tremendous amount of people.

But population density doesn't necessarily create wealth. Think of India. With roughly 600 people per square mile, India is one of the most densely populated countries in the world. In the United States, population density averages about 60 people per square mile. When you have people come into a community who are industrious, who have the ability to do things, and who may have a little bit of money, then you are creating wealth. Population alone can be a detriment, but population combined with industry creates wealth.

Japan has been successful because of its industry. But that country has a very rigid economy. A handful of people at the top of the government oversee all of the industries, and they decide what is best for the country. One of the reasons Japan has been an economic success is that industries are integrated there, and a small group of people has the authority to tell the rest of the citizenry what to do.

That explains why they have such severe trading and immigration laws. But as a consequence of this, Japan doesn't have the infusion of new energy and ideas that we get from people who immigrate to the United States. In countries that are controlled from the top down, people are told what to do more than anything else. In America, people are allowed to think. They are allowed to participate. They are given the opportunity to, for example, invest in property and build an estate.

Despite all the hoopla about the Japanese's ability to save, they still are nowhere near as well off as Americans. The average person living in Japan has a much-lower standard of living than the average American because they do not have the distribution of wealth or the natural resources that we do. Most of the land in Japan is not arable. Their opportunities, their housing, their way of life are all compromised.

We read in the newspaper how we have slums and a growing number of poor, but the middle-class is what really makes America the great power that it is. And the American middle class lives in superb luxury compared to the rest of the world.

Our inflationary economy makes it relatively easy for wage earners to buy big-ticket items on credit. If you have a job and make $40,000 a year, you can buy a new car without making a large down payment. You can buy a new house and you only have to put a modest amount down on it. If you wanted to furnish the house, you can go to the furniture company and say, "Look, I've got a brand-new car. I've got a brand-new house. I'm a success. Why don't you loan me some money to buy the furniture?" And, if you have a good credit history, they will.

I've traveled all around the world, from Africa to Eastern Europe, from South America to remote destinations in the South Pacific. Citizens of other countries can't get credit like we can here in the United States. In fact, it is easier to obtain credit in the United States than it is in any other major industrialized country I know, easier than in Canada, Australia, Germany, France, Japan, or Great Britain.

If the United States nullified some of its antitrust laws so companies could work together and do research and development to their mutual benefit, they could take on competition anywhere. Companies together can do some pretty remarkable things. But when they are hampered in ways industries in other countries are not, that can tip the scales.

Many people think our antitrust laws are obsolete. I tend to agree. We're dealing in the world arena now, not just on a domestic front. Leading corporations such as GM, AT&T, and IBM are tailoring their products and services to meet the needs not only of US customers but international clients as well. But with so many restrictions on business, corporate America has a hard time keeping pace with the rapid changes in the world economy.

I have great faith in America. It's a wonderful place to live. Of course, we have our problems, but if you travel to other continents, you'll find that most countries have it a lot worse than we do. Why do you think people from around the world want to live here?

Many people are frightened by the national debt, the sum of all the debts that the government has amassed. Yet the gross domestic product of the United States is about $10 trillion. Plus, if you were to calculate the present market value of all the assets the federal government owns, you would arrive at a figure also in the trillions. This puts the national debt in proper context.

The federal government doesn't do its bookkeeping like a business or individual would. How do you measure the market value of Yosemite National Park, Yellowstone, or Glacier? You can't measure the value of these national treasures. Even the assets that can be measured—public housing, military bases, millions of acres of land not a part of the national park system—all of this is valued and on the books according to the cost at the time of acquisition or construction.

In the depths of the Depression, when Franklin Roosevelt came to power and implemented his New Deal, he took the government off the monetary standard and switched it to gold. Roosevelt maintained that we have to spend money in order to be successful, so he created national workforces.

He created Conservation Corps around the country so that when people couldn't find jobs, the government would give them something to do. They built a lot of construction projects for public uses, including state capitals, schools, library buildings, universities and cultural institutions. Instead of putting people on welfare, the idea was that they would work on these various projects, be paid by the government, and eventually these projects would be publicly beneficial, which is exactly what happened. Public works projects on that scale aren't being undertaken much anymore. Yet this type of federal spending is extremely important. It is the kind of thing that makes America strong.

The construction of the Grand Coulee Dam on the Columbia River, the largest concrete structure in the world, was extremely costly and time consuming (construction lasted from 1933 to 1942) because it is situated on difficult terrain. But once the Grand Coulee was up and operating, the arid land of the Columbia River basin in Washington state became a blooming oasis. In addition to being an enormous source of hydroelectric power, that dam now provides a water supply for the irrigation of over one million acres of land previously used only for dry farming and grazing.

The Hoover Dam is another example. Located on the lower Colorado River on the Arizona-Nevada border, the Hoover Dam is one of the most efficient electricity-generating plants in the country, providing water for domestic, industrial, and municipal use as well as creating the largest artificial lake in America, Lake Mead, which is now used for recreational purposes. It is very difficult to put a dollar value on these types of assets, yet they create astronomical wealth.

The Grand Coulee and Hoover dams have turned desert lands into fertile areas, creating thousands of jobs and enhancing the economies of entire state and regions. The dams have also created wealth in the form of produce and other crops that can be sold around the world. Many people regard public works projects such as the Grand Coulee and Hoover dams as the unsung heroes of World War II. The electricity generated from these power plants provided energy for building warships, cargo vessels, ice-breaking ships, aircraft, rubber and metal products, and a host of other materials necessary for the war effort.

Other public works projects, such as boat harbors, rural electrification systems and highways also create value. Any well-planned public transportation project is bound to enhance value. The ability to move goods, services, and people is very important to the economy. From an investment standpoint, the important thing about public works projects is to analyze whether they are prompting change in a positive direction. Buy real estate when you can be assured of change in a positive direction and when you know that the subject property will be in the path of growth.

I believe the nation's railroad systems will be improved over the next 10 to 20 years. Similarly, during the Eisenhower administration, the freeway systems were improved with the passage of the Federal Aid Highway Bill. If rail systems are upgraded throughout the country, it will create more mass transit, and that in turn will create value. In Los Angeles County, the county assessor has started to assess the properties located near the new Metro rail subway stations at a higher rate than normal. The assessor's office recognizes how the Metro rail project increases the value of the sur-rounding properties.

The construction of highways, freeways, and railways affects housing prices because it provides easier access to more areas. When you have a shift in transportation activity, it creates tremendous value. But property can also lose value if there is a negative impact from that shift. Look at all the little towns along old Route 66, which stretched from Lakeshore Drive in Chicago to Ocean Park Boulevard in Santa Monica. Many of these towns were doing superbly before they put an interstate in. All of a sudden a good number of them went bust.

Aerospace spending is extremely important because space is unlimited, and we can explore it literally from here to eternity. That explains why the space station is so important. To distinguish between space and defense, space exploration is not like the defense industry. You don't get your money back from building war machines. But you do get your money back from space exploration, maybe not in dollars, but in other ways because the sci-entific and medical experiments the astronauts conduct in space improve our living conditions and ability to do things on the ground.

I remember when the astronauts' main mission was to take pictures of Earth using infrared photography from various points in space. By analyzing the photographs, oceanographers discovered a barrier shelf just beyond the Gulf of Mexico that prevented fish from getting into a huge area of about 500 square miles. So a project was initiated to remove part of that barrier so fish could get into the giant feeding area. This one action, by the added fishing it allowed, created hundreds, if not thousands, of jobs and fed hundreds of thousands of people.

Free-Trade Agreements

The North America Free Trade Agreement (NAFTA), which phases out tariffs and restrictions on most goods and services traded between Mexico, Canada, and the United States, is having a tremendous effect on real estate. In my estimation, it will continue to have a positive economic impact on the border states of Texas, New Mexico, Arizona, and California. The easier it is for businesses to move back and forth across the border, the more economic activity will be generated within those states. And with more business activity comes more employment opportunities, increased population, and overall prosperity. Once average income levels start to rise, real estate values will increase because people will demand a higher standard of living.

Attitude Toward Taxation

To my way of thinking, the move toward higher taxes destroys incentive. I think that what must be done on a macro level is to curtail government spending. I think that no matter how much money there is, for Congress it will never be enough. And I think the more you give to Congress, the more it will spend, and the more it spends, the deeper we will get in debt. It's really disturbing when Congress raises taxes but doesn't cut spending. Like they say, a penny saved is a congressional oversight.

Higher real property taxes remove the incentive for people to buy property in an area. That is one of the reasons why I recommend acquiring existing housing in an established area; there is no guarantee people and jobs will move into a newly established area, especially when taxes are higher due to financing all of the new roads, facilities, and public buildings.

One of the best things about our tax system is that it keeps the money supply circulating. A person can make all the money possible while living, but after death, the government claims most of it through inheritance tax. If you make a tremendous amount of money and are put into a higher bracket where the taxes are severe, you might not like it, but that also puts money back into circulation for others to make. The tax system also encourages the creation of charitable trusts, endowments, scholarship funds, nonprofit foundations, and other innovative financial vehicles.

As money recirculates through the economy, a growth pattern occurs as new money becomes available. The big problem in many developing countries, such as Brazil and Argentina, is that a tiny fraction of the population controls virtually all of the wealth. There are only minor tax laws on the books, doing little or nothing to mitigate this fact. Few developing countries have a substantial income tax or inheritance tax.

So the elite continue to inherit money from their families, and they are the only ones who can afford to attend college and become well educated. Because they know more, they continue to drain the country of all its wealth and the weak tax laws ensure that the wealth will never be evenly distributed among the people.

COST OF GOVERNMENT

The more you take out of the gross domestic product and invest to stimulate growth, the more long-term prosperity you can expect in return. So if the government is spending a lot of money on public works projects and private/public partnerships, that activity is inevitably going to stimulate the private business sector and create more opportunity.

The effect of an increase or decrease in spending depends on what the government is spending the money on. If the government spends money on housing and employment programs that people can use to elevate their position, they are likely to benefit the economy. If, on the other hand, money allocated for social services is distributed in the form of handouts to people who then squander it, then I don't see how it benefits the economy or even really helps the people it is designed to assist.

If the government were to spend less money for nonessential services, services that don't enhance the community, and more on projects that add to community growth, that could be very advantageous. It's easy for the government as well as individuals to spend money in the wrong places. If you or anyone else who invests capital puts it in the wrong place, it isn't going to do anybody any good, and the government is not immune to that.

At the regional level, some states have strict rules governing what public funds can be allocated for. The tidelands (coastal regions) in Long Beach, California, are a great example. The City of Long Beach was able to buy the Queen Mary, build a surrounding break wall, and set up the storied ocean liner as a tourist attraction largely through the use of tidelands money—profits that came from oil wells located in the tidelands.

Fortuitously, the Long Beach City Council was prevented by state law from taking those monies and depositing them into the general fund. They had to be spent from whence they originated. Over time, the city accumulated a huge fund and was able to buy the Queen Mary and spend all the money necessary to convert it into an attraction. By spending the tidelands money wisely, the city council enhanced the city's reputation and attracted new business to the community by acquiring an asset that is known worldwide. Strategically, it was a sound move. Such thoughtful public investments greatly enhance land values in the surrounding area.

FEDERAL PARTICIPATION IN HOUSING

Subsidized Housing Programs

Subsidized housing programs are intended to improve the living conditions of people with moderate, or minimal, means. The general problem with housing programs is their political nature. The billions spent on these projects address only one aspect of the total need—shelter. Other considerations should include the development of community services, education, and employment-assistance programs to improve the outlook and socioeconomic position of the recipients who occupy these buildings.

The sad part of subsidized housing programs is that these building projects often become slums. Typically, public housing developments are in the downtown district of a city or in low-income areas. The theory behind most public housing projects is to provide adequate shelter for people of moderate means to help get them on their feet and find jobs, thereby contributing to the local economy and helping to improve the city. However, it often doesn't work that way.

In many major cities, housing projects have become havens for drug dealing and gang activity. It's terrible, but it doesn't have to be this way. In Philadelphia and other cities around the country, tenants are starting to organize with the goal of buying back the public housing buildings they live in from the city with funds from the federal government.

In St. Louis, several families recently united to reclaim a public housing project that was virtually destroyed over the years by tenants who had no concern for the property. The building in question was originally built as part of an urban renewal project in the 1960s. These families asked the government for help in clearing out problem tenants and rehabilitating the building so that responsible tenants could once again enjoy living there. They then created a board of directors and picked new tenants who agreed to follow the rules. Those who didn't adhere to the new guidelines were kicked out. The building association enforced their conditions to the letter of the law and in a very short time turned a once woebegone project into a desirable place to live.

If the government invests in a lot of subsidized mass housing projects, it generally does not improve the growth potential of the surrounding real estate because of this pattern of neglect. However, smaller subsidized housing projects—for instance, housing for senior citizens—may enhance a community. If new housing is built in an old residential area, it generally improves the neighborhood.

Regardless of income, how people live is a matter of mental attitude. The condition of the beach in front of the property I own is a matter of mental attitude. If the hordes of people who visit the beach every weekend during the summer leave garbage on the sidewalk and throw their trash in the sand, pretty soon the beach would look atrocious. This is exactly what happens every Memorial Day and Labor Day—the beginning and end of summer. Fortunately, county maintenance crews come by the next day and rake the sand clean with giant tractors. Concerned residents pick up the rest. Yet, if people's attitudes were different, this effort and expense would be unnecessary.

Once, while visiting Leningrad (now St. Petersburg), Russia, I took a stroll on a Sunday afternoon through a park adjacent to the Neva River on my way to a sightseeing trip. People were sprawled out everywhere in this park, sitting on the grass and having lunch. When I came back at night, you couldn't even tell that the place had been used. There wasn't one speck of trash anywhere. Now if this had been a weekend at the beach in front of my apartment complex, you could imagine how the place would have looked. It's all a matter of attitude.

Insured Mortgages

The federal government, through the Federal Housing Administration, or FHA, insures many types of home mortgages by providing mortgage insurance to private institutional lenders for construction and home loans. The FHA charges the borrower a 0.5% annual premium on the average outstanding loan balance to insure the lender against loss. If a mortgage is insured by the government, the lender is assured that its money is safe and will be repaid. This enables the bank or savings and loan association to borrow against this secured asset, thus allowing future growth.

To ensure liquidity, most institutional lenders package their mortgage loans along with other mortgage loans and sell them to the secondary market, namely, the Federal National Mortgage Association ("Fannie Mae"), the Government National Mortgage Association ("Ginnie Mae"), and the Federal Home Loan Mortgage Corporation ("Freddie Mac"). Portions of these loan commitments are then sold as securities to the public, backed by a guarantee from the US Treasury. The lenders, in turn, get their money back and are able to offer it for other people to borrow. In this way, a steady supply of money remains available for future transactions.

Mortgages that do not meet government requirements are not insurable. Second mortgages usually aren't insured by the government because they are a junior lien to the first mortgage and typically involve very little collateral. As such, they are a far riskier investment. Because they aren't protected, uninsured mortgages and second mortgages command a higher interest rate than insured mortgages. Private-party mortgages from so-called hard moneylenders also fall into this category.

Money Supply

If the government is a machine and the economy its engine, money is the grease that makes its operation possible. The supply of money is vital to economic activity. Fluctuations in entrepreneurial activity due to the availability of financing affect the health of the economy nationwide.

The money supply is determined largely by the actions of the Federal Reserve Bank through the buying and selling of US Treasury securities. The Federal Reserve Board controls the fluctuation of prime interest rates, which in turn determine consumer lending rates. Interest rates in large part influence economic growth. High interest rates tend to restrict expansion while lower interest rates typically stimulate economic activity.

Dr. Schumacher comments on how national trends affect local investment. Much that deserves commentary has happened since he first wrote those words. Many changes, which have affected the real estate market both nationally and locally, will affect where you invest and also underline the wisdom of the buy-and-hold philosophy.

The National Debt

First, the national debt has tripled from around $3 trillion in the early 1990s to over $10 trillion as of this writing. The national debt was held to under $1 trillion until the early 1980s. If deficit spending continues at this pace, besides being highly inflationary, more government revenues will go to interest to service the mounting debt burden. In addition to the increasing legacy costs of Social Security, Medicare and other health care for an aging population, there will be less money available from the federal government to help cities grow their infrastructures.

Be very aware that cash-starved governments look at property owners as revenue sources.

Cities That Overspend

It is important that the local government in the state where you invest remains solvent. You have to watch out for local and state governments that have stayed within their budgetary restraints, especially when several cities have gone bankrupt in recent years. If you are in a city, county or state that is tax starved for revenue, you as a property holder may be in for higher property taxes, income taxes, business license fees and the like. The roads may not get patched and the police and fire departments may be understaffed.

Sometimes front yards can double as graveyards for broken-down cars, appliances and who knows what, all partially obscured by waist-high weeds. Postal workers won't deliver mail because the streets are in such bad shape. Cities such as these can undergo Chapter 9 bankruptcy, the municipal cousin of Chapter 11 bankruptcy for corporations. New York City and Vallejo and Orange County, California, are just a few of these municipalities that have had problems in the past.

Future problems will exist for other cities as they try to deliver on the salaries and benefits negotiated with public-employee labor unions. And some states, few of which are accumulating financial resources sufficient to fulfill pension promises they have made to their employees, will be looking to raise property taxes to combat their budgetary shortfalls.

One of the cities wherein I bought several houses was not insolvent but had problems before I bought there. It was a transitional neighborhood in a bad time of the California real estate market—the early 1990s. I knew I was investing in a tough area on the mend and mine happened to be the last drug house on the block. The area had just gone through a tough time.

But following Dr. Schumacher's guidance, I talked to the neighbors, the police department and other local investors to see about the growth arc of that neighborhood. That was when I found out that city's police coverage of that area was woefully lacking because of the city council's apathy and budget cutbacks. Local gang activity had produced an environment wherein stolen cars were brought in to be stripped on darkened avenues and pushers patrolled the streets to guard their territory. In addition, a large amount of residents were welfare recipients.

Normally, I would have been scared stiff to invest there but I knew change was in the air because everybody's attitude had shifted. In an area that was mostly rental houses, the owner occupants had had enough. They called for a series of meetings with the newly elected mayor and the police chief. Over time, new street lights were installed, more police cruisers patrolled and the city allocated more resources to clean up this trashy area. It helped that property tax revenues were increasing since local property values were on their way up.

The house that I cleaned up helped the neighborhood show more pride of ownership. It is safer, with no drug houses and no vagrants walking up and down the streets. All it took was a shift in city resources, more tax revenue and local residents getting fed up.

But don't try to be a one-man beautification committee and try to change the neighborhood by yourself. Neighborhoods undergoing transition take time to come around, so you need all the help you can get.

REAL ESTATE VALUE
AND THE ECONOMY

When you invest in real estate, you are buying the present worth of *contemplated future benefits*. This means that you are looking into the future and assuming what the world will be like or what you will be able to do with this piece of real estate over the period of time that you own it. In other words, as you see it today, contemplated future benefits means that you will one day have those financial benefits that you project to be buying now.

Measure of Market Value

Real estate is heterogeneous; no two parcels are exactly alike. You could subdivide the Sahara Desert into large tracts of land and one would be worth more than the other because it would be closer to the equator or closer to the Mediterranean Sea or whatever. But it is ridiculous, of course, to make an assumption like that.

But since no two parcels of real estate are exactly alike, there is no true measure of market value of real estate. Every time there is an economic event or an unusual development, it can affect the market value of real estate. But there is no way you can measure it exactly because real estate, being unique and influenced by the prevailing conditions in a specific geographic area, restricts the market value of a property to a specific location.

Real Estate Is Negotiable

When you buy and sell real estate, it is a negotiable item because there isn't any proof that the market value is established. Market value is the present worth of contemplated future benefits to be derived from that piece of real estate. Present worth means how much you would be willing to pay today to receive contemplated benefits from that property over the long period of time that you would own it. Now because there are very few sales of comparable, let alone identical properties, this becomes a negotiable asset and everybody has a difference of opinion as to how these benefits would affect them. That is why the price cannot be truly established or accurately measured.

The value of real estate depends on market conditions and how they will influence the subject property. When investing, it is important to be cautious and do a thorough analysis of whatever you are contemplating to invest in.

Buy-and-Hold Strategy

The *buy-and-hold* strategy is extremely important in this because by taking a measured approach to investing, a person will study a neighborhood and contemplate how future actions of the marketplace will affect the economic status of the neighborhood.

It is extremely important to understand this. Neighborhoods change dramatically, either advantageously or detrimentally, depending upon the type of activity occurring in the neighborhood. The capital appreciation of real estate is affected by the surrounding community and the actions, attitudes and thinking of people. People can create and destroy value. Property must be analyzed from the standpoint of the neighborhood, the economy of the community, the growth factors and all those elements that have an effect upon the total appreciation of real estate within a community.

LET INFLATION WORK FOR YOU

The United States of America, one of the most dynamic economies in the world and a capitalistic country, would not be able to survive if we did not have inflation. Inflation is the key to economic growth and prosperity.

Start Early

The important thing for a young person who wishes to retire with adequate wealth is to think about inflation as early as possible. Young people should understand and make investments in things that act as hedges against the inflationary trend. For example, the other day I had an opportunity to talk to a friend whose young boy, Charlie, is seven years old. Charlie is interested in collecting stamps. He is also thinking about his future.

Inflation-Proof

I had the chance to outline to the boy how he could become independently well off when he retires after a lifetime of labor. I suggested that the young boy, even at the early age of seven, become interested in items that are inflation-proof. For instance, when I was a kid I used to collect stamps, first-day covers, and coins. I believe that a young kid today should collect, say, gold coins, whenever he can get some or even just one, and put the coins aside as an inflationary measure. The important thing is for him to realize that *gold or even silver coins, because of their scarcity and their demand,* will go up in value as long as inflation exists in our country. Other items such as precious jewels also increase in value.

Cars

As a child grows into a teenager, he or she will consider buying an automobile. If you purchase an automobile, you know you are paying substantial interest on the purchase. When I was a teenager, my mother and father told me to buy a small piece of real estate with the money that I was planning to put down on a car and the real estate would buy the automobile. That is exactly what happened.

When I was 18 years old, my mother and father found a two-unit property for $500 down. We bought the property and over a period of about two years the property was paying for itself and making extra money, which we were able to use to buy the car. The real estate paid off the car in full. Lots of people will buy antique cars or cars that have value over and beyond their sales value because the vehicles become scarce and they are in great demand. In my opinion, the young investor should look for and be aware of this type of investment.

Antiques

As a child gets older he should consider buying things that are useful and which have value over and beyond their use. For instance, after the child grows up and eventually marries and moves into a home, he could buy antique furniture that has not only useful value but intrinsic value as time goes on. If you purchase a new fabric couch, after 10 to 15 years that couch will deteriorate and you will have to pay to have it sent to the junkyard.

If you were to buy a couch with antique value, such as a wood carved settee and you took care of it, the couch could very well be worth more than what you originally paid for it. Usable antique furniture is a far better possession to own in your home than ordinary contemporary furniture that becomes obsolete and unfashionable after a few years' use.

Real Estate

The best investment is real estate. If you purchase real estate in the proper location, under the proper circumstances and with the right timing, that property should increase in value far beyond the rate of inflation. Remember, you can make a low down payment, sometimes 3% to 10% on a piece of property. As inflation increases over the years, the real estate value will increase to compensate for the inflationary trend.

Inflation

The young person should be fully aware of how inflation works and how they could be in a position where inflation will work for them instead of against them. As a young person, you work for dollars. As a more experienced person, you expect your money to work for you in the form of creating assets that are inflation hedges which will make money continuously during your period of employment, whether you are making a large salary, small salary, or something in between.

6

How National Trends Affect Your Region, Metropolitan Area and Community

THE REGION

> Generally, a segment of the nation set apart from other areas by geographical boundaries, which typically comprises a cluster of states such as New England, the South, Southwest, Midwest, Atlantic Seaboard, Pacific Northwest, and so on.

One of the most salient indicators of regional growth is the current and anticipated population trend of the region. In my opinion, there will be continued migration to warmer climates in the West and Southwest because it's an easier life. There will be more opportunities there than in the slow-growing Rust Belt regions and industrial North. Data from the 2000 census confirms that the nation's population continues to move west and south, as it has since the 1940s. California's population swelled by more than four million people over the last decade, from 29.8 million residents in 1990 to 33.8 million in 2000.

Las Vegas and Phoenix are the fastest-growing cities in the USA, while California and Texas are the fastest-growing states in the union. Florida, also rapidly growing is the third fastest state. Despite this growth, California is nowhere near its maximum population density. Information from the state department of finance projects that several million more people will be moving into the five-county greater Los Angeles area over the next 10 years. This influx represents the greatest migration of people to an American city since New York at the turn of the last century.

As mentioned, population combined with industry is what creates wealth, and there is an abundant supply of both of these vital factors in the Golden State. If California were an independent country, it would rank as the seventh-largest stand-alone economy in the world. I think Southern California in particular is the garden spot of the garden spots of the world.

Where to Buy and Hold Far Into the Twenty-First Century

Big population shifts are coming to the United States and the makeup of each region is slated to change dramatically. We are 300 million strong now and we will be at 400 million by 2043, according to the US Census. Some demographers say the US population will double to 600 million by the year 2060 due to the huge influx of immigrants from Asia and Latin America.

By 2025, Hispanics and Asians will account for over a third of the population in a dozen or more states.

Following the teachings of Dr. Schumacher, I have invested in the Sun Belt areas of California, Las Vegas, Phoenix and Oklahoma, where there has been a tremendous population surge. Consequently, my houses stay full and in high demand.

Now, demographers project more will live in the Midwest—Colorado, Tennessee, Illinois, Oklahoma and Texas.

What About the Rest of the Country?

Great opportunities are to be had throughout the United States.

Interior Boomtowns

Each of the ten biggest cities once lay within 500 miles of the Canadian border. Now, seven of the top ten are Sun Belt cities, closer to Chihuahua than Toronto.

Domestic inflow was over 200,000 in the Inland Empire, Phoenix, Atlanta, Las Vegas and Orlando. These are economic dynamos that are driving much of America's growth. There is less economic polarization there than in the coastal megalopolises.

- Dallas is now larger than San Francisco.
- Houston is now larger than Detroit.
- Atlanta is now larger than Boston.
- Charlotte is now larger than Milwaukee.
- San Antonio has more domestic than immigrant inflow even though the border is only a three-hour drive away.

The interior boomtowns generated 38% of the nation's population growth in 2000 through 2006, as opposed to the coastal cities. This can be ascribed to:

- Problems with families in an urbanized setting.
- Kids not being able to walk anywhere because of the traffic.
- People not knowing each other.
- Parents not being able to stay home with their kids or continuing to send them to public schools.
- In interior boomtowns, people can actually afford a beautiful house in a nice neighborhood.

The highest-growing locales since 2000 have been:

- McKinney, Texas, which lies in the path of the outward expansion of Dallas. This is the fastest-growing of any city, with a population over 50,000. It has nearly doubled in size since 2000 to 107,530.
- Gilbert, Arizona (increased 73.9% to 191,517).
- Northern Las Vegas (increased 71.1% to 197,567).
- Port St. Lucie, Florida (increased 61.9% to 143,868).

Economic Considerations

In times of economic prosperity or distress, different regions of the country are affected differently. Take the recession of the 1990s. Regions like the Pacific Northwest held their own while New England experienced considerable hardship. The dot-com bust of 2000 hit California and the West Coast particularly hard. In this chapter, our focus is on how important trends affect the region, metropolitan area, and community you are planning to invest in, so you can decide whether that area shows enough promise.

Southwestern states, including Texas, Arizona, and Colorado, are prime examples. The housing market in those areas is strong in spite of a mild recession. Between 1988 and 2005, Nevada and Arizona are projected to have growth in personal income, employment, and population. The US Department of Commerce predicts that Arizona's population growth will increase over 20%. Just a few years ago, these states were supposedly "dying on the vine."

More than any one factor, a positive attitude can bring about a boom. If people think in terms of wealth and the success of the economy, then we will have a robust economy. Only a handful of people ever got rich during the Gold Rush of 1849. But people flocked to Sutter's Mill in California because they thought they could get in on the action. If everyone thought we were in a depression, it wouldn't matter what the actual economic conditions were; we would be in a severe crisis. People would adopt a siege mentality. They wouldn't spend their money. Instead of eating porterhouse steaks, they'd be eating franks. People would conserve electricity. Our country is very wasteful, but when we go into a depression mode, people double up. They live in apartments together. They don't turn on unnecessary lights. They start figuring out ways to conserve. It's a state of mind as much as anything else. On the other hand, if people think times are good, they go out and spend money; they buy new cars; they purchase new homes; they take trips around the world.

Over the past few years, there has been a tremendous housing boom in Las Vegas, spurred mainly by retirees from California and the East Coast seeking a more affordable and comfortable lifestyle and no state income tax. Las Vegas is unique. If the economy flattens out or goes bust, the housing market there could collapse. At the very least, it would be very dramatically affected. There's not much industry there to keep the economy going except tourism and gambling. California recently enacted a legalized gambling law on Indian reservations. It's starting to have an effect on the Las Vegas economy.

In the next ten to twenty years, if the United States normalizes relations with Cuba and Cuba becomes a free country, there's no question that it will go back to what it was before Castro. It will be one of the hot spots of the Caribbean. If the US trade boycott is finally lifted, Cuba's economy will get moving again.

In my estimation, hotels and casinos will be built that are very comparable to what you see in Las Vegas right now. Before Castro's revolution, you used to be able to go to Cuba by ferry from Key West. If that returned, imagine what would happen to the economies of Miami and the Florida Keys. They would be bolstered by an influx of tourism. On the other hand, Atlantic City would probably suffer, similar to the impact of California gambling on Las Vegas.

LEGISLATIVE ACTIONS

Environmental Regulations

Political trends and legislative decisions at the national and regional levels can have a tremendous effect on the value of real estate. Environmental legislation, such as the Clean Air Act of 1990, has had a dramatic impact on smokestack industries—oil refining, auto making, steel manufacturing, and so on. If the EPA (Environmental Protection Agency) or Congress imposes restrictions on emissions for automobiles, the car industry is affected.

Other types of environmental restraints include restrictions on the fishing industry off the Pacific Coast, the timber industry in Oregon and Washington, mining operations in the Sierra Nevada, controls on California's water supply, and the debate over nuclear power plants for electricity. All these actions either create jobs or destroy jobs. They either enhance the economy or undermine the economy. In Southern California, there are severe air-quality regulations, which has driven out some business. Whether you have a change for the better or for the worse, it affects the market value of real property.

In addition to regulatory policies, the actions and attitudes of people create as well as destroy value. Sometimes it happens overnight, sometimes it happens over a long period of time. Slow-growth attitudes have a dramatic impact on property values, usually causing existing properties to increase in value. Disputes between slow-growth advocates and developers can take years to resolve.

Environmentalists can also have a monumental effect on the market value of land. I once did an appraisal of one of the largest privately owned parcels of land in Oahu, Hawaii. A Japanese group wanted to buy and develop this property, which extended for thousands of acres. This parcel included about 1.25 miles of beautiful frontage along the beach, with a big ranch and a little village. About 80% of the land was in an environmental preserve.

The investment group wanted to build a yacht harbor, two or three golf courses, condominiums, and a hotel development. The owners of the property wanted $32 million for the estate. This was about 35 to 40 years ago. The buyers asked me to do an appraisal of the property and tell them how much they should pay for it. So I flew to Hawaii, studied the problem, and figured out that if they were able to develop the land in the way that the sellers said they could, the property would be worth $30 million. But despite the fact that the owners said they could develop this preserve, the environmentalists were so strong there that the would-be investors couldn't do a thing. Thus, slow-growth attitudes can curtail economic activity in a community.

Environmental restraints are very important to watch. If restrictions are imposed on cutting down trees to protect certain endangered species, then the lumber industry is going to suffer. The lumber industry is going to affect the value of real estate because it will cost more to build houses. If no new houses are being built, existing properties are going to increase in value.

On the other hand, for a city like Seattle, part of the attraction is that there are a lot of forests and mountains in the area. So if the logging companies cut everything down, that would hurt the value of the property too. It works both ways. You have to have a balance.

Here is another controversy. In California, there is a very serious water problem. If it continues to worsen, regional authorities aren't going to issue any more water meters, and that will impede growth of huge tracts. Subdivisions would not be built in the growing Riverside and San Bernardino areas. If this occurs, the value of existing housing is going to increase sharply. Several years ago in San Clemente, along California's central coast, a development group started a housing project and laid out all the subdivisions. But the city decided that the water shortage was severe enough to curtail development and refused to issue permits for water meters. The developers had millions tied up in the project. It was really brutal. Consequently, values of existing houses in the adjacent tracts have started to skyrocket.

With the diversity of the Southern California economy and its proximity to the Pacific Rim, many people have high-paying jobs, and that means that they can afford to pay a high price for prime real estate. At the same time, millions more people are projected to move to the area over the next 10 to 20 years. Every decade, California's population increases. In fact, 50% of the US population lives within 50 miles of the West or East coast, and net coastal population increases by over 3,000 people a day, according to some estimates. That's an amazing statistic, if you think about it. If the water shortage continues and it is not possible to build new housing to compensate for this influx, you will have a situation like you have in Tokyo, where houses are worth millions and millions because of the shortage. It changes the nature of financing. If you get into hundred-year loans, it can have a tremendous effect.

Environmental restrictions by regional agencies, such as the South Coast Air Quality Management District in Southern California, limit the amount of toxic pollutants in the air and are driving a lot of business out of the area, resulting in corporate relocation to Georgia, Arizona, Texas, Oklahoma, Missouri, and other less-restrictive and cost-prohibitive states. In the short-term, this may have a detrimental effect on the regional economy, but other people will move in with other types of businesses, compensating for the outflow. It is important to be aware of environmental factors and what affect they are having on the housing market and the economy.

People often think the mineral deposits under their land are extremely valuable. For instance, if you had an oil well producing a gusher proportion of oil, that would no doubt make you rich. There is a possibility of having gold or other precious metals underneath your property. Today, however, another thing you must look out for, which is far more serious, are the detrimental things that you find underneath the ground.

A young man I knew acquired a piece of desert land through an inheritance from this father. The young man had never seen the property and didn't know where it was. He finally found it through a metes and bounds description and the tract map and area. There were no streets, sidewalks or thoroughfares to the property; it was totally locked in by other parcels with no development in the area whatsoever. However, over the next 15 years, the young man and others built homes and started a community.

One day, though, the young man was visited by an environmental engineer, who explained that there was a problem with the land his house was built on. Evidently, many years before he acquired the property, a silver plating company, unbeknownst to anyone, had disposed of large drums of toxic waste on that very piece of land. The drums on his land had been the target of motorcycle gangs and others who had used them for target practice. Consequently, the fluid in the cans had leaked out through the bullet holes, down into the desert sand and into the subterranean soil.

Eventually, after five years or more of seeping into the underground water system, the drinking water supply for people in the community, as well as the water for land irrigation, was affected.

Because the environmental problem had started on this young man's land, he became completely responsible for cleaning up the mess and for imposing hazards on other people. The young man ended up liable for a $1.5 million bill to clean up the mess on the property, which was probably worth only $5,000! Of course, he couldn't pay the $1.5 million. They foreclosed on his house, took all his assets, his business and he filed for bankruptcy. Eventually, his wife left him, taking the two children. He appealed to the environmental agencies to be reasonable, but he was unsuccessful.

The young man tried to trace the barrels back to the company who had dumped them in the first place. But the company had anticipated the problem; they had removed all traceable markings from the metal drums.

As this story illustrates, it is very important that if you own land, you inspect it periodically to ensure there are no detrimental factors affecting it. As the owner, you are liable. A person who buys a piece of real estate should be extremely careful to check the underground facilities to see if there are any hazardous wastes or materials.

A piece of property I was familiar with was going to be purchased by the county for a truck depot. This property was ideal because it was across the street from the county yards, in an ideal location. The property had originally been used as a truck repair yard, with all kinds of parts and junk on the site. Before the county purchased the property, they decided to have an analysis of the underground material. They hired an environmental company who conducted borings of the site and found three underground fuel tanks that had been there for many years and were completely rusted out. A lot of toxic material had seeped into the ground.

The county figured it would cost $1 million to eliminate the problem before they could use the site for the purpose they had intended. The surface land had been negotiated at a price of $500,000 so if they purchased the property it would have cost them $1.5 million. The county walked away from the deal. The property owner was now faced with all the problems on the site and there wasn't any way he could sell it to anyone without disclosing this tremendous hazard.

Before you purchase a property, check adjacent types of businesses or industries that might produce toxic waste. Check the soil conditions of the subject property and ascertain if the site was previously used for underground gasoline, fuel oil, toxic waste, or other materials that might create an environmental hazard. It is very important for you to realize what the problems are. If you are not extra cautious, your purchase could be totally disastrous.

CLIMATIC CONDITIONS

Generally speaking, if you have a nice recreational community in an area where you have sun most of the year, property values are going to increase. Housing prices are generally higher in temperate climates. Look what's happened in Honolulu, Hawaii, where single-family homes sell on average for $388,500, compared to Green Bay, Wisconsin, where the median price for a single-family residence is $128,000. The competition to find a good investment in Honolulu is tremendous. On the other hand, not too many people want to invest in Green Bay. You need a polar bear instinct for at least part of the year to live there. In my opinion, Florida is a fabulous place to invest. Personally, I don't like the bugs, but many people don't mind them. Palm Springs and Las Vegas are other examples of how warm weather can enhance the housing market.

One way of gauging how climatic conditions affect land values is by analyzing the median price of homes in different regions of the country. Also, look at the strategic decisions made by local industry. Corporations such as Disney, which decided Anaheim, California was the ideal spot for Disneyland and Orlando, Florida, the best location for Walt Disney World, don't invest in a given location blindly. Both Anaheim and Orlando are densely populated areas with highly desirable climates. Disney's recent $1 billion expansion of Disneyland in Anaheim speaks volumes about the continuing potential of the Los Angeles area.

Climatic conditions, therefore, can have a direct effect on the regional economy. In addition to hospitality and tourism, the sporting industry thrives in warmer regions. Southern California is able to host practically more sporting events than any place else in the world because of the temperate climate. The facilities can always be used, and because of that, more sports arenas and stadiums have been built to accommodate the year-round demand for indoor and outdoor sporting events. Although Florida has mild weather for most of the year, it does have a hurricane season, which makes coastal development difficult, and freezing temperatures in some areas during the winter months, which puts a damper on economic activity.

Smog conditions also have much to do with the value of real estate. About the only area that is smog-free in Southern California is the beach, where some of the highest property values are found. Much of the appeal of states like Oregon and Washington has to do with their clean air and pristine environments.

Harsh-climate states have an inherent disadvantage in my opinion: The climate is not as conducive to industrial development as that of the southern states. A manufacturer can build a plant in San Diego, California, and, provided that the pollution level isn't too high, operate it every day of the year. In some of the Northeastern and upper Midwestern states such as Maine, Vermont, upstate New York, and Minnesota, there are certain days when the weather is so severe that people can't even get to work. The high cost of construction in order to protect workers and equipment from extreme weather is an added burden of doing business in harsh climates, whereas in most of the western states you can practically build a hut and work there year-round without adverse effects.

AGRICULTURAL PRODUCTION

Agriculture production can be absolutely essential to a state and region. In California, agriculture production is an important segment of the state economy. If a region has a lot of agricultural activity, it can create tremendous wealth.

> *A friend of mine bought 100 acres of land in rural Indio, California, a few years ago for $100,000. Today, it's probably worth two to three times that amount because other landowners in the region have developed irrigation systems. The regional authorities formed a water district, and now this investor has the opportunity to make use of the water on his land. That makes his property considerably more valuable than it was before the water district was formed.*

In a stable farming community that grows truck crops—vegetables such as potatoes, tomatoes, celery, lettuce, and cucumbers that are hauled to market by truck at regular intervals—the economy is usually quite stable because (most) everyone eats vegetables. Farming communities that grow oranges and lemons and other citrus crops are more exposed. If a serious drought or freeze occurs, it can affect the economy of the whole community. People will have a difficult time paying their mortgages, and it could impact the local or regional economy.

The United States is the only country in the world that has two crops of wheat—winter wheat and summer wheat (hard wheat and soft wheat). America has enough farmland to feed the world, so we always have a surplus of certain crops. And with modern technology, we're always improving our ability to grow crops and to grow more on smaller parcels of land. We have mechanized agriculture to the point where the system favors the large farmer because of cheaper labor costs and a higher production volume.

Sometimes there's a tremendous profit in agriculture, but sometimes it's very risky because of insects, weather, harvest rates, demand—a whole slew of unpredictable and uncontrollable factors. Locusts can fly across the plains and eat up all the wheat fields in their path. Or the Mediterranean fruit fly may contaminate an important crop. The result in either case can be disastrous.

On the other hand, when there's a surplus, farmers can't always make enough money to survive. Agriculture in a way is speculative, which explains why commodity markets and farm subsidies were established to help stabilize the markets. If farm subsidies are lifted, many small- to medium-sized farmers are going to get caught in the fallout, and that's going to have an impact on the regional economy.

GOVERNMENT ACTIONS

Subsidized Industries

Although it doesn't contribute to the extent that other industrialized countries do, the US government subsidizes many important industries, including agriculture, aerospace and defense, aircraft production, utilities, waterways, and (at times) even auto makers such as Chrysler. As long as government subsidies continue and there is proper growth and economic development from these subsidies, they will enhance the value of property in the area.

When the government closes or curtails spending at military bases, it has shifted the economy dramatically because the government pours millions and millions of dollars into these facilities. The bases have provided a tremendous amount of direct and ancillary employment. Many of these bases are so valuable that, if they were handed over to the cities in which they are located, the real estate they occupy could be put to immediate use.

The California State University campus at Monterey Bay, the former Army base of Fort Ord, is just such an example. Such base closings may result in a loss of jobs, but they also create a lot of opportunity. The greater the change, the more opportunity that is created.

Drastic cuts in defense spending, which led to cutbacks in the well-paying aerospace industry, lessened the demand for new homes and created more demand for apartments in communities that were dependent on defense. If homes are not selling and financing is hard to get, then the market for apartment housing gets better.

Taxation Policies

A growing number of states are experiencing serious deficit problems. Increased taxpayer demand on public services, combined with growing expectations for an ever higher standard of living, has seriously challenged state governments. At least 30 states faced shortfalls in their 2002 budgets attributable to the sluggish economy and growing demands for spending. At the same time, state governments are obliged to make infrastructure improvements, to highways, roadways, water systems, and utilities, to keep commerce competitive and prosperous.

States with a constant influx of people, particularly in the West, call for new taxes that can discourage new business activity. Moreover, if companies already in business decide they can no longer afford to operate in the state because of tax increases, they may relocate to other states, thereby weakening the economy and hurting the housing market. This partly explains why the legislatures in many states with budget deficits decide to raise or create taxes on consumer items rather than taxing industry.

THE METROPOLITAN AREA

A metropolitan area is defined as a large center of population including one or more central cities and their adjacent satellite communities.

Population Trends

In the years following World War II, Americans participated in the greatest migration of people from one area to another in the history of the world up to that time. Millions of people relocated from the East Coast, Northeast, and Midwest to the southern and western states, most notably California, which is now the most populous state in the union. The desirable climate and great opportunities afforded by post-war commercial and industrial activity stimulated the mass relocation.

People are always looking for a better life, both within and outside of the confines of their own region, state and country, and will relocate to areas where this is possible. Witness the recent migration of people from Mexico and Central America to the United States, as well as the exodus of Eastern Europeans to Western Europe.

Since the Census Bureau started tracking demographic shifts, it has been evident that home building closely follows population trends. If population levels increase, residential building and land values generally increase proportionately.

The quickest way to solve a housing shortage in a crowded or growing area is to erect new housing. Subsidized housing is another answer, but governments these days are hard pressed to find sufficient resources to fund that type of activity. When new housing is built, people in higher income brackets tend to move up, creating a supply of available, lower-priced, existing housing for people in the middle and lower brackets. A marked population increase in a metropolitan area therefore creates demand for both new and existing housing.

ECONOMIC ACTIVITY

Active vs. Dormant Industries

Whether influenced by recession, global competition, or overproduction, industrial activity often goes in cycles. Heavy industries such as auto making, metals processing, building, and construction are prime examples. Whenever there is a glut of oil on the market, oil prices drop and petroleum production activity wanes. Right now there isn't much demand for copper, and most of the copper mills in Arizona are shut down.

If you are interested in buying in an area with dormant industries, make sure there is some anticipated spark that will eventually stimulate the local economy. New technology may make many of these dormant industries all but obsolete. The large regional steel plants in Pittsburgh, for example, may never be able to compete with steel manufacturers that are more internationally oriented. The same is true of shipbuilding. On the other hand, industries that are globally competitive, for instance, high technology, media, and entertainment, may have bright futures. It is important to do considerable research before making an investment decision.

Labor Market

A prolonged strike can have a detrimental effect on the local economy. The old *Los Angeles-Herald Examiner* once had the largest circulation of any afternoon newspaper in the country. Then, in 1967, the paper's unions decided to go on strike, resulting in a prolonged labor action that lasted for 10 years. Advertisers fled, circulation plummeted, employees left or lost their jobs, and the local economy suffered. The strikers made their point, and they sounded the now-defunct paper's death knell. A prolonged labor action can put a company out of business and result in the loss of jobs.

Job actions can have a dramatic effect on the area economy. When people are out of work, they can't afford new housing and the real estate market slows. It's important to invest in an area of diversified industry. Greater Los Angeles is ideal in this respect because of its size and diversity. In addition, the region has the resources, land, entrepreneurs, and utilities to do a lot of things. There are many basic industries in the area offering goods or services that people from outside the area want to buy. This, combined with the abundance of small- to medium-sized businesses, allows the local economy able to withstand periodic downturns. Southern California is unique in the sense that there's such a diversification of industries.

The important thing, when deciding on a location, is to select a community that has a good, solid economic base that will grow with the needs of the country over the next 20 years or more. Such a base could consist of the service and information industries, which are presently competitive and are likely to remain competitive over time. Next to growth industries, look for stable industries, such as wholesale trade and distribution, transportation, agriculture, and health care, that aren't subject to wild fluctuations and that will provide a source of reliable employment.

Given the shift in the national economy from an industrial/manufacturing to a high-tech/service orientation, it has become increasingly important to look for areas with companies that employ thinkers or "symbolic analysts," in Robert Reich's phrase. A thinker makes more than someone who works in a steel mill. A service, consulting, high-tech, or think-tank type of business is a clean business. It doesn't create smog, pollution, or much waste. But it does generate new ideas and solutions. Those kinds of businesses are ideal, in my opinion. They produce high-paying jobs, help to keep property values up, and enable homeowners to obtain loans, get better credit, and make their payments. And as the wages of the employees go up, you'll find that real estate values will go up in harmony, only more rapidly.

Southern California is probably one of the best places in the world to invest in because, for all its growth and activity, this area really hasn't taken off yet. There are so many advantages, and there are so many things that are planned and proposed that the future growth is going to be monumental.

Not too long ago I did an appraisal of an automobile junkyard in the Los Angeles Harbor area. The railroad was putting a turning radius in the location of the junkyard. From that analysis, I figured that the dynamic growth in the Long Beach/Los Angeles Harbor area is going to be astounding. With increased activity in the Asian markets coming to the United States and the trade activity that has been improving around the harbor, the Los Angeles Customs District recently surpassed New York as the nation's busiest commercial gateway. Given it's bound to the Greater Los Angeles area's inevitable expansion, it isn't a question of whether growth is going to continue—it's bound to.

The factors are in place. There are now calls to operate the Los Angeles Harbor 24 hours a day, as the world's business ports—Hong Kong and Singapore—already operate. Knowing information like this is in itself worth money. If the L.A. Harbor expands its operations, as it inevitably will, what do you think this will do to the properties in the surrounding areas? Long Beach and Los Angeles are the only major port cities in the world that aren't flanked by high-rise office buildings, except for the recently constructed World Trade Center and a few other buildings in downtown Long Beach.

Some cities are dependent on one or two companies and industries. Take Seattle, whose biggest employers are Boeing and Microsoft. If Boeing's doing well, then Seattle's doing well. If the company has lucrative contracts, then money's running out the front door. However, if Boeing loses its prized contracts, people will be standing in the street. Despite the presence of Microsoft, that's still a mostly one-industry town if you ask me. Many towns are dependent on jobs provided by the city, county, or federal government. That's not the best situation to invest in either.

Up through the dot-com bust of 2000, areas with high technology industries were doing very well. Today, many of these areas, such as Portland and California's Silicon Valley, are struggling. But over time they'll come back.

To find out about an area's economic activity and growth potential, basic industries, and the outlook for them, contact:

- City planning departments
- Area chambers of commerce
- State departments of finance or revenue

- Economics departments of major financial institutions
- Area real estate boards
- Utility companies

Be sure to read:

- Newspapers
- Business publications
- Real estate journals

Recreational Facilities

The building of a large sports arena can also change the character of the area. Sometimes it serves as a physical barrier that limits or alters development, such as Hollywood Park in Inglewood, California, or Wrigley Field in Chicago, Illinois.

When they finally installed lights at Wrigley Field, that changed the character of the neighborhood. Not surprisingly, the people in the surrounding area fought tooth and nail against it because they didn't want the noise, traffic, congestion, and everything else that comes with night baseball games. Ideally, you learn about these developments before they happen, when they are still in the discussion phases, so you can plan your investment strategy accordingly. There's always a way to find out about up-and-coming projects and developments if you do your research.

CONSTRUCTION COSTS

If shortages of materials or strikes cause construction costs to rise dramatically, then existing housing and buildings are going to go up in value, provided there's a demand. A labor shortage usually means that it will cost more to build. If it does, then prices go up. When the airport authority built the north runway at Los Angeles International Airport, there was a strike by concrete workers. Because of the shortage of concrete and demand from builders, the price of concrete went out of sight.

The time of year also affects labor efficiency. When I need some painting done on my beachfront property in the summer, it takes twice as long than in the winter because there are more visual distractions and activities like volleyball tournaments going on. Because of the extra time involved, it costs more to have work done in the summer. Conversely, in cities like Minneapolis or Buffalo, repair costs are much higher in the winter due to the harsh working conditions.

MAJOR IMPROVEMENT PROGRAMS

Redevelopment Projects

Many cities have redevelopment agencies. Often, members of the city council sit on the agency or have direct influence regarding the actions of the agency. Redevelopment agencies are entities established to improve the quality of life for the residents of a community or to improve the business or industrial climate of an area. Well-planned redevelopment projects can enhance the growth pattern of an area. If the nature of the community is enhanced by a redevelopment project, the project is justified. If not, the project shouldn't move forward.

Redevelopment plans that improve "blighted" or run-down areas generally raise a neighborhood's growth potential. In Baltimore, the city's historic waterfront area was improved through an impressive redevelopment project that gave the dilapidated docks a new lease on life. In Santa Monica, an area known as Pacific Ocean Park in front of the boardwalk was once the subject of a city redevelopment project that cleared about 10 blocks of rundown housing to make room for two high-rise apartment buildings.

The Bunker Hill redevelopment project in downtown Los Angeles, started in the early 1940s, made room for the many highrise buildings that today constitute the city skyline. The development of the Bunker Hill project has had a positive effect on growth in the central business district because it put a once blighted area to a higher and better use.

My brother and I did a reuse appraisal determining the highest and best use of each designated land parcel surrounding the University of Southern California for a development known as the Hoover Street project. The study area was enormous, encompassing approximately 10 city blocks. At the time, there was a lot of privately owned land on the south side of Jefferson Boulevard that the university wanted for expansion of the campus.

In order to implement the project, the City of Los Angeles Redevelopment Agency had to condemn all the land and improvements in the vicinity of the university so the campus could be expanded and a buffer zone created for student housing and a community shopping center. The city had the legal authority to do this on the grounds of eminent domain, the right of a government or public utility to acquire private property for public use through the condemnation process, provided that just compensation is awarded for the taking of the property. In other words, the redevelopment agency is required to pay fair market value for property it acquires. Once acquired, the redevelopment parcels may then be sold to private developers who are entitled to low interest loans as an incentive to develop the site.

> *In the early 1970s, I did an appraisal of a redevelopment project in National City, California, a community located on the outskirts of San Diego. In the mid-1960s, San Diego was whole heartedly dependent on the aircraft industry. When Convair, a defense contractor and maker of military aircraft, went out of business, the area had serious unemployment problems. So the city went out into the suburbs and bought large tracts of vacant land for commercial and industrial use. They then sold it to businesses and based the price on potential employment.*
>
> *If you were going to purchase the land and build a warehouse where you had only two people working, the cost of the land would be extremely high. But if you were going to employ 100 people, you could get it for almost nothing. The city of San Diego practically gave away the land because they wanted employment. In this way, the city was able to attract new industry into the community and diversify its economic base. That's happening now in such states as Arizona, Arkansas, and Georgia.*

Sometimes growth can be measured in the time it takes to travel to certain places rather than the distance covered. My uncle was 91 years old when he passed away. First he walked to work, then he rode a horse, then he rode a bicycle, then he drove a car, and then took the Red Car train. All the while, it took him about 30 minutes to get to work. Most people live about 30 to 40 minutes from where they work. If a freeway is built enabling people to live farther from work, it's going to change the whole transportation pattern. If you put in a high-speed rail, it may increase land values in outlying areas.

With an existing freeway, you know where the growth is. A proposed freeway is speculative because you don't know when or where they're going to build it. Most cities don't like the idea of having a freeway running through their town, such as South Pasadena, which has successfully blocked the extension of the 710 freeway to the 210 freeway. Major improvement programs such as boat harbors and gateways, downtown office buildings, a world-class subway system, and redevelopment projects generally increase area property values, but may have a short-term negative impact on the immediate community in which they are built. When the city of Redondo Beach started building the breakwater in 1963, they condemned a large area adjacent to the harbor to start a redevelopment project. The surrounding property in the immediate vicinity was for sale for practically nothing, presumably because it was an undesirable area to buy.

Yet if you went down to the city planning department, you could see that the city was committed to going ahead with the redevelopment project; they had the rocks for the breakwater into the water and were starting to tear buildings down and condemn the land. That was the perfect time to go in and buy residential property because of the obvious potential that existed.

Once a commitment is made and the city starts building, you can project into the future and envision how the area will look after the 10 or 15 years that it's going to take to fully develop the project. Often, you can see that a certain development is going to be fabulous when they get through with it, and you're going to be sitting on top of a gold mine.

If there was a private development that had an impact great enough to change the character of the community, then I would have as much faith in it as a government project. Not many major projects are started that aren't completed.

> *After analyzing the Redondo Beach breakwater project, I decided to buy an empty lot for $12,000 with $500 down. It wasn't a pretty sight. It was close to the harbor development and there was a lot of dirt and rubble and trucks going by. But I knew that the property would double in value after the marina was built. I wasn't looking at the mess sitting in front of me, I was looking at the long-range potential created by a harbor that would be there 30 years from now. Sure enough, today that property's worth over three-quarters of a million dollars.*

Although residential real estate is a good investment around a redevelopment project, commercial property in these instances may be a little speculative. In Pasadena, there was a massive redevelopment deal called the Pepper Street Project, which encompassed about 10 city blocks. The city took an interminable amount of time—probably four or five years—setting up the project, obtaining all the necessary approvals, appropriating the money, appraising and condemning the properties, making the architectural drawings, and realigning the streets.

During this time, the properties adjacent to the project really suffered. The supermarket adjacent to the development went broke, and the dry cleaners and nearby small businesses lost their leases because of it. If you owned residential property, you may have taken a short-term loss. However, when the project was finally finished your losses would have seemed insignificant compared to the rents the market would bear.

For all of the big projects that are proposed, very few are ever completed. Yet once a project gets started, the odds are in your favor that it will be finished. So it was obvious with the growth factor that was occurring around Hermosa Beach, even though the crumbs weren't spilling over from economic activity in surrounding communities, that we had a terrific advantage. When you see a substantial positive development of a community and there's no way that the community can turn back, then that is the time to buy. Visualize what a major development project will do for a community once the deal is committed, and take advantage of it today.

However, the investor must be concerned when purchasing property that he or she will own for a long period that there is no threat of imminent condemnation to the property or the immediate vicinity of the property. I once represented the airport commission as an appraiser when the Los Angeles International Airport needed to condemn entire tracts of residential properties to build a new runway north of the existing airport grounds. In all, about 350 houses north of the airport were condemned for demolition. When the Federal Aviation Administration granted the local airport authority permission to expand the runway, it stipulated that no houses could be within 750 feet of the runway.

Some friends of mine were planning to purchase a single-family residence in Westchester, a suburb near the airport. They were really enthusiastic about the house, which had a beautiful backyard and was ideally located near a high school. But it was only a matter of time before the airport authority was going to expand and acquire homes in the area where my friends wanted to live.

I told them that in 10 years, they would not be living in the house if they bought it. They refused to believe me until I obtained a map from the airport commission of the proposed acquisition showing where the new runway was planned. After locating their house on the map, I discovered that it was the second house from where the condemnation project stopped to acquire the land for the runway expansion.

We then pinpointed a location on the map that was about the same distance from a presently existing airport runway as their residence would be when the new runway was in full operation with airplanes taking off every few minutes. We then drove to the designated spot on the map and spent about an hour sitting in the car listening to the noise pattern.

I am sure you know the rest of the story. The noise was frighteningly loud. So they bought a beautiful residence in a suburban area about 12 miles south of the airport. Today, their house is worth well over 10 times what they originally paid for it. The place they once had their sights on still sits adjacent to the airport runway and isn't worth all that much more than they would have paid for it.

Although the acquisition of sites for building projects may enhance a community and make it more desirable, it is important not to get caught in the condemnation trap by failing to foresee any adverse factors that might affect your purchase. On the other hand, there have been other instances when condemnation has benefited investors.

A close friend of mine and fellow instructor at UCLA Extension once owned a large parcel of vacant land in the San Gabriel Valley. Located on a main thoroughfare, this particular parcel was ideal for an automobile dealership. A few years after he purchased the land, the adjacent city annexed the community where his property was. After the annexation, the city decided it needed a new school site.

To everyone's amazement, the city decided my friend's property on a busy highway would be suitable for a grade school and, after initiating condemnation proceedings, *offered $2 million for it. The price was conservative, so my friend said to the city negotiator, "I don't think this property is good for a school. If you want to buy it, I won't fight over the price. But I want to put a clause in the sale document to be recorded that the property is to be used for a public school only. And if the city does not use it for that specific purpose, I reserve the right to buy the property back for $2 million."*

The city purchased this property, but for a variety of reasons, never built a school on the site. Fifteen years later, the city gave up and sold the property back to my friend for $2 million on account of the agreement they made. Due to appreciation, he was able to purchase a $20 million piece of real estate for a tenth of the price. And he didn't have to pay any real property taxes for the 15-year period while the property was appreciating in value because it was owned by the city. Condemnation was beneficial in this instance. My friend's measured approach paid off handsomely. Of course, this was an unusual situation. There is no substitute for knowing what you are doing. Think the problem through and consider the long-term effects.

Infrastructure Obsolescence

In addition to redevelopment considerations, It is equally important to check with local and regional planning commissions, city councils, boards of supervisors, and the like, to find out what building restrictions may apply to a given area. Environmental considerations, like overloaded sewer and water systems or inadequate parking, could lead to building moratoriums and downzoning efforts in overcrowded areas, causing the value of land to rise. From an investor's standpoint, these form a favorable set of conditions in which to become a property owner.

On the other hand, if you want to buy a "tear-down" property for a low price and either remodel it or build a new structure, severe building restrictions can hinder the project's approval or result in exorbitant fees for building permits. You can never be too informed about the area you are buying into. With real estate, there are many factors that affect value. You have to take into consideration all of them to understand why something is happening.

THE COMMUNITY

That part of the metropolitan area composed of a number of neighborhoods that have a tendency toward common interests and problems.

Geographical Pattern

Natural terrain separates and defines community boundaries. Natural barriers, such as hills, valleys, rivers, forests, lakes, and ravines, tend to distinguish communities, providing a distinctive feel and enriching them with natural beauty. They create a unique condition beyond geographic markers. Proximity to an ocean, lake, or river can also increase value if it is desirable.

Conversely, a swamp or cesspool will detract from a property's appeal. With a river, you always want to live on the most desirable side, which is generally away from industrial plants, obnoxious odors, and other pollutants. The top of the hill is usually worth more money because it typically affords a sweeping view. When you buy property, be sure to get a sweeping view, not a view of the sweepings!

> *O*n the other hand, if you live on any unstable cliff in Malibu, California, your house could slide into the ocean after a big storm. Or a rockslide could shut down the highway. A big boulder once fell on Pacific Coast Highway, forcing people to drive 35 miles out of their way into the San Fernando Valley just to get to Santa Monica. The roads were so bad you couldn't drive on them for a week. That situation, to me, is geographically undesirable.
>
> I wouldn't buy in an area like Malibu. A friend of mine bought a house that sits out over the ocean. He and his wife are raising three children. Malibu has an extremely narrow beach and Pacific Coast Highway is right at their back doors. Where are the kids supposed to play when the tide comes in—on the highway?

Natural barriers are often employed to partition industrial properties (business parks, factories, and the like) from residential real estate, although artificial barriers such as highways also serve this purpose.

Barriers between different types of real estate are important because they limit the encroachment of one type of development or another. Typically, if a residential development encroaches on an industrial property, the industrial property gives way.

Unlike other natural barriers, undeveloped land areas are changeable. When undeveloped land is developed, it changes the whole complexity of the community. It probably will enhance the adjacent neighborhoods. When considering an area, try to figure out what type of improvements will be made and how those improvements will impact the surrounding area. Find out who owns the property. Developers can't build without approval from the city or county planning department. If plans or drawings have been filed, carefully examine them, then talk to the developer to learn more about the project.

Some developments may be detrimental. For instance, a furniture maker or auto body shop might create noxious odors. Positive developments would depend on the type of property you are looking at. If you are thinking of acquiring an apartment house and someone wanted to build a recreational facility or health spa across the street, that might add to the desirability of your property. A tasteful shopping center could have a similar effect.

Satellite Communities

In Los Angeles County, there are 88 separate cities, including the City of Los Angeles. Regional shopping centers—major shopping centers that service a satellite community—and industrial complexes have a tremendous effect on values in suburban areas. If an industry or business is not smoke-producing, toxic, or noise polluting but is instead clean and enhances the community, such as a semiconductor plant, it can be an asset to the surrounding area.

In my opinion, the best types of industries are the high-tech industries because they are relatively clean and have fairly high payrolls. Aerospace, computers, biotechnology firms, and virtually all of the high-tech industries are fantastic as far as land values are concerned because they are usually kind to the environment and contribute to a higher average family income level. Think of the possibilities if a company such as Boeing and Northrop Grumman in Redondo Beach, which employs engineers, who are planning the future and designing communications satellites, more efficient credit systems, space transportation systems and the like, were to double its staff.

Wow! It is self-evident what would happen to real estate values in a community should this occur.

> *What do 100 new factory workers bring to a town over the course of a year? According to the US Chamber of Commerce, 359 more people, 91 more schoolchildren, 100 more households, 229,000 more bank deposits, three more retail establishments, and 331,000 more retail sales. For every 100 aerospace workers, an estimated 67 jobs in ancillary industries are created. That's substantial. Now look at it in the other direction. What happens when a high-tech employer closes and 100 people lose their jobs? All this is taken away, or most of it. So, if you are going to invest in real estate, you must consider these kinds of situations and assess the growth potential of the community.*

CIVIC GOVERNMENT POLICIES

Assessments

If city or county governments impose taxes and assessments on your property, it doesn't necessarily help you. Hermosa Beach, the city where I live, is a bedroom community, so the city has to provide services such as police, fire, health, schools, and utilities. If a city has industry or large amounts of commercial activity to generate tax revenue, it can be very beneficial to the community. But cities that are dependent on residents for a tax base are bound to have problems because they can't provide enough services that people want and expect in proportion to what they pay. The tax rate in the nearby community of El Segundo is about half what it is in Hermosa Beach because El Segundo has so much industry.

Rent Control

Rent control has a tremendous effect on property values. Rent control limits the amount of rent that property owners can charge for the use of their rental units. It isn't based on economics or market conditions, but rather on legislative activity. When a community is totally developed and saturated, and people claim they can't afford the rent, legislators sometimes respond by enacting a rent control ordinance. However, any time legislative activity is separated from economic conditions, there is a tremendous spread and the property owner usually winds up losing financially. Landlords need to raise the rents in order to keep pace with the spiraling costs of properly maintaining the building.

Affordable housing is a victim of controls. If you put rent controls on property, you're not going to have equally accessible, affordable housing because you won't have free enterprise. Depending on how hermetic the controls are, some people may have cheap rent, while others are excluded. When cities impose zoning restrictions or height and density limits, they make affordable housing more expensive because developers can't build housing of adequate quality or quantity.

> *A friend of mine owns a six-unit apartment building in a rent-controlled city. It's a really nice place in one of the premiere locations in all of Southern California. But rent control allows him to get only around $450 a month for a one-bedroom apartment. Without rent control, he'd probably get about $1,000 a month for the same unit. I remember once, when he had a vacancy, he put an ad in the paper, and it was an absolute circus. He literally had hundreds and hundreds of people lined up, waiting to apply. How can you make a selection? In my opinion, it would be better for the city to build housing for the elderly rather than interfere with private enterprise.*

Rents can only go as high as people can afford to pay. That's why rent control doesn't work and is artificial. When governments crimp or disrupt the free economy, it can have a tremendous impact on the natural flow of goods and services and can also impede growth.

For instance, the establishment of the California Coastal Commission in the 1970s, which has planning jurisdiction over any property within 2,000 feet of the coastline, has resulted in such severe building restrictions that many people have gone bankrupt. If the ocean damaged your house, the Coastal Commission wouldn't let you place rocks in front to protect it. They maintain it would impede the beach, even though the ocean was destroying your house. And if the tide did destroy your house, they might not let you build it back the way it was.

A great example of this occurred in Malibu. After a certain point, you couldn't build any more apartments along the coastline. If an apartment already existed, it didn't have any competition, so the real estate values soared. It was a boon for the existing apartment owners, but it left everybody else high and dry. Some people had purchased lots figuring they would eventually build a couple of units, but they weren't allowed to do so.

The point of this is to think about real estate in terms of the overall picture and for the long term. Economic, legislative, environmental, and man-made forces can have a tremendous impact on the value of real estate and should be carefully considered before an investment decision is made.

7

How National Trends Affect Your Immediate Neighborhood

THE NEIGHBORHOOD

A residential area with distinguishing characteristics comprised of people with similar interests. A neighborhood can consist of a city block, a street, or a handful of houses, as long as it is an area where there is an identifiable group of people.

PHYSICAL CHARACTERISTICS

Overall Trend of the Area

Having narrowed down the likely location of your real estate investment to a specific community, it is important to determine the growth potential of the immediate neighborhood. The surrounding neighborhood has just as much influence on the value of a property as the property itself.

As with the outlying area, it is important to assess the neighborhood trend. There are really only three things that happen to real estate values at the neighborhood level: Values remain stable, they increase, or they decrease. When a neighborhood reaches its peak growth stage, the cycle is upward. After that, values plateau. At the end of the plateau period, they begin to drop off. Eventually, at some later date, they may begin to increase again if conditions are favorable. Every neighborhood goes through this cycle.

The best time to invest in a neighborhood is at the very lowest ebb of the cycle, when it has deteriorated but when you can see future growth potential because of the surrounding communities and activities.

If a neighborhood has already started to deteriorate, and we can see that it has more or less bottomed out and is now at a point where growth is likely to occur, then that's actually a good time to buy. You should not be interested in what will happen today; you should be interested in what will happen 20 or 30 years later.

To understand the cycle of ownership, you have to look at the history of the area. Sometimes property becomes more valuable as multiple residential real estate is developed and land values rise. Sometimes not. The only thing you can be assured of is change. And every time there is change, it either creates or destroys value. Neighborhoods make up a community, so if the larger trend in the community is toward development, you can reasonably expect development to continue.

When I decided to invest in Hermosa Beach, the two larger adjacent communities had tremendous growth potential. Redondo Beach, the next city over, was constructing the King Harbor boating marina, while Manhattan Beach was removing hazardous railroad tracks. Hermosa Beach sits in the middle of these two cities, so I concluded that even if Hermosa wanted to go back to a sleepy little town, it couldn't because the pressure from all sides wouldn't permit it. The adjacent areas simply wouldn't let it deteriorate any further. When I bought in 1960, I determined that the city's condition had hit rock bottom and couldn't get any worse because of the surrounding activity.

There are a lot of areas around the country where you can see this type of thing happening. But you have to do your homework, and you have to understand a little about the local economic conditions. Know what to look for. There is a plenitude of information and material available about almost every city, so you must be careful not to place too much weight on irrelevant details. There are only a few indicators that are truly important in your analysis. Don't get lost in the trivia.

Before anything can happen, you have to decide you're ready to do it. The easiest thing to say is, "I won't take a chance because it will hurt me," or "I'm sticking my neck out too far." We all see great opportunities, but may be afraid to take a risk. That's the biggest problem many would-be investors face—their own reluctance.

William Zeckendorf was one of the greatest entrepreneurs of the century. After World War II, the United States government commissioned Zeckendorf to locate and acquire the property for the United Nations building in New York. So he went along the East River and found a site which had been a hog ranch and advised the UN to build their new building on this site. While he was negotiating a price, he bought a number of properties surrounding the subject site himself. Land that he paid $3 or $4 a square foot for before the UN building was built ballooned to $300 per square foot after it was constructed. And so Zeckendorf made a fortune on the deal.

Granted, he knew something that nobody else did. But it was possible to extrapolate the facts and come to the same realization just by reading the paper. Anybody could have found out, but not anybody was willing to follow up on it. A similar development recently transpired in Long Beach, California, with the building of the World Trade Center. Local economists were projecting that it would become the hub of downtown business activity as well as the focus in international trading activity for the ports of Long Beach and Los Angeles. But the point isn't to just be aware, it's to do something about it. In some locales, land is becoming scarce; there just isn't any more available for development. But some people have a hard time seeing an opportunity when it presents itself and acting on it.

When I heard they were going to build a new World Trade Center building in Long Beach, I drove down there and found a 34-unit apartment building that was up for sale within two blocks of the soon-to-be-built skyscraper. The developer had boxed off the construction site and had just dug the hole to lay the foundation. The apartment building was in terrible condition, a real dog. The people who owned it were letting it fall apart and didn't believe the area would ever turn around, even with the World Trade Center right at their front door.

I told my wife that we ought to make an offer on the apartment building and try to buy it because I knew we could make a few million off it. But she said, "Oh, no, no! I don't want to go near the place. I don't like the people. I'm afraid." I can guarantee you, whoever bought that building would have been able to rehabilitate it, double or triple the rents, and change the tenancy dramatically.

It would be pretty hard to lose on a deal like that if you could get it at a realistic price. As soon as the World Trade Center building was constructed, people started scrambling. Once a new building like that is standing, the potential is obvious. What you want to do is get there before the potential is plain for all to see.

QUALITY, CONVENIENCE, AND AVAILABILITY OF FACILITIES

A key indicator of the overall trend of a neighborhood is the quality, convenience, and availability of facilities that improve a community. If public schools, public transportation, shopping centers, cultural, recreational, and religious institutions are not top quality or don't work properly, they're not going to do the neighborhood and surrounding land values much good. The reputation of a school district can have a direct impact on the desirability of a particular neighborhood. An effective local transportation system can have a positive effect on real estate values and so can a substantial performing arts center or civic amphitheater. The availability of utilities also has a direct bearing on a neighborhood's growth potential. Some rural areas don't have sewer systems; they still have septic tanks. Not all areas have natural gas. The availability of cable television might even be a consideration. Today, a big consideration is whether an area has DSL (digital service line), a line available for rapid Internet service.

LAND AND IMPROVEMENT CHARACTERISTICS

Street Patterns

When considering a neighborhood to invest in, look for a homogeneous street pattern. Irregular subdivisions that conflict with each other don't have through streets, causing frequent traffic jams and congestion. In London, England, streets often run into funny alleyways and drivers can end up at someone's backyard or on a main highway. That city had a number of topsy-turvy growth patterns, and subdivisions were laid down without regard to each other. Unpredictable streets create an unpredictable traffic flow.

Boston, Philadelphia, and Baltimore are also like that. They are all old cities that have had unique and unusual growth. The patterns are such that access is prevented from certain directions. How you get in and out of a neighborhood obviously is a matter of convenience. On the other hand, if you have poor street patterns, it might be an advantage to a family with children precisely because it prevents access and therefore reduces street traffic. It's always advantageous if a family can live on a cul-de-sac because there is no through traffic, and people are more careful when they drive.

A few years ago, my wife and I joined the Orange County Performing Arts Center in Costa Mesa, California. Because the center is too far for us to drive for an evening, we started looking in the surrounding area for a condominium so we could attend the opera and ballet and have a place to stay overnight. I attended a local National Association of Realtors, Certified Commercial Investment Members meeting where the marketing director for the South Coast Metro Association spoke about a development that was planned for the community over time.

She had a number of statistics, so I sat there and listened. She talked about how they were going to build more high-rise office buildings and expand John Wayne Airport in nearby Irvine. After she was through, I asked what they were going to do about the traffic problem caused by all this planned development. She said, "We're thinking about widening the streets, or not allowing people to park on the streets, or changing the stop signs and signals." I told my wife that they were going to create one of the worst traffic jams in history. The apartments close to this huge, new employment/commercial center were going to be worth their weight in gold because the people living there would not have to commute to work. That was when I decided to buy my first condominium in Orange County. Now I own 30!

In 2003, Orange County population is currently around three million. By 2020, another 400,000 or so residents are expected to be living in the area.

> Orange County is already looking to the future with a proposed elevated monorail type or light-rail transportation to serve John Wayne airport to the Civic Center and beyond.

Current plans propose a light rail system along Bristol Street to Santa Ana Boulevard. If this is developed, it will have a significant impact on our condominiums, which would be in close proximity to this project.

> The added access this gives to my residents will ensure my condominiums will be worth way more than what we paid for them.

These are already among the most reasonable rents in the community and they are bound to rise significantly in the future due to all the activity in the area.

Similar Land Uses

A well-planned community generally has land uses that are well-defined. For instance, a residential neighborhood might have main thoroughfares surrounding it so it is completely separated and insulated from industrial property. Ideally, you want to find a homogeneous neighborhood where the land uses are more or less the same, where the homeowners are in the same basic income bracket, and where there is a similar family mix so that the attitudes are harmonious. This scenario lends itself to growth far more readily than areas with an incongruous mix of people and property.

As for lot shape, it is important to have a shape that is usable. A long and narrow, or irregularly shaped lot might present problems and prevent optimum use. A lot for commercial use that is only 25 feet wide is really difficult to use because it doesn't allow for adequate frontage. In many cases a buyer won't even know what the actual dimensions are until a surveyor is hired to physically determine them. As mentioned, I've been in many situations where people thought they were buying something they didn't get. Concerning lot orientation, it's generally considered desirable to have a house facing east with the bedrooms toward the west because it allows sunlight to filter into the bedroom in the afternoon while allowing you to sit in the coolness of the living room, where you are more likely to be at that time of the day.

Percentage of Area Developed

A neighborhood usually reaches its peak value and will begin to plateau when about 85% of the area is developed. That's when the initial enthusiasm will start to subside and when the original families in the neighborhood will want to start looking for something better. When that happens, the secondary owners move in. The second wave of owners generally will keep land values at a constant level for a period of time.

After that, property values will either go up or down, depending on what happens to the community. If the neighborhood deteriorates from undesirable activity, property values will go down. If people start acting in a negative manner—parking on lawns, installing cheap awnings that detract from appearances, letting yards get overgrown, not fixing potholes, changing their car oil in gutters, tolerating excessive loitering and untoward behavior—the neighborhood will cease to be a desirable place to live. Conversely, if everyone in the area has an attitude toward bettering the neighborhood, then the neighborhood will improve. Just as negative attitudes and actions will make property values go down, positive attitudes and actions will make them go up.

A neighborhood that is about 85% developed may still continue to rise in value, but you know that the potential is there for values to start leveling off. If the neighborhood is fully developed, then some of those people are going to think of moving somewhere else. Americans are always looking for the next best thing; they're always trying to design a better mousetrap or achieve a better life-style. In my opinion, the only way to solve the problem of affordable housing is to continue to build new houses, because the people who live in the upper level generally want to live in new housing. That can start a chain reaction all the way down the economic line.

In performing a neighborhood analysis, you don't measure the real estate as such. Instead, it is more important to measure the actions, attitudes, and thinking of people. It may not be as easy to do, but if you think of psychology as part of the business of real estate, then you will be ahead of other investors.

For example, I own five apartment buildings with a total of 26 rental units on the oceanfront. When I have the opportunity, I ask people why they choose to move here because it gives me a better idea how I can advertise and attract the right type of tenant for the area. I want to know why they want to be here, why people buy houses 150 feet from the beach, why they will pay almost as much for a house on a walk-street up from the beach as they will for a house right on the oceanfront. If you can commingle the attitudes of the people who live in a neighborhood, you'll have a much greater understanding of the forces that determine value.

Harmony of Development

Monotonous tract development, where there are hundreds or thousands of homes built all at once in uniform fashion, turns me off. It's like tenement housing; every building is practically the same. I think it destroys the beauty of the landscape. I like to stay away from it unless you can get a real bargain, because mass-produced housing projects usually appreciate at a slower rate than custom homes. When there isn't a feeling of uniqueness, your options are limited. This also applies to condominium projects that take on the appearance of row houses. Developers are just creating future slums by building structures like that. A unique design is going to be worth more over time, not a prefabricated, mass-produced one.

I've always felt that buying a unique property in an established area was much better than buying something that made you feel as if you were part of a mule train. A neighborhood where the properties are roughly the same size, quality, and price but are different in design has a more desirable aspect than a monotonous tract development, because it gives property owners a feeling of individual expression. When the neighborhood is established and has a certain reputation, people of the same income and socioeconomic status will generally go there.

The right location is the key to the whole thing; but you need the foresight to see the added potential. When you have a piece of real estate that is well located, it's probably better to own that property than build a new one if you're not sure what you're doing. The reason is that you can study a past performance of what has happened to an existing building. With a new building, that type of information doesn't exist. You only have similar, newer buildings to refer to.

Generally speaking, if you have a tract of homes in a desirable area, the value of those homes will reach their peak when the last property is sold. At this point, people who bought in first begin to want something more desirable and start looking for something else. If the neighborhood doesn't have true amenities to hold values—adequate employment opportunities, good schools, parks, recreational facilities, shopping centers, churches—it will generally deteriorate. The only thing that makes property in a monotonous housing tract valuable after that is a superb location. Otherwise, values become static and in some cases will fall.

If a city added a stop signal to a corner, the house or apartment building next to that corner would be affected. The crossing might be safer, but the noise would increase because people would periodically be compelled to start their cars and motorcycles from a standstill. A friend of mine once told me that she had to move from a particular house facing a thoroughfare because the motorcycles would shift gears at a point adjacent to her property and the noise became irritating over time.

When a city imposes traffic regulations, it directly affects residential real estate, many times in a negative fashion. But with commercial real estate, such as restaurants or retail stores, new traffic patterns can easily enhance values because motorists are obligated to stop, look around, and see what's in their immediate environment. What might be a disadvantage in one situation might be advantageous in another.

Other potentially negative developments may include a mini-mall or convenience store, which may add to the congestion problem and attract patrons who litter the neighborhood. But even these developments wouldn't deter me if I were able to buy a property in a good location at the right price. There's always a price at which a property is worth purchasing.

Some of the condominiums we bought in Costa Mesa face the boulevard. Because of this, we were able to pick them up for only $45,000 each. Even so, all these units still rent for around $800 a month, nearly the same amount I get for my other units inside the complex. Many people like to live on a busy street because they think there's something going on there. Again, it's the attitudes and thinking of people that determine value. You might find one person who thinks it's great and another who thinks it's terrible.

If you buy a house or apartment building in the center of a neighborhood, the surrounding houses will act as insulation and keep undesirable property uses away. Commercial and industrial property and multiple residential properties won't encroach. If a property is located on the edge of a neighborhood, it could have an encroachment, especially if the property is located next to a highway, used-car lot, or other type of commercial establishment. If a house is next to the corner, there could be a service station adjacent to the property that does body work on Saturday morning at 7:30 a.m. right under the bedroom window.

Zoning ordinances also act as artificial barriers. If a property is commercially zoned, developers are prevented from building any more houses in that area. But buying a property next to another property with a different use can sometimes work out over the long term. An office building is an example of a positive development, particularly if people want to live near their work.

Another example is a proposed hotel development in a desirable beach community adjacent to an existing residential development. One of the houses directly across the street from a proposed hotel where I live now rents for $2,500 a month. It was originally purchased in 1963 for $16,000 with no money down. If it takes two years to build the new hotel, then after three or four years the value of the residence, which originally cost $45,000, might go as high as $500,000, depending on the economy and the state of the housing market. You only need one opportunity like this in a lifetime to get you going.

If a property is commercially zoned, that serves as a barrier. You can't build any more houses in that direction. Or if a property is zoned for low density, you may be prevented from building multiple units on that site.

Recently, we built a new house on a lot I've owned for 30 years. In 1961, I could have built two units on the land. Today, because it's been downzoned, I was only able to build one single-family residence, and a scaled-back one at that. The city is trying to do everything it can to reduce the population density. If there are too many people, it's too hard on the utilities, it strains the maintenance budget, and it's difficult for the police and fire departments to provide an adequate level of service. Most cities in areas of fairly heavy density are having these problems and yet I think they are some of the best areas to invest in because the restrictions eliminate competition.

Before you buy anything, you should have as many facts at your disposal as possible. Bernard Baruch was a businessman and personal advisor to several presidents. From a humble beginning, he rose to become one of the wealthiest men in America. He used to say that if you have a very important problem, you should gather all the facts and information about it. The weight of the facts would answer the question for you or at least point in the direction of the solution. (Baruch was nicknamed "Dr. Facts" by President Woodrow Wilson.) In other words, the more careful the research, the more meaningful the final analysis.

It's important, however, not to go crazy over facts. Dwell on the important details and use the unimportant details for background. What's important and what isn't depends on the circumstances and the problem. The only way to know what's vital and what's extraneous is through education, knowledge, and experience. You just have to get out and do it; be proactive in your research and don't leave any important stone unturned. Remember also that the smart investor knows when to stop researching and arrive at a decision.

ECONOMIC CHARACTERISTICS

Degree of Home Ownership

In a newer single-family residential neighborhood, or "bedroom community," the odds are reasonably good that the homeowner will live in the neighborhood. But after the neighborhood has stabilized, homeowners start to move out and tenants start to move in. At this point, the neighborhood may start to deteriorate because renters don't have the same pride of ownership that owners do. They generally aren't of the mind to sweep the gutters, keep the yard maintained or pick up stray trash. And why should they be? They don't have a long-term financial stake in the neighborhood.

Most lending institutions will bend over backwards for homeowners because they represent stability, mom, apple pie, a white picket fence, and so on. They are substantial members of the community. On the other hand, banks aren't too enthusiastic about speculators or absentee landlords because they tend to be less reliable.

If you're in a rental area and the properties are only half-rented, the area will deteriorate. This has happened in numerous communities around the country, including parts of Kansas City, St. Louis, Detroit, Chicago's East Side, and New York City (just to name a few), where many housing projects are largely unoccupied, even though there is a housing shortage, because the area has become so dilapidated and run down. Unattended property naturally detracts from the value of the surrounding real estate. To change things for the better, you have to give people a stake in determining their own destiny.

If you are in an area with high rental rates and can see that the rents are increasing, then you know that the value of real property is increasing along with them. Whenever I see a sign for a rental, I always ask how much the rent is. And then I note how long it takes to rent it. I used to write this information down and keep track of it pretty carefully. Rental rates are especially important when you have a lot of competition and you need to keep your own rents slightly lower than the place down the street because you're just getting by and need the rent to make your payments. In many situations, real estate values will increase more rapidly than the rents. It only takes one person to pay a high price for a property, but it takes a large group of people to pay higher rental rates, pushing the average up.

FAMILY INCOME CHARACTERISTICS

The income levels of people in a community directly influence real estate values. If people in a community are prosperous, then values are generally high. When the oil market bottomed out, the local economies of Galveston, Midland, and Houston, Texas, as well as Oklahoma City, all took a real beating. Moreover, many industries that were dependent on the oil industry went out of business, so all types of workers lost their jobs and their homes and had to foreclose on their real estate. When contemplating an investment, make sure that people in the area are gainfully employed and will continue to be employed. Ideally, find a location where the incomes are substantial and diversified and where the conditions exist for steady growth. If you consider the demographics of the community and the influx of people into the area, you'll find that as the wages go up, so does the price of real estate.

Percentage of Families on Public Assistance

Generally speaking, the more people who are on public assistance in a neighborhood, the less likely that properties will rise in value. When I did an appraisal of a redevelopment project in National City, California, I discovered that 50% of the people in the area were on public assistance or welfare of some kind or another. That kind of data, which is readily available from the county and state, if not the local newspaper, is a red flag for the potential investor. The local real estate prices in these areas may be cheap, but they're not likely to appreciate.

An important thing to consider when buying investment property is how much spendable income the people in the neighborhood have and what their attitude is toward living. Are they gangsters who bring in $200,000 a year by selling crack cocaine or are they mechanical engineers making $100,000 a year designing high-speed transit or the national aerospace plane?

SOCIAL CHARACTERISTICS

Density of the Population

With 20,000 people in 1.4 square miles, Hermosa Beach is one of the most densely populated cities in California. The density, in my opinion, is destroying the area. Even before the current wave of municipal budget crises, Hermosa always seemed to run a deficit budget. Hermosa is an old city with inadequate parking and a dated infrastructure. And because the city has very little industry to provide a tax base, it lacks the necessary funds to run the city in a manner in which the community would like to have it run. High density can be a detriment in that respect, but when you own property in a highly populated area, density increases land values because of the demand.

For the past few years, the city council has been trying to downzone everything in an effort to reduce the number of residents, so they make it extremely difficult to own a business, build a house, or remodel an apartment building. Plans for building a new house in Hermosa Beach may sit in the city building department for a year. The drawings for remodeling one of my buildings on The Strand took nine months to be approved. Then, I had to seek approval from the state coastal commission, the city planning commission, and the city council. Although this is an incredible inconvenience, it is also extremely beneficial because the city's downzoning efforts make the existing properties worth much more.

Composition of the Population

If you find people with approximately the same income and same mix of family arrangements, whether it is the traditional family, singles, single parents with children, or senior citizens, then you have a harmonious neighborhood because everyone is more or less thinking on the same terms. The outside appearance of property also helps shape and define the neighborhood, but mainly it's the homogeneity of the inhabitants.

Incongruous economic and lifestyle patterns will create the potential for deterioration because of the lack of similar attitudes and values. Say you have a $300,000 house with a husband, wife, and three kids. In the house next door are five political activists who never fail to argue with each other into the early morning hours. Next door to that you have three bachelors. Next door to that you have a small, family-run day care center. The house next door to that doubles as an auto body shop. An incongruous mix like this tends to hinder the neighborhood from reaching its full potential. Consider the composition of the population before you buy.

Harmonious Attitudes

In order for there to be harmony, everyone in a neighborhood has to think somewhat alike. Most people like the idea of flowers in the garden, clean and maintained streets, and not having cars parked on the front lawn. With harmonious attitudes, chances are that people will take pride in their neighborhood and see that it improves or maintains its current character rather than deteriorates.

When people allow their properties to deteriorate, they almost always have a deteriorating attitude toward themselves. As a property owner, if you allow people to leave their trash in the front yard and park their cars, boats, and RVs on the lawn, you are contributing to the demise of the neighborhood because that type of activity detracts from property values. If everyone around has trashy attitudes, including property owners, then you're going to have a trashy neighborhood.

Don't be misled, however. The income level and outlook of the inhabitants are far more important than the outside appearance of the neighborhood. Remember, you want to invest in an area that has growth potential. If you see a neighborhood that has substantially declined but is in an area where the surrounding communities are good, these are growth factors that will eventually increase the value of the depressed neighborhood. The investor has a slightly different outlook than someone who wants to buy a piece of property for shelter.

If you go into the worst neighborhood and buy the best house there is, you will lose money. But, if you go into the best neighborhood and buy the worst house, you can always make money. You can always improve a house, but you can't by yourself impose your will to change a neighborhood. A group of people may be able to, but you can't do it individually.

The investor should not be concerned with what a piece of property is like now, but what it will be like 30 years from now. Your objective should always be forward-looking. Buy something today and estimate what the property will be worth 20 or 30 years hence. If you can find a dilapidated district, that might be a real opportunity because neighborhoods change. They go through different phases as peoples' attitudes change.

PRIDE OF OWNERSHIP

Pride of ownership is defined not only by the way people maintain the interior and exterior of their property, but also by the attitudes they have toward ownership.

> *My brother used to own a 14-unit apartment building in Hermosa Beach. In 1965, the building, which he had purchased with pretty high leverage, had a negative cash flow of $2,000 per month, which was a lot of money at the time. It was costing him that much to own it. But for him it was worth it. He used to sit across the street and say, "Gosh, I own this property!" The satisfaction he derived from knowing that he was the owner of this big, impressive complex tickled him to no end. That's pride of ownership. Plus, the building's now worth about 20 times what he paid for it.*
>
> *It makes me feel pretty good when I can walk on the beach and look up at my building, which sort of reminds me of a smaller version of a private beach club. That's pride of ownership, too. I felt it the first day I bought it. I liked it from the very beginning. I was thrilled to pieces—even though it was vacant, in terrible shape, and there were big awful-looking curtains in the front window and faded red carpets on the living room floor. I knew I could always fix the building and the interior and if I did, someday it was going to be worth something.*

Civic pride is slightly different than pride of ownership. With civic pride, people may be proud of the fact that they live in a certain area. It's more a pride of accomplishment, a feeling that you've arrived. These attitudes can also have a positive effect on property values.

For instance, if a group of people band together and start a neighborhood watch program to see that law and order are preserved, that tends to have a positive impact on law enforcement and helps to minimize crime. If something does happen, people will be up in arms and take action instead of shrugging their shoulders and saying, "Well, fortunately, it didn't happen to me, so I'll forget about it."

When people actively participate in neighborhood activities and show concern about their homes, they generally have a good attitude toward maintaining and improving the neighborhood. Similarly, if there are high enrollments, memberships, and participation in educational and cultural institutions, you can be assured that people want to improve themselves, better their condition, and strive for a higher standard of living.

Absence or Presence of Vice

If you get a bad feeling from an area, look at the crime rates. Crime rates can affect real estate values, drive people away from business districts, and take away revenue. Even so, it's important to weigh the amount of criminal activity against other salient factors, such as plans for new developments. If the city government is building a new hotel and convention center, expanding the harbor, or building a new sports arena, then I would be interested in buying a nearby property no matter how seedy the area is. Once the developer commits and gets these plans going, he can't go back. In this type of situation, I wouldn't give the crime factor much weight unless it's widespread.

Every area has crime. Just the mere fact that money is around will instigate it. Look for a neighborhood where you feel comfortable and can control the situation. I've never been afraid to walk on the beach at night. When I bought my home in Hermosa Beach, I figured that a burglar or attacker would only have one way to exit—inland (east). I thought about that very carefully when I was younger so that when I got older I wouldn't have to worry.

Sometimes, you can face the crime issue head-on by yourself. I once knew a fellow who bought a 30-unit apartment building in one of the most notorious parts of South

Central Los Angeles. It was in really bad shape, so he fixed it up. Before he started renovating, he put a fence around the place and got a few guard dogs to patrol the property. The front entrance sat about four feet above the street level for some reason, so he had a ramp built across the sidewalk to the front entrance so that the dogs could run under the ramp and not disturb the tenants.

That simple solution solved a lot of problems. Even though that place was in a high-crime area, it never got burglarized, and he was able to find good tenants. He transformed a run-down, dilapidated property into a desirable asset and turned it into a good-paying proposition. It took a lot of determination, but it paid off for him. Not only that, he wound up helping the people who lived there, and they appreciated his efforts.

Make a list of all the positive things that will make the property go up in value in 20 years. After you can imagine these things, consider the negatives. If you think of the positive qualities enough times, the negative attributes won't seem as bad as they did at first. But if you start listing the negative aspects first and begin to dwell on them, you'll never finish making your list. Unfortunately, that's what many people do. They find something to criticize and drum up an excuse for why they don't want to do it. That's the wrong approach. You should approach your investment program with a positive attitude like my friend did, and watch as wonderful things start to happen.

REAL ESTATE SALES ACTIVITY

Number and Prices of Homes for Sale

Before investing in a neighborhood, consider the number and price of the homes that are for sale to determine if you're in a buyer's or seller's market. This information should be available from your realtor or the local Board of Realty. But don't lose sight of the fact that you want to consider what the area will be like in 30 years. That's where you could make a critical mistake. If it's a buyer's market with a glut of properties listed for sale, you might be able to negotiate better terms. If you can get favorable terms, it could be well worth your while to buy even in the middle of a downturn.

> *If properties that are for sale in a neighborhood sit on the market for a long time, they are probably overpriced. If so, you can probably negotiate a good deal. The down payment and the terms of sale are more important than the purchase price. Say a seller has a residence for sale for $300,000. He or she has a $100,000 loan on the property and wants $200,000 cash out of the deal. You can come along and offer $300,000, offering to pay $100,000 in cash if the seller agrees to take back a second mortgage for $100,000. You go to lenders and refinance the property. If you get a $200,000 first loan and the seller agrees to carry the $100,000 second loan, at this point, you haven't got a dime invested, except closing costs.*
>
> *Now, supposing he or she is very anxious to sell and is willing to take no interest or principal payments for 10 years on the second. How much will that note be worth if you tried to sell it on the open market? Probably only about $25,000 because of the terms, so you're really buying the property for $225,000 not $300,000. You never know what a motivated seller will do. For more on creative financing, see chapter 13.*

SALES CONDITIONS

Willingness of Lenders to Participate

The willingness of recognized institutional lenders to participate in the neighborhood says a great deal about the value of the property. If a lender, which is supposed to be conservative by nature in its lending practices, is willing to make a loan, then that is a major vote of confidence in the subject neighborhood. Also, if your real estate agent is on the ball and keeping track of what's going on in the community, he or she should be able to find out whether substantial down payments are being made on purchases. This suggests that the people moving into the area are solid citizens.

Number of Foreclosures

The number of foreclosures has an effect on the overall trend of the neighborhood. If people no longer have the ability to make their payments, they'll be foreclosed on and the property will deteriorate, which is bad for the quality of a neighborhood. If there are a lot of foreclosures, it indicates that the neighborhood is in a recessionary trend, although foreclosures don't necessarily occur together unless the people who live there are all employed by the same industry and that industry is in the midst of restructuring and mass layoffs. Similarly, if there are a lot of people in a neighborhood with delinquent taxes, they don't have the money to sustain themselves and they don't think much of the property. If you have a good broker, he should know these kinds of things. Watch these neighborhoods, because when they turn around they will make great investments.

GOVERNMENTAL CHARACTERISTICS

Taxation Policies

In most cities and counties, the assessed value for real property acts as the basis for determining the property tax rate. Real property taxes are the best revenue bases for governments because property is always there. It is always possible to get a lien against a property because real estate is secure; it doesn't move. On the other hand, you can take a car across the state line and all your creditors can do is hire a skip-tracer.

If property taxes increase, there is far more expense in owning real estate. When taxes go up, it takes money out of the income stream of property owners. However, higher property taxes probably won't result in lower housing prices. Usually, when property taxes go up, it is a sign that the neighborhood is improving. Taxes aren't usually raised in areas that are declining.

Recently, I consulted some property owners whose real property assessments doubled over a two-year period. Incensed, these home and apartment owners formed an action committee to fight the dramatic increase. Amazingly, the county assessor's reassessment proved to be correct. As a result, land values, as well as real property taxes, increased dramatically. Property owners were subsequently compelled to improve their rental units to bring in more income to pay the higher tax rate. There was an upside to these higher assessments, however; in the process of making improvements to their units, the property owners stimulated the local real estate market and were able to ask for higher rents.

Municipal Fees and Assessments

Municipal fees and assessments are another burden on property owners and occur when a city decides to make general improvements to municipal infrastructures such as roads and utilities. Even the smallest city governments have regulatory and taxing authorities, which make them powerful. In many cities, property owners now have to pay an additional trash-collection tax to fund recycling programs. The installation of new sewer lines can also result in a new assessment.

If a city has too much indebtedness caused by the passage of too many bond issues for public works projects, it could have a low municipal bond rating. Since the bonds are riskier, investors who buy them are entitled to more interest. That means property owners would have to pay more money to accommodate that higher interest rate. If, in this situation, a city were to put new initiatives on the ballot to build new schools, resurface streets, and undertake a massive redevelopment project and all the measures were approved by voters at the same time, all city services would be placed in jeopardy on account of the precarious revenues.

Zoning Ordinances

When selecting property, obtain a zoning map and see how the area is zoned. If you're looking at an R-1 residential lot but the house next door is zoned C-2 commercial, you're going to want to know about it, because someday the owner could tear down that C-2 house and replace it with a muffler shop or convenience store. You want the owner to know that you have this information so the price will be right. Figure 7.1 shows a typical zoning map.

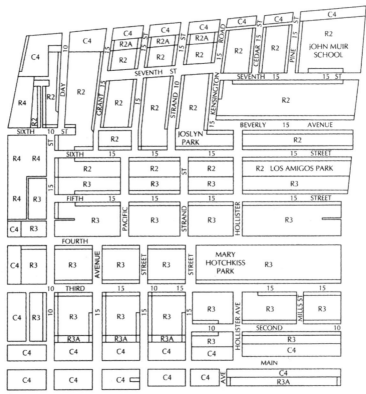

FIGURE 7.1
Sample zoning map showing permitted land uses. (C = commercial; R = residential; R-A = parking; R2, 3, 4 = allowable density, e.g., two units, three units, four units.)

If I were going to buy a property with questionable zoning, I would make the deal contingent on zoning approval by the city council. That is a standard practice if you want to change a zoning designation. Unless, of course, you can buy the property for so little that it doesn't matter. The problem with zoning matters is that you need a seller who's willing to wait months to sell to allow enough time for the zoning process to complete.

Typically, if a zoning change is approved, the property will become more valuable, in which case the seller could ask for more. Say a parcel is rezoned from residential to commercial. A buyer would probably pay at least 25% more to build a restaurant or shopping center in place of a house or apartment building. But since these kinds of changes aren't guaranteed, you need to agree on a price assuming that the property will be rezoned. If it isn't, you might want to reconsider your purchase.

Wherever there are heavy population densities, there tend to be slow-growth movements that advocate downzoning. An elevator designed for 10 people can't hold 15 because it's dangerous. The same thing is true for a city. If a city's public services—streets, schools, utilities, and the like—are designed only for 10,000 or 20,000 people but 40,000 move in, you're going to have a colossal problem, and that is exactly what's happening in many popular areas, especially on the coasts. Cities in these instances have no choice but to downzone. If a city decides to downzone an area, it generally means that existing properties become more valuable. Say you owned a single-family residence that was 5,000 square feet on a lot, and the city changed the setbacks so they had to be 17 feet from the alleyway before you could put in a garage. And they've added setbacks on the side, so now you can build only 2,000 square feet on the same lot. The existing building, which now becomes "legal non-conforming," could be worth much more than a new one.

Legal-non-conforming properties that aren't burdened with the factor of functional obsolescence enable property owners to utilize the property to the greatest extent. The six-unit apartment building I live in, which became legal non-conforming in 1956 when the city changed its zoning ordinance, is not functionally obsolete in the least. Even though it was built in 1938, it accommodates six groups of tenants as well now as it did then.

Everything manmade is a depreciating asset; as soon as it's built, it starts to deteriorate and go down in value. But my building, even though it is 65 years old, is worth more now than when it was built partly because of downzoning.

I have two lots in Redondo Beach zoned R-3. Each is only big enough for a single-family residence, but together, I could build three units. However, I cannot do so because of a zoning ordinance that prevents accumulation of lots to gain plottage. Since it isn't possible to assemble adjoining lots for construction purposes, you aren't going to see any big apartment buildings erected in Redondo Beach anytime soon. Single-family residences, therefore, will rise in value. In these examples, external influences from governmental bodies have had a marked effect on real estate values.

Creative Rehabilitation

Creative rehabilitation is the act of improving the present use of a building to a higher and better use by eliminating such negative factors as obsolescence and physical deterioration. Many older buildings are structurally sound but lack modern amenities, including modern electrical wiring, plumbing, heating systems, and insulation. When the basic structure is sound and modern facilities are installed, the value of the property is sometimes enhanced beyond what a new building would be worth on the same site.

Oftentimes, you can get more money out of an older building that can be rehabilitated than you can by constructing a new building, especially if the older building is legal non-conforming and has more units than the current zoning ordinance allows. There are examples of this in most areas. Typically, the city allows property owners to renovate a building that doesn't conform with current zoning laws without a special permit or variance as long as the renovation doesn't change the exterior of the building or add to the overall square footage. In high-density areas, a remodeling job often makes better sense than building from the ground up because you don't have to provide all the parking necessary for a new building.

Building Codes

Building codes are designed to provide the city building department with a uniform method of regulating the construction of buildings in keeping with health and safety requirements. These regulations are stipulated in the form of construction standards. In high-density areas, such as New York City or Manhattan Beach, people attempt to modify and rent illegal apartment units, such as converted garages, basements, attics, and bedrooms. If building codes are vigorously enforced, this helps preserve the quality of the neighborhood. Still, many renters and owners do things without a permit. If you have any questions about a specific site, check with the city building department on building permits. They are a matter of public record.

Health and Fire Regulations

Health and fire regulations, such as laws that require smoke detectors, fire extinguishers, and sprinkler systems, can really become a costly issue in a high-density area. Several years ago, the City of Los Angeles passed an ordinance requiring all high-rise buildings to install sprinklers. It is very expensive to comply with a fire code like that. Many older office buildings have asbestos in the ceiling, and in order to install sprinklers, the asbestos has to be removed. Sometimes conforming to new regulations can cost as much as rehabilitating the whole building. That's why investors who know the law and can work efficiently within it are going to be successful. The more you know, the more you can take into consideration when putting an offer on a property, whether a residence, apartment building, or commercial building.

A lot of people don't know what an asbestos ceiling is, let alone how to deal with the city when an inspector comes out. Asbestos is a hazardous material used for fireproofing before it was discovered to be dangerous, and its removal is governed by strict regulations. When an inspector walks through a building and notes that it has an asbestos ceiling it and you can't put in sprinklers until you get rid of it, then some owners might get desperate, especially if the building isn't paying for itself at the moment.

When investing, strive to become educated and knowledgeable enough to realize what the important factors are that affect the value of the property you are interested in acquiring. Learn what contingencies and events might occur that will advantageously affect the value of that property the long haul. Also, become aware of the detrimental factors that can undermine the value of the property over that period. Those are the important things; the rest is secondary.

Dwell on these kinds of things and look at them in the form of a trend. When you see that the trend is going in the right direction, act on it. When you see it going in the wrong direction, move on to something else. Understanding what factors are important is a matter of studying the problem. As we'll see in chapter 9, the surest sign that the value of land will rise is if average income levels are on an upward trend. Two other key indicators of long-term growth potential include population estimates and employment projections.

Knowledge is more important than money. Once you're in an area with growth potential, you don't have to do nearly as much research and analysis. Once you've found a neighborhood with a strong growth trajectory, you can hop on the bandwagon. But it is important to go through a reasonable process of assessing a neighborhood's long-term prospects to be assured of a solid investment location.

Neighborhood Decay: Disaster or Opportunity?

One of the most brutal episodes in the history of crime occurred in 1888 in the East End of London, in an area known as Whitechapel. From August to November of that year, five women were brutally murdered and their bodies were mutilated. This was the case of Jack the Ripper. Many stories have been written about him and how brutal he was. Scotland Yard was never able to find the murderer or bring anyone to justice, although many theories have been formulated over the years.

It is interesting to note that this area in London was an underprivileged area of the city. Even now, over 100 years later, the area is pretty much in the same state of decline as it was in 1888 when the murders occurred.

One of the most important things about real estate values is the actions, attitudes and thinking of people. They create as well as destroy value. Because this community has not been improved due to economic constraints, the area has been a difficult place to live in for over a century and therefore has been a problem investment for real estate investors.

Most major cities in the world have the same problem. In the Whitechapel example, where the community does not have large sums of money to spend for improvement of the area, the actions and attitudes of the people who live in that community must improve in order for any real estate investment to appreciate in value.

People who invest in communities like this, if they understand the problems, can acquire the property very cheaply. The investment can be successful if they know how to rent properties of this kind and how to deal with the people involved. The investment requires people who understand the area and who are willing to put in the hard work necessary to collect the rent and maintain the properties.

In my opinion, it is extremely important to look at areas where real estate values have deteriorated dramatically and where investors are reluctant to invest, even though millions of federal, state and even city funds might go into redevelopment efforts to enhance it. The attitude of the people in these communities is vital to making the area safe so business can prosper and residents can live in security without fear of gang wars and random killings.

You must analyze a district with the intent of buying real estate where you would expect to get capital appreciation over a reasonable period of time, say over 20 or 30 years. It is necessary to find out what kind of influences might occur to enhance or retard the economic development during this time.

These areas of difficulty can be found in most major cities of the United States and other parts of the world. It is a Herculean task for cities and even communities to change the attitude of people within these areas to be more concerned about the neighborhood and to have a desire to improve conditions for a better way of life than what previously existed. This very important factor should be considered. If you expect a neighborhood to improve and decay to be eliminated, the people within that area must improve their thinking. Spending money on rebuilding buildings is a step in the right direction. Even then, the improvement will be far from complete.

Real estate investors should be cautioned that if they are looking for capital appreciation in any type of real estate investment, they must find a community with a good attitude that is trying to improve itself, where rules of self-discipline and concern toward other people are appreciated. It isn't easy to find communities that are willing to change in that direction. There has to be some type of outside influence that will aid in the change. A major problem today in redeveloping underprivileged communities is their poor financial conditions of municipalities due to the recent recession.

But good opportunities do exist if you are an informed investor. So keep looking and you may have an opportunity for an investment to increase enormously in value.

In sharp contrast, consider Central London England, where real estate prices have gone out of sight in recent years and traffic has become so clogged that city officials have taken drastic measures to try and resolve the problems.

A "congestion charge" fee was introduced in February 2003 in an effort to curtail traffic through the city during peak hours. The fee back then was the equivalent of about $8 per day per car passing through a certain area of London between the hours of 7:00 a.m. and 6:00 p.m. Monday through Friday. Taxis and motorcycles are exempt. Rates in 2009 are the equivalent of $15 per day, with fines for nonpayment ranging between $98 and $295. The area also has been expanded to include West London. Residents within the restricted area are allowed a reduced fee rate for one car per family. The system runs on CCTV cameras erected at all the streets leading into the restricted area. Each license plate is photographed as the car enters the restricted zone. This is a good example of how density of population affects real estate values. It's a question of supply and demand. Housing prices in Central London are continuing to go through the roof.

8

Use the Internet to Buy Real Estate: Getting Started and Continuing Your Education

Getting Started and Continuing Your Education

I use the Internet a lot. It is a great tool to find properties, get familiar with the economic potential of an area and find good vendors—real estate agents, fix-it people, property managers and the like. I advertise for renters using several Web sites that you will find in this chapter because the classified-ad sections are not being used as much anymore.

In fact, I bought several REO bank foreclosures in 1999 before the Internet was as popular as it is today. Before that, many VA foreclosures were bought by my company using the computer. I am a big believer in the time-saving benefits the Internet provides.

Be the Virtual Man on the Street

Here's something current. You want to look at a property, travel down the street and look at the neighborhood? Then use maps.google.com and see a virtual "man on the street" view for most every major city in the country. Type in the property address and use the little man icon to be transported right in front of the house. But that street view is dated to the day, years ago, when Google sent their truck out to view that location.

But there is no substitute for getting out there and being on the streets, using your wits, making offers and meeting sellers. The Internet can get you in front of what the house looked like years ago and deluge you with torrents of information, but what you do with it determines your success. Too many budding real estate entrepreneurs use the computer as a crutch; it seems they are afraid of people and want to take the lazy way out.

You need to use the common sense you are learning in this book to be successful. Anticipating why a neighborhood will be worth more years from now, seeing a property become distressed and then jumping on it, figuring out how much it would take to rehab it and screening for the right tenants are just some of the talents you will need to acquire.

Use the Best Web Sites

Many of the Web Sites on the following pages are the ones I use or are the tools of some very successful investors I know.

1. WWW.HOMESALES.GOV—I have bought 11 houses because of this information! Foreclosed homes for sale from the US government. They are from the US Department of Housing and Urban Development (HUD), the Veterans Administration (VA), the Department of Agriculture (USDA) and the Small Business Administration (SBA).
2. WWW.GOVSALES.GOV—I love government auctions! Surplus government property of all types—washers, dryers, furniture, file cabinets, vehicles, etc., all sold very cheaply.
3. WWW.REALTYTIMES.COM—this free web site is a repository for realtor newsletters nationwide. It is a great source for local knowledge in a specific neighborhood. Although realtors are salespeople and their newsletters can be a bit fluffy there is no substitute for having somebody "on the ground" with whom you can cross check information.

4. WWW.REALTOR.ORG—click on the research bar and get the appreciation rates for the top 100 metro areas nationwide!

5. WWW.OFHEO.GOV—the Office of Federal Housing Enterprise Oversight. A great research site. Gives housing prices and appreciation rates for states and most major metro areas.

6. WWW.CNNMONEY.COM—this one-stop Web site has it all! Very current business info and a very complete real estate news site.

7. WWW.ZILLOW.COM—to check the value of almost any property in the nation. You get a satellite map of your property and the sales prices of all other houses on the block.

8. WWW.INMANNEWS.COM—a paid-subscriber site that gives very good daily real estate news.

9. WWW.NEWSPAPERS.COM—access the nation's newspapers online. Scan the daily business pages for updated economic information.

10. WWW.REALESTATEJOURNAL.COM—brought to you by the folks at the *Wall Street Journal*. Learn about the current real estate/business environment from the Wall Street perspective.

Learn and Find Out About Foreclosures and Bank Repos Near You:

11. WWW.ALL-FORECLOSURE.COM—one of the best sites for REOs. and government foreclosures. Not only do they have extensive info about how foreclosures work, but they have actual bank repos listed for sale. I bought 3 as the result of finding this site. And the banks will deal with you!

12. WWW.FORECLOSUREFORUM.COM—San-Diego-based foreclosure specialist. Good chat room, free sample grant deeds, lease agreements, notes and purchase contracts. Very informative on how foreclosures work, evictions and more.

13. WWW.FORECLOSURES.COM—tells about foreclosure procedures in each state and has a service that will track foreclosures in most areas.

Locate Investment Property Nationwide and Find Out How Much It Is Worth:

14. WWW.REALTOR.COM—this National Association of Realtor Web site gets you in contact with member realtors and their listings. Find contractors, movers and local real estate vendors. Good background resources.
15. WWW.DQNEWS.COM—Data Quick's Web site has very current info regarding changes in median home prices. It covers all metro areas in California and ten other cities.
16. WWW.ZIPREALTY.COM—online comparables. Personal info required.
17. WWW.HOMERADAR.COM—good articles and online comparables.
18. WWW.EBAYREALESTATE@EBAY.COM—this Web site will e-mail you sales as they happen in any area. The lazy man's guide to riches.
19. WWW.TRUIIA.COM—has a nationwide database of varied listings in all areas. Easy to use. I use it.

Great Places to Find Out Job Growth and to Where People Are Moving:

20. WWW.FEDSTATS.GOV—great Web site for you data dogs out there. You can find out where people work, how much they make and how many live in a given area.
21. WWW.BLS.GOV—from the US Bureau of Labor Statistics, this very huge and voluminous database is for serious data dogs only!

22. WWW.BEA.GOV—this Web site summarizes the complex data from the BLS data above. It gives nice a synopsis of all states' most recent unemployment data, personal income growth, types of industries and current area GDPs.

23. WWW.CENSUS.GOV—from the US Census Bureau Web site, you can find out the cost of living (CPI) in any area, the types of industry and vacancy rates. Demographic and economic data and much more!

24. WWW.CHAMBEROFCOMMERCE.COM—access local economic information from the group most responsible for promoting the area's business interests. If you know nothing about an area, this is the place to start.

25. WWW.BESTPLACES.NET—criteria-best appreciation, lowest home prices, best schools, lowest crime, etc.

26. WWW.RREEF.COM—a paid-subscriber site but has a terrific free economic map that graphically displays US economic activity state by state. Great research from Deutsche Bank.

Other Commentators on the Real Estate Scene Nationwide:

27. WWW.LOCALMARKETMONITOR.COM—a very good survey for future economic trends in over 100 different metropolitan areas. Somewhat dated but has enough free information to be useful.

28. WWW.ERC.ORG—future job growth in different areas of the country. What makes this site unique is that it surveys human resource professionals who do the actual hiring for major corporations and finds out when and where they hire, how many jobs they will have, and how much they will pay.

Free Property Profiles Are Worth the Money:

29. WWW.TITLEADVANTAGE.COM—run your own property profiles and sales comparables for free. This is the same as having your own account at a title company.

How to Find Out About Your Credit Score and Repair It:

30. WWW.MYFICO.COM—get your credit score and a copy of your credit report online from this secure site. Best Web site to get the straight scoop on how they compute credit scores straight from the horse's mouth, the Fair Isaac Co.
31. WWW.CREDITINFOCENTER.COM—Lots of free information revealing credit scores and how to repair credit. Highly recommended.
32. WWW.BANKRATE.COM—Well-regarded Web site gives loads of info about how credit works, credit cards for people with poor credit, how to complain to credit bureaus and much, much more.
33. WWW.MORTGAGE101.COM—a beginner's guide to mortgages.

You Must Learn About Local, National and International Business and Economic Trends:

34. WWW.MONEY.COM—recommended reading for general financial news.
35. WWW.YAHOO.COM—Yahoo.com finance.
36. WWW.CNBC.COM—great site that tells you all about the happenings on Wall Street.
37. WWW.FORTUNE.COM—recommended reading for general financial news.
38. WWW.FORBES.COM—recommended reading for general financial news.

39. WWW.ECONOMIST.COM—find out what is happening globally.
40. WWW.ITA.DOC.GOV—this International Trade Association site gives oodles of trade and export data from all states in the US to show international trade activity. Very important info that reveals that no place is isolated in our growing global village!

My Best Gurus, Where You Will Get the Best Knowledge Without Paying an Arm and a Leg:

41. WWW.CASHFLOWCONCEPTS.COM—long one of the brightest minds in the creative real estate business, Jack Miller has done it better and longer than most and writes a great newsletter.
42. WWW.DAVIDTILNEY.COM—everything you need to know about managing the tenant-landlord relationship. My property management guru.
43. WWW.JOHNSCHAUB.COM—John will teach you everything you need to know about the house biz. A very good teacher.
44. WWW.PETERFORTUNATO.COM—Peter Fortunato has a very informative style that focuses on people, documentation and negotiation. His Paper Course sets a standard in the industry.
45. WWW.LOUISBROWN.COM—Louis Brown has the best and most complete paperwork in the business. A knowledgeable and down-to-earth investor/teacher. Somewhat more expensive but worth the money.

Screen Your Gurus:

46. WWW.REALESTATECOURSEREVIEWS.COM—go here to read Amazon-type reviews of some on the above gurus from real real estate investors.

Use Your IRA or Retirement Plan to Buy Real Estate:

47. WWW.ENTRUST.COM—entrust has been around a long time and gives great service. They have very detailed training programs, so I like to use them.

48. WWW.TRUSTETC.COM—Equity Trust is the granddaddy of self-directed IRA investing. You Want to Explore Commercial Real Estate Investing?

49. WWW.CCIM.COM—a commercial real estate investor Web site.

50. WWW.HOUSINGFINANCE.COM—a Web site for apartment financing.

51. WWW.VANDEMA.COM—all about commercial real estate.

People Active in Real Estate— Industry Trade Groups:

52. WWW.NMHC.ORG—the National Multi-Housing Unit Council represents the interests of the nation's larger and most prominent apartment firms. NMHC conducts apartment-related research and encourages the exchange of strategic business information. A great free newsletter tells you where all the big money is going.

53. WWW.NAMB.ORG—National Association of Mortgage Brokers. Since mortgage brokers participate in more than 68% of home loan originations, homebuyers' interests are also important to them. A great place to start if you want to get into the business.

54. WWW.A-E-A.ORG—the American Escrow Association. This industry trade group Web site has a great Q&A section that demystifies the escrow process.

55. WWW.ALTA.ORG—the American Land Title Association (ALTA).

56. WWW.BOMA.COM—the Building Owners and Managers Association.
57. WWW.FANNIEMAE.COM.
58. WWW.FREDDIEMAC.COM.
59. WWW.HUD.ORG—the Department of Housing and Urban Development (HUD).
60. WWW.INFOVILLE.COM—the National Council of Exchangers. A great way to find a licensed 1031 exchange accommodator.
Nationwide Neighborhoods—Find out What's Going on in Any Town Nationwide; Neighborhood Information—Demographics, Desirability Indexes, Crime Statistics, Schools and How They Rank:
61. WWW.EPODUNK.COM—iF you don't know what is going on in an area, this is the place for just about any town in the country, no matter how small.

So You Want to Be a Landlord—Find out the Rental Market:

62. WWW.REALFACTS.COM—an excellent resource to track multiunit vacancy rates nationwide.
63. WWW.RHOL.ORG—nearly anything related to the rental housing business.
64. WWW.LANDLORD.COM—a great resource for forms. Over one million members nationwide.
65. WWW.MRLANDLORD.COM—has links to landlord-tenant laws in all fifty states.
66. WWW.AOAUSA.COM—the Apartment Owners Association, An excellent resource. Has a tenant-screening service for credit history, bounced checks and previous evictions. Membership includes a very informative monthly newsletter.
67. WWW.RENTLAW.COM—one of the best multifaceted landlord resources I have seen. **Highly recommended.** Has landlord-tenant laws state by state as well as info on 1031 exchanges, Section 8 vouchers and limited liability companies (LLCs), sample lease agreements and much more.

List Your Houses for Rent at Low to No Cost— Check Your Immediate Area for Best Results:

68. WWW.RENTALS.COM.
69. WWW.FORRENT.COM.
70. WWW.EZRENTLIST.COM.
71. WWW.RENT.COM.
72. WWW.RENTALS.COM.
73. WWW.WESTSIDERENTALS.COM.
74. WWW.CRAIGSLIST.COM—this is the one I use the most. Find renters for free.
75. WWW.RENTREADYINC.COM—California only.

Know Thy Law—Legal Web Sites:

76. WWW.STATELOCALGOV.NET—a great governmental resource that lists all state and local.
77. WWW.BRBPUB.COM—Government Public Records Online. Access US government information online. Look up all state and federal laws.
78. WWW.IRS.COM—the Internal Revenue Service (IRS).
79. WWW.LEGALWIZ.COM—Bill Bronchick. Informative attorney specializing in creative real estate. Highly recommended.
80. WWW.LEGALZOOM.COM—a great Web site that has legal information in all areas. Create your own living trust, limited liability corporation or corporation.
81. WWW.NOLOPRESS.COM—great free newsletters for whatever legal situation you are in.

Find a Home Inspection Company:

82. WWW.NAHI.ORG—the National Association of Home Inspectors.

Meet With Other Investors— Find a Real Estate Investors Club in Your Town:

83.   WWW.REICLUB.COM—National Real Estate Investment Clubs.

Talk Virtually to Other People Like You— Real Estate Chat Rooms:

84.   WWW.CREONLINE.COM—Creative Investment Clubs of America. Informative discussions with a good following of regulars. Good newsrooms and information regarding legal issues, financing, mobile homes and legal issues.

85.   WWW.LEGALWIZ.COM—discussions of the legal aspects of real estate, hosted by Bill Bronchick.

Government Grants to Help You Buy Your First Residence:

86.   WWW.NCSHA.ORG—the National Council of State Housing Agencies. Find out the government agency in your state that will provide financial assistance or maybe even a free down payment for your first home.

Miscellaneous:

87.   WWW.CAR.ORG—the California Association of Realtor's Web site is a very good source for raw economic data for state trends in housing affordability and housing strength in all California areas.

88.   WWW.DOF.CA.ORG—this State of California Department of Finance site offers very good demographic data. It is very detailed and will tell you to where people are moving, population data and the kinds of jobs and how much they pay.

Take a Ride Down the Internet Highway— An Example of How I Use the Internet to Build Wealth

Suppose I want to buy a house. There are myriad ways to find properties to buy:

1.   They can fall into your lap (this will happen once you build a name for yourself).
2.   You might see one while driving around—a property in distress, or maybe you just like the neighborhood or the city.
3.   A friend or real estate broker tells you about a it.
4.   The banks are in distress—you want to buy an REO.

If I don't know much about a city, I will go to www.chamberofcommerce.com to get a fix on the kind of businesses in the area. Let's say it's close by, in my case Los Angeles. Perhaps I go to www.newspapers.com and find local, neighborhood papers to keep up with the business activity—who is hiring, who is being laid off and what companies seem to be prospering the most. I want to buy near those firms that are doing well. Why? Because those well-paid tenants need to rent from me!

If I want to know how much a house in that area would rent for, I go to www.zilpy.com to see what the rents are for the same size house. The numbers of bedrooms and bathrooms have to match. Then I would call a local property manager to verify the information. Property managers are great sources of what a property is worth rent-wise.

If I am satisfied that the city has good prospects, I verify that with employment data from www.bls.gov to see how that city's unemployment rate compares with rest of California. If there is sustainable job growth, I want to have a long-term relationship with that city in the form of property ownership. I will have a stake in the long-term prosperity of Los Angeles.

It's time to zero in on a neighborhood. Not all areas of a city are the same and I want to be in the path of progress. I need local knowledge of the investment potential of two or three areas of the city, and you don't get this on the Internet. Local real estate investment clubs are full of longtime landlords, property flippers, contractors, real estate agents and others who serve the real estate investor community. By going to www.reiclub.com, I find them listed. Maybe I talk to the president of the club about where the best areas in town are, ask who the successful long-term buy-and-hold investors are (I want to talk to them!) and where he would invest. Maybe he knows of a hot deal right now or can refer me to a wholesaler who finds below-market deals for a living then sells them to investors.

By this time, I am getting a flavor of the locale—job growth, where are the hot areas of LA are, how the rents are doing, the kinds of tenants a neighborhood attracts and where the successful landlords are making the most money. I am also finding people I will use in the future.

Now I can use the Internet to find a property to buy. The local multiple listing service on www.ziprealty.com or www.homeradar.com is where I start. Then I compare the values I see on www.truilia.com to see how good a deal they are. Maybe by this time I have found a real estate agent who can help me run the property comparables and he can lead me to some special deals.

If I want to find bank foreclosures, I can find all the REOs I want on www.all-foreclosure.com. Since I have bought VA and FHA foreclosures in the past, I might start with www.homesales.gov. All these foreclosure Web sites allow you to select properties by state, city and possibly as specific as by ZIP code.

Once you have several specific neighborhoods in mind, wait. Good deals go fast, so you need keep your power on your microscope. Keep monitoring your Web sites, have locals looking for you, and you will find what you are looking for.

When you find something you like, go to maps.google.com and map it. Click on the icon that affords you a street-level view. If it looks good, turn off your computer and GO SEE IT.

This is where you get off the Internet highway and start to walk. The World Wide Web can only do so much; you have to walk it before you buy it. If you can't afford to walk the property, you can't afford it.

Make the offer—how much to pay is up to you. Just make sure it is rentable because once you buy it, you will want to get it filled with a paying renter as soon as possible.

Many new purchases need repairs before you rent them out. When you are close to having it done, start advertising to get a renter on www.craigslist.com and on the other landlord Web sites I have listed. I like Craig'slist the best; right now it is used the most by younger, Internet-savvy renters.

Once you have several applicants you like, check their credit, bounced checks and eviction histories on www.aoausa.com or www.mrlandlord.com.

You don't have to ride the Internet road exactly as I do; you do not even have to get on the Internet. Some of the most successful investors I know don't even have e-mail addresses.

Conclusion

If you want to purchase a home or investment property, you can easily access the Internet and get an incredible amount of information about an area ir the value within specific regions, and find a realtor or lender. All this can be done from the Internet search engines.

Learn to browse and surf the Internet sites that I have given you and you will be light years ahead of the average buyer. Use your common sense, your savvy and the knowledge you gain in this book and you cannot be stopped from building wealth far into the twenty-first century.

9

Select the Right Property and Make an Analysis of Its Growth Potential

After identifying the right neighborhood for your investment, the next step is to select the right property to buy and analyze its growth potential. Besides physical appearance and other visible signs, a key consideration in determining the desirability of a piece of real estate is its zoning designation, whether high- or low-density industrial, commercial, or residential. Knowing the lot's size and precise boundaries can also influence the sales price.

The first thing you should do is find a good real estate market where you know there is great potential. Most people find a place where they want to live and buy a piece of property there, and if they like the area, they might buy another one. When I came to Hermosa Beach, I studied the area very carefully before buying anything. It was rundown at the time, but I always looked at it with a long-term perspective. I wasn't so much interested in what the property was like when I bought it as what it would be worth 20 or 30 years later.

Ideally, you should spend a few months investigating as much as you can about a community. Before you buy, maybe rent for a little while, and give yourself some time to do a study and determine what you really want, what your objectives are, and how they fit into your overall program. It's always better for you to make an analysis of a community firsthand than to hire someone to do it, because you know what you're looking for.

Table 9.1 lists the many characteristics to be aware of when judging the value of income property.

TABLE 9.1
Factors that Affect the Value of Income Property

Land	Services	Facilities	Conditions
Location	Paving	Schools	Zoning
Topography	Sidewalks	Churches	Percent developed
Street width	Street lights	Proximity to mass transit	Type of development
Alleyways	Phone service	Neighborhood shopping	Appearance
Corner lots	Cable TV service	Regional shopping	Present use
Drainage	Internet access		Highest and best use
Soil conditions	Utilities		Deed restrictions
Size and shape	Transportation		Assessed values
Filled ground	Fire protection		Easements
	Police protection		

A few years ago I spoke with a real estate broker who moved to Belmont Shore, an upscale residential community south of Long Beach, California. This broker told me that he spent two years studying the community, real estate market and local economy before he decided to open his office there. He took it upon himself to become thoroughly informed about all aspects of the community before he completed one transaction. During the next few years, he advertised the fact that he had become an authority on Belmont Shore and would invite property owners, prospective buyers, and other interested parties to attend seminars where he shared his knowledge of the area. Needless to say, he developed a thriving business.

In 1960, during the construction of King Harbor in Redondo Beach, I chartered a helicopter to survey the best land to invest in along the South Bay coastline. Since there wasn't any beach frontage in Redondo, I decided on Hermosa Beach, a dilapidated (at that time) seaside community whose proximity to the ocean, beach front lots, and run-down condition suggested that things could only get better. I started at a time when Hermosa was so deteriorated, there was nowhere it could go but up.

Another advantage to Hermosa was the fact that the city—not the state or some other distant entity—owned the beach, so the chances of local authorities confiscating property to build a parking lot for public access to the beach, as had happened in neighboring Manhattan Beach, were minimal.

Most buyers are not aware of everything going on around a property. People don't generally think about real estate in that sense. They don't explore it in that depth. They say, "Well, I can ask my broker if I have a question."

In Manhattan Beach you can talk to 80% of the brokers selling real estate and you won't find many who know that the beach is a state park, and therefore owned by the State of California and not the City of Manhattan Beach. Most people are dumbfounded when I tell them that. What difference does it make? About 30 years ago, the state decided to put a car park in front of several houses in the north end of town and there was nothing the homeowners could do about it because they found out too late. If the state wanted to do that in Hermosa Beach, they would have to wrestle control of beach access away from the city, and people would find out about it and protest. But if you're dealing with the state, by the time you find out who ordered it, the parking lot would already be built. That's exactly what happened in Manhattan Beach. The few residents who rallied at the last minute against the parking lot were too late.

At one time, Hermosa Beach didn't care if it grew because the residents liked the village atmosphere. The surrounding cities of Redondo Beach, Manhattan Beach, Torrance, and El Segundo are entirely different. Redondo built a marina and substantial hotel and the South Bay Galleria, which is a very successful shopping mall. Manhattan Beach has its own Manhattan Village Shopping Center and a rebuilt pier. Torrance is home to the largest shopping center in the world under one roof, and El Segundo has allowed the construction of several high-rise office buildings.

Today the city of Hermosa Beach downtown business district has been revitalized with the building of a new hotel, a plaza with new shops and restaurants, and substantial plans for redevelopment of the pier.

> They have just completed 200 Pier Plaza, an upscale office building that is attracting high-end tenants.

The economic repercussions of this development have had a tremendous impact on the value of properties. That is why Hermosa was such a valuable area to invest in during the early days. Even if they didn't want their city to grow, the residents couldn't do much about it. So even though the city was falling apart, everything else was falling into place.

In addition, several major aerospace contractors set up operations within a few miles of my house. The most dramatic thing to happen to this community has been the influx of the aerospace and defense industries. These high-tech companies have created jobs of substance. In the early 1960s, the average income of people in this area was about $15,000 a year.

> Today, it's close to $81,000.

The main reason is the number of well-paying professional jobs that have been created by companies such Boeing, Northrop Grumman, Aerospace Corp, Xerox, and Computer Sciences Corp., plus the fact that it's a desirable place to live. More recently, the entertainment industry has realized that the South Bay is a desirable place to do business.

Another reason that the land near me has gone up in value so much is that there's no vacant land left to build on; there's no room for expansion. When this happens, you have two choices: either build up or tear down the old structures and build new ones. Either way, property values increase on account of construction costs and the tremendous demand. Owing to the influx of population with high incomes in an area of high density where there is little supply, the demand becomes astronomical.

> We almost bought a house that fell down a hill. Before I tell you about that, let me say that you must become familiar with the inventory if you are going to find a good deal in an area you like.
>
> When we bought our principal residence in Laguna Beach, California, we became familiar with the area by renting there first. We got to know the neighborhoods and streets and acquired a feel for the community. The entire inventory for sale on the market became familiar to us by our doing five things:
>
> 1.   We went out one or two days a week and looked at every house that was listed for sale in our price range.

2. We had two or three real estate buyer's brokers who knew exactly what we wanted looking for us. They knew about the brand-new listings and some gave us "pocket listings"—houses that are for sale but not listed in the MLS for some reason.

3. Once a week the local realtor association usually has a "broker's preview" wherein all the local agents look at what is new on the market and at houses where the price has just been reduced. (Isn't that great info to know?)

4. On Sundays we went to all the open houses, talked to the agents and sometimes waited for the prices to come down if we wanted the houses badly enough.

5. We made offers.

One Sunday we saw an open house, dropped in, saw the price and made a full-price offer that was accepted that night. It was such a great buy that an offer priced $80,000 higher came in the next day, but it was too late. It did not hurt that we gave the listing broker both sides of the commission. (He made a double commission because he represented the seller and us, the buyers).

Another realtor did not have our best interests at heart on a previous offer we'd made. We were in escrow for three months before we found out that the house was on top of an ancient landslide. A geological inspection revealed there was a possibly unstable rock formation thousands of feet below the surface. In the case of an earthquake, the geologist said the house could shift. I could not sleep at night knowing I could be shifting down the hill.

We called to cancel the deal but the realtor tried to minimize the problem, saying that Laguna Beach is full of ancient landslides and that we will never find as good a deal as that one. I could not believe my ears.

That geological inspection saved us. Six months later, that house slid down the hill and became a debris pile at the bottom of a ravine. The house we own today is worth three times what we paid for it.

Here are the three tips that saved us:

1. We did our inspections
   a. Geological—the house was located on a slope
   b. Soil—we needed to know the erosion potential when it rained
   c. Property—the house was in good shape, but there is nothing like a second set of trained eyes to catch a defect that we might have missed
2. We became intimately knowledgeable about the neighborhood where we wanted to live and invest
3. We did not trust everything we heard

My brother and I once did an appraisal of the California Rock Salt Company located in the Mojave Desert near Amboy, California. Amboy, a sleepy little town, had a population of about 500. The population of Amboy could probably double in a year or two, and it wouldn't affect the market value of land there. However, if you doubled the population in a confined area like the beach cities south of Los Angeles, real estate values would go out of sight, like Tokyo, because there wouldn't be room for expansion.

From an investment point of view, people make big mistakes when they go to outlying areas, where there are huge tracts of land, and buy houses for 10% down. When the house is built, the contractor moves on to the next tract. Pretty soon there are thousands and thousands of houses in that area, and they're all competitive with each other. If there is a slight recession, a portion of those living there are going to lose their jobs and won't be able to make their mortgage payments. Foreclosures then appear on the market, and people will be able to come in and buy properties for less than what the original owners bought them for. The original buyers are left with the realization that they overpaid for property that may not realize much appreciation.

That scenario won't occur when there's no room for expansion because competition like that will not exist. When there isn't a lot of room for expansion in a desirable area and people in that area have good jobs, you can be assured that land values in that area are going to rise.

Another reason I decided to invest in Hermosa Beach is that I knew there was a scarcity of land. There are only about 200 beachfront properties on The Strand. Land values were destined to go up. And, sure enough, I haven't lost any money on the real estate I've invested in. It's all gone out of sight! Properties I purchased with $3,000 down or less at a price of $35,000 to $85,000 in the early 1960s are worth over $3 million today. It's easy to sit here now and say with hindsight that it was inevitable, but I am convinced that similar patterns will emerge in the future if you just pick the right area to invest in. Today, you can't even buy a lot on or near The Strand for less than $1.5 million. The dollar keeps shrinking. There has to be 3% or 4% inflation a year just to keep the economy going.

In addition to the scarcity factor associated with land in high-demand areas, there's also foreign investment. Many foreign investors can afford to pay more and afford to pay all cash. I've had a number of Asian buyers look at my properties. They're looking at the long haul. What you've got to remember about real estate is that you pay today for what you expect to get from that property years later. I refer to this as the contemplated future benefits of real estate.

Most investors are interested in the return they're going to get today, not what they're going to get tomorrow. Real estate is not that type of investment. In my opinion, you have to look at the long term. There are opportunities everywhere, areas all over the country that are going to be good. When I decided to invest at the beach in the early 1960s, I couldn't have gone to downtown Manhattan in New York City at 42nd Street and Broadway and bought a piece of property. This was all I could afford. But 50 years before, 42nd and Broadway might have been ideal and affordable for a guy like me.

As I've said before, I believe in buying and holding. What you have to do is find an area that has a strong growth pattern and be correct in your analysis.

LOCATION

Since the immediate, surrounding neighborhood has just as much, or more, influence on property values as the condition of the subject property itself, select a property where the neighborhood has the greatest potential for economic growth. Unless you just want to live in a particular neighbor-hood because of its charm, I would recommend going into an area that is established and built up so you can see the results. I wouldn't recommend a brand-new development.

It may seem wonderful to buy a new luxury house in a new area if you can afford to, but if you're going to pay $400,000 or $500,000—or more—I think you could do just as well to buy into an exclusive community that's already established. In addition, if you look at the tax rates in many parts of the country, they tend to be higher in newer areas because it costs local governments more to maintain a new community.

A few years ago, I had a tenant who, when he got married and had two kids, decided to move to Palmdale, California, where he could buy a five-bedroom house for an affordable price. The problem was that he worked at Xerox in El Segundo, about 60 miles away. Can you imagine that? That kind of daily commute is a tremendous sacrifice and one that I don't think is a good idea because over a period of time I'm sure it placed a lot of stress on him and his family. I think he should have tried to find something closer to his job, in a fringe area.

First-time buyers should look at property in fringe areas because fringe areas are usually older. As the greater metropolitan area continues to grow, these fringe areas are likely to become more valuable. In areas that have a history of growth, things tend to get better, not worse.

Not too long ago, I did an appraisal for a redevelopment agency in Compton, California. The subject property was a two-bedroom, one-bath house of about 1,000 square feet that was built in the 1920s. It was in very good condition but it was located in a rough area and was therefore only worth $70,000. Compare that house in Compton, which is about 12 miles from the beach, to a comparable property on The Strand, 12 miles west, that would sell today for about $2 million—and that's just what the land is worth. There is a range between that $70,000 and $2 million where you will be able to find a property that fits your pocketbook.

If you plotted two-bedroom, one-bath houses from Compton to Hermosa Beach every mile or so and had 10 comparable sales to support your opinion, you would know what you could afford and the quality of the neighborhood of each subject property. Say you decide to buy a house for

$350,000 in the City of Carson, about five miles from the beach. If the South Bay real estate market continues to rise to the point where prices continue appreciating as they have done, that property in Carson is going to go up, too. Pretty soon, the property in Compton is going to be worth more as well, because it's at the lower end of the same scale, where people who can't find affordable housing in areas where they want to live, have to live.

With tract homes in outlying areas, there can be dramatic changes in the value of property over a period of a few years once the houses are built. The stabilized value of real estate can be maintained by upkeep and physical enhancements. Even financing can change the market value. I wouldn't buy a tract home, however. I would prefer to buy a house in a seasoned community where the surrounding area is already developed, where everything is established, where the schools are good, where I know what the community's like, what the people are like, and where the stores are.

With the condominiums I bought in Orange County, people living there can walk to restaurants, buy their groceries or even take care of their medical needs without ever driving a car. Right now, they are ideal for college students or single people. But as our population ages, there will be a tremendous demand for retirement communities. Ten or fifteen years from now, these places will be ideal for retirees. And because the amenities are so fabulous, we'll be getting double the rent. Over the long pull, these units will do more than pay themselves off. But one of the main reasons I bought there was that the area was established.

When developers build a tract of houses in an outlying area, they have the tract down the road to contend with. That tract may extend into the desert or rural countryside for 25 or 50 miles. And there will always be competition to sell and rent for a lower price than your neighbor or the seller down the street. Until the area becomes established, the only thing you can count on to increase the value of that property is inflation.

> That area will not become established until the commercial growth catches up to the residential. Every major city has sprawl, and the outer edges of that sprawl are risky areas in which to invest. The good-paying jobs may be far away, so tenants have to drive a long way—or move closer into town, to better spots.

> The further out of town you are during hard times, the more your rents will slacken. But with each recovery following a recession, those outer-ring areas firm up because the commercial infrastructure catches up; the local economies become stronger.

The person who goes into a newly developed area and buys a new high-rise office building is also making a big mistake. They're pioneering and that's okay. But I don't think investors should take those kinds of risks unless they have a lot of holding power and can afford to lose money on their investment for 15 or 20 years. The opportunities for the person who isn't wealthy are much better in already established neighborhoods because you can see what direction the neighborhood is going in.

In some of these new communities, appearances are deceiving because what you may think is a jewel of an investment might be a disaster. The entire tract can go bust. Consider the example of Colorado Centre, a 3,000-acre housing development and planned community southeast of Colorado Springs. In 1985, this tract of sparkling new homes with Rocky Mountain views seemed like an idyllic place for first-time home buyers to invest in for the future—for as little as $600 down and $730 a month.

By 1989, these $75,000 homes were worth literally nothing because the local municipality and tax district went bankrupt. One homeowner who was interviewed on "60 Minutes" said his home was appraised at a negative value of $5,400. The hoards of people who were counted on to buy lots and build houses, along with the big companies that were supposed to relocate there and pay taxes, never came. And so the 130-odd families who did buy into the tract got struck with the bankrupt tax district's entire debt burden of $25 million. Some deal! Between 1993 and 1995, VA foreclosures in that area were again selling for around $75,000 to $80,000. The state had stepped in and paid for the utilities. Today the area is doing well, but only because taxpayers' money bailed out the local agencies. You can't count on an investment like that.

On the other hand, if you own property in an established area, you eliminate the risk of unknown variables and wishful projections. If you buy a house in San Francisco, for instance, an increase in land values can be attributed to a number of factors: the attitude and actions of the city government, which may be attempting to downzone; the regional high-tech industry may hire more people at a higher salary; or increased demand may come into the neighborhood. These are the types of pressures that create value. There are more pressures on prices to go up in areas that are already built and already have an infrastructure in place.

*M*y friend's father was a respected attorney in Philadelphia, and used to handle legal matters for Kress & Woolworth's. Around 1910, my friend's father and his law partner each decided to build a new house there. He bought a lot in the suburbs to build on for about $12,000. His associate bought a lot in town, for which he paid $8,000. They both used the same architectural firm and built about the same size house. The guy who lived in town didn't have too far to go to the office—a great advantage at the time. But the guy who lived in the suburb was in a growing community with fairly nice homes.

When their estates were settled some 30 years later, the heirs of the suburbanite received $150,000, while the heirs of the city dweller, whose property was now in an industrial zone, received a pittance by comparison. After three decades, the house in the suburbs was worth 10 times more than the downtown property because the downtown site was encroached on by an industrial development, which forced the owner to tear down the house. What remained was just a vacant lot. The buildings were almost identical to begin with but their end value after 30 years was dependent on their location. If you have the choice of buying one lot over another, you shouldn't be concerned about what they cost in today's dollars. Instead, focus on what they're going to be worth in 20 years, and carefully assess the factors that affect value (see Table 9.1).

Many people make the mistake of buying in the wrong location. In the above example, it took 20 years for an encroachment to occur. But when it did, there was nothing the owners could do.

Just because certain properties are high-priced doesn't necessarily mean they have some inherent advantage. One property may cost more than another today, but will it still be worth more tomorrow? It might be subjected to condemnation, in which the government claims the property for public use for a redevelopment or street-widening project—or a new highway, school, or park. Unforeseen encroachments, such as zoning changes, can dramatically alter the use and value of property.

Real estate that is scarce is in great demand, such as oceanfront property or a property that has favorable access or scenery—whatever determines value according to the attitudes of people in the area. Of course, some locations, such as Beverly Hills, Park Avenue, or Palm Beach, will probably never be zoned for different uses than they are now.

ANALYZING GROWTH POTENTIAL

When analyzing a property's growth potential, it is important to find out as much as you can about a community and isolate the factors that contribute to growth. Selecting the right area to invest in is paramount. By conducting research, you can find out what the city and regional governments are planning to do and if there are any projects on the drawing board.

Another sign of growth is the addition of new area codes by the regional phone companies. The area I live in was recently assigned a new area code because of the increase in business and residential phone use created by the growing number of fax machines, computer modems, and multiple phone lines. This is a concrete sign of growth in progress. It forced me to modify all my stationery, but it's very reassuring.

When contemplating a purchase, the best method of weighing the benefits and drawbacks is to write down everything you like about the property. Get a piece of paper, draw a line down the center, and write the property's positive attributes on one side and negative ones on the other. List everything about the subject property and surrounding area. This will help make your decision as objective as possible.

Start with the positive, then write the negative. (If you write down everything that is negative first, you won't ever get past the first step.) Then cross off the things that counterbalance each other; there might be one positive quality that outweighs all the negative things put together.

The three most important factors in determining growth potential are:

- family income
- population growth
- the duration of that growth

Everything else is important, but not as important.

You can draw all kinds of references from data, but it is worthless if you don't know what to do with it. The surest sign that the value of land will rise is if average income levels are on an upward trend. If you can foresee how long these trends are going to last, then you have an important indicator for selecting the right community. But other factors and details come into play when selecting the individual property that represents the best value in the community.

As mentioned, population on its own does not create wealth. You need population combined with industry—and the industry should have expansion potential. You can learn about this in the pages of the *Wall Street Journal, Business Week, Fortune,* and the business section of your local newspaper.

> Or you could go to www.newspapers.com. That is an excellent Web site where you can find a newspaper from anywhere in the world.
>
> There are many national radio and TV programs, like *Marketplace, Nightly Business Report* and *Wall Street Week,* wherein you can learn about general business trends that will affect your real estate. As a matter of fact, the more you can become an amateur economist—the more you know where your tenants work, how much they make and what kind of jobs are moving into the area—the more astute your decisions will be.

When I first moved to Hermosa Beach, I bought a big street map of the city to track the local real estate activity to become as informed as I could about the community. I hung this map on the wall and made notations with differently colored pushpins to track different developments. I used red to indicate sales, yellow for listings, blue for assessments and street improvement projects, white for new buildings, and green for other important activities, such as zone changes. Then I numbered each mark, wrote an explanation of it, and kept it in a loose-leaf binder for easy reference.

I also used the multiple listing service and put citations from that on the map as well. If the city was planning to do something, I'd write it down in a reference book. In this way, I was able to keep very close track of what was going on in the community and had a visual picture of the local real estate activity. When you see a property coming on the market and you know what the other properties have sold for in the last three years, you can make an informed offer.

Pick an area, say, five city blocks, that you like, get a big map, and put it on the wall. Put every bit of information you know about the community on that map. When something comes along that you think you want to buy, you will have all sorts of data to help determine what you think you can afford to pay for it. From this, you can also see what the trend is.

If you see a large number of new single-family residences in the area with apartment buildings, you can probably conclude that that particular strip's been downzoned to R-1. But you should always check with the city planning department to make sure.

The important thing is to look at these factors in search of a trend or pattern. When you see that the trend is going in the right direction, take action. When you see that it's going in the wrong direction, go on to something else.

When you're organized, it's pretty easy to figure out whether and how the community is growing. I find it useful to pencil everything out to better visualize the various pieces of the puzzle. This work is a problem for some people; it's not easy. If it took little or no effort, all the people lying on the beach in front of my building would be multimillionaires (they're not). My mother used to say that luck is 90% hard work and only 10% chance; it's work that makes you successful, not chance.

When I started my real estate investment program, I was working full-time as an appraiser at Marshall and Stevens and was taking care of my properties. You have to like real estate or it's going to burden you. For me, it was always fun. I looked at it as a hobby and spent most of my spare time in some real-estate-oriented activity or discussion.

A Digital Update to Ease Your Search

While there is no substitute for being on the streets to see the developments in your town, there are many online sources that can tell you what is going on. My previous chapter is full of Web sites that will aid your search.

Corner Lots

A corner lot isn't always desirable in a normal single-family residential area, but when you have a multiple residential situation, a corner lot becomes valuable, especially if the city is planning to change the use and require more parking per apartment unit. A corner lot also becomes valuable if it is vacant and you want to build on it, primarily because of easy access. Lot orientation can also enhance the property value.

Lot Size and Precise Boundaries

It's worth repeating that most buyers are not aware of everything going on around a property. A lot of people aren't even informed about the actual zoning of the subject property—let alone the precise boundaries of the piece of real estate they're thinking about purchasing.

The size of the lot is extremely important and should conform with the neighborhood and the community. You can look for this on a tract map. If you have a larger parcel than the standard-sized lot, that's actually good. But you don't want a smaller one, unless you can buy it cheap, assuming everything is equal, because you can get into a situation where a lot is substandard. With a substandard lot, if you have two units on your property and something happened to the structure, or if you wanted to tear it down and rebuild, you might only be able to put one back. If it were really small, you might not even be able to put one back.

If you're going to buy a piece of land, you ought to get a metes and bounds description of the parcel, which describes the boundary lines, as well as a survey of the land to physically locate points, so that you can go out and see what you're buying. This can cost a little extra, but it's worth the expense. I knew a couple who bought a restaurant on a two-acre parcel of land. The broker assured them that the property they were buying was two acres and came with a restaurant, an orchard, a house, and a yard. They bought the property and closed escrow, thinking they had found the deal of the century.

Well, one day the new owners (my friends) went over to the property and started working in the orchard, and the real owner told them to get off what they thought was their property! Only after this incident did they obtain a metes and bounds description, which showed the true extent of their lot, which turned out to be only 3/4 of an acre. They wound up suing the former owner and the broker. The whole thing was a disaster that could have been avoided if they had simply hired a surveyor to physically locate the property lines from the legal metes and bounds description before the escrow closed.

If you put an offer to purchase property through escrow (which is common in western states), the seller has to give the escrow company a proper legal description. But not all states have escrow laws, so it is frequently incumbent on the buyer to obtain one independently. With real estate, you're buying the property based on the legal description, not on what you are told you're getting. To see the legal description of the lot, simply visit the county recorder's office and make a copy of the deed. If it's too complicated, have a professional read and interpret it for you. If there's any doubt, hire a surveyor while the property's in escrow, or before the deal closes, and put up some flags so you know exactly where the property's lines are before you buy.

To estimate lot boundaries, look at the telephone poles. Usually, they're located on the property lines, but not always. Sometimes you can see the pins in the street or in the sidewalk where the surveyors have laid them. In California, surveyors put their identification numbers on their surveying pins so a record of the survey can be kept with the local city hall.

I once bought a three-unit building and discovered that one of the units encroached on the side yard of somebody else's property. When I made an offer, I wrote on the deposit receipt what I thought the dimensions of the property were. The owners counter-offered, saying that the lot was bigger, and that they wanted more. So I said, "Okay, I'll buy it at your price if it is bigger, but I'll buy it at my price if it's smaller." Needless to say, I bought it at my price, which was 20% lower than theirs, because they didn't know what they were talking about. They were also desperate to sell and couldn't find another buyer.

There is no substitute for knowledge in a negotiation. Everybody has an opinion about what to do, but you have to be right on your facts. The sellers of that property were probably told what the size was when they bought the place and assumed that it was the honest truth. But it didn't matter. I did my research and proved them wrong. I even brought them a tract map to illustrate my point. If you find an encroachment, always try to make an adjustment in the purchase price.

In 1968, my brother Paul decided to buy a four-unit building, but the city claimed that it was legally a three-unit. After intensive negotiations with the owner, Paul was able to get the seller to lower his required down payment. My brother wound up buying the property for $65,000 with $5,000 down—only 8% of the purchase price. Eventually, I bought the property from my brother and was able to prove to the city that the property was a legitimate four-unit apartment building and not a bootlegged triplex with an illegal fourth unit.

Just as you want to be sure that there are no legal discrepancies or encroachments on your property, you also want to ensure that you are not encroaching on somebody else's property. A stairway once encroached onto a property I bought in Hermosa Beach by about a foot and a half. After I made the purchase, the people who had built the stairway put their property up for sale. I didn't think it would cause much concern, so I asked the owners to remove the steps. They told me that they had a right to it and that I could go jump in the ocean. Finally, they sold their property, and the new owner and I got together: I paid him $1,500 to have it removed. That was a cheap price to pay, because after that I was able to get the necessary permits to build a new house on my lot!

One-Horse Towns

If you have an area that is reliant on one industry, you have some unique considerations that will affect your chances for success. I have bought properties in many areas that have given me a view as to how this works.

In Jacksonville, North Carolina, where I have a property, the main employer is the Camp LeJune military base. The economy is reliant upon the happenings of the Marines. When there is a military engagement overseas and the Marines are being mobilized, I encounter a soft rental market. Even worse, if the base ever closes or is downsized, my renters will leave or not be able to make the existing market rent.

When the war in Iraq started, we had problems finding renters for a while. As more Marines were cycled back, it became easier. Also, due to the Soldiers and Sailors Civil Relief Act, I may have problems collecting rents if they get mobilized. Check the provisions of the act if you rent to the military.

Also, I have found that most military towns have low to moderate appreciation if the area is not supported by other industry. How the military does will be how you do.

In Las Vegas I had trouble renting houses because gambling revenue went down. The casinos start laying off people in 2007, when economic hard times hit. Less people were traveling from Southern California to gamble.

I had more turnovers in two years than the previous five years. When the casinos laid off card dealers, pit bosses, cocktail severs and other hotel workers, less people moved to Las Vegas and the rental markets became soft. I had to rent to tenants that were Section 8. Not my favorite.

Section 8 renters have their rent subsidized by the Department of Housing and Urban Development (HUD) based upon financial need. Financially needy clients probably will have problems taking care of the house, but I felt had no choice. It happens in areas that go through tough times, like California did in the 1990s.

In my opinion, Las Vegas is a special case of a one-industry town that it is OK in which to invest. There is more going on there than just gambling and it will be one of the cities that will prosper far into the twenty-first century. No state income tax, a business-friendly environment, a low cost of living and its proximity to California will make this a Mecca for a long time to come.

One-horse towns wherein one industry dominates the local economy can be problem. A broad mix of industries is what you want because if one sector is having problems, you have others to pick up the slack.

Changing the Use Changes the Value

About 25 years ago, an investor from the East Coast decided to travel throughout the Midwest and the Pacific Northwest. He came to a town without freeways, situated in a valley with two fairly good-sized mountains on either side. The state where this little town was located decided to build a freeway through the area to connect with the Northwest part of the United States because the traffic through this valley area was extremely heavy.

The state had planned to alleviate the traffic problem by bypassing the city and building a new freeway that would attract more visitors and tourists to the community. The town involved was reluctant for the state to construct a freeway because they felt it would hurt the downtown business district, through which all traffic had to pass.

The investor drove through this area on a Saturday afternoon, and the traffic was so heavy it took him over and hour to go through the central part of town. He decided this was not very satisfactory for the people in the community.

On Monday morning, he went to the city hall, saw the city manager and two city council members, and asked them what they planned to do to relieve the city ingress and egress problem. They said the only possible solution might be to make the main street a one-way road through town and design another road for access in the opposite direction.

The real estate investor considered this possibility. There wasn't anything else that could be done to expand the roads for a freeway. He got a huge map of the community and set out a program to figure out how the city administration would decide where to locate one-way streets. The investor studied all possibilities and talked with city planners, the city council members and the city manager. He came up with a plan whereby the northbound traffic would go through the city center on the main street and the southbound traffic be directed to the side street, west of the main thoroughfare. He submitted this information to the city council, and everyone thought it was a good idea.

About two weeks later the city council accepted his plan. So the investor found some excellent sites at the proposed new one-way streets, and made a lease option purchase on five southwest corners, the most ideal location if the one-way street was adopted because the city would have to rezone this area as commercial.

Eventually the changes were made and the traffic congestion eased quite dramatically from the main thoroughfare. The newly constructed one-way street going south became the main ingress through the city. The investor, of course, was buying the corner lots as future gas station sites.

As the city prospered, tourists could more easily pass through the expanding city. The change in street patterns created tremendous prosperity for the city businesses and the properties along the one-way streets. In addition, the real estate investor who had purchased five of the corners along this area made a tremendous profit. He later sold the five gas station sites to major oil companies.

Often when a street pattern in a city is changed, the new pattern may create added wealth for some properties and location, but it may also create a loss in value in other areas. People's actions, attitudes and thinking can create real estate value as well as destroy it.

10

Forecast Your Property's Market Value in 20 Years Using Available Data

In the last chapter, we discussed how to select the right property and make an analysis of its growth potential. The next step in determining a property's growth potential is to make a long-range forecast of its market value in 20 or 30 years based on available data. Long-range forecasting basically entails making an analysis of a property's anticipated value by carefully considering the factors that influence its long-term worth. By analyzing the economic and environmental factors affecting a property, it is possible to project its future market value and, hence, its attractiveness as an investment. Successfully investing in real estate requires a long-term outlook that isn't subject to the ups and downs of short-lived adjustment periods. By evaluating what has happened to a given market in the past and making a realistic projection based on available data, it is possible to predict future market value. In fact, it is often easier to predict the market value of a piece of real estate 20 or 30 years from now than its value next year or the year after.

A n appraiser I knew was asked in the early 1920s by Northwestern Mutual Life Insurance Company to make a 50-year projection of the Stevens Hotel on Michigan Avenue in Chicago, at that time, the largest hotel in the world. I spoke to him in 1970, and, although he couldn't foresee the Great Depression, he had come very close to predicting the market value of that property 50 years hence.

> *About the only factors he hadn't taken into consideration were the inevitable ebbs in the economy, which he had no way of predicting.*

Even so, he was able to predict the long-range market value of that property. He had researched the growth pattern of the area and knew that hotels were going to be popular and commerce would be coming to Chicago in the Roaring Twenties. The second largest city in the United States at the time, Chicago was a boomtown, and it was fairly easy to make an estimate. But the dips between 1920 and 1970 were such that the original owner of the hotel wound up losing it in a downturn.

The first step in putting together a forecast is to gather all the information pertinent to a specific site's growth potential. There are numerous factors that are important to consider when forecasting a property's future market value. These include:

- Local population trends
- Average family income level and its projected growth or decline
- Local and regional economic trends
- Comparable property values (or "comps")
- Past real estate appreciation rates
- City redevelopment plans
- Applicable zoning ordinances
- Local street-widening and public works projects
- Utility improvement plans
- School enrollment projections
- Plans for new civic and/or commercial developments that will enhance the community, such as regional shopping centers, parks, schools, and recreation centers
- Plans for city or county annexations
- Plans to expand residential subdivisions
- Other relevant building, redevelopment, and real estate-related information that the city and county planners can provide

A city is not going to put in more schools, parks, and utilities if it doesn't have a growth pattern. If a city is going to expand, it must plan 10 or 15 years in advance. It can't expand without a growth plan, and such plans are a matter of public record. But you need to take the initiative to learn about them.

Armed with this knowledge, you can then make an informed decision, one that is in your long-term interest. Remember, the best real estate investment strategy is the one that relies the least on chance and emotion and recognizes that planning and patience make for profits—what you owe today, you'll be worth tomorrow.

If you are willing to buy something and sit on it over the long haul, the odds of your losing are remote. But most people can't do that. They see a $5,000 or $10,000 profit and grab it. Or, they think the whole thing is collapsing, so they run for it. The key is to find the right piece of property and not stick your neck out too far.

Short-Term Thinking

The benefit of holding real estate is that it is a forced savings account. Short-term thinking, grabbing the quick buck and not keeping the right property are the death of many a new investor. I know because I've seen it happen over the many years I have been speaking at real estate investment clubs and other groups. The most common laments I hear are:

1. "I wish I hadn't sold my house."
2. "I lost my money because I frittered it away."
3. "Property is so expensive that I can't afford it now."

Cash is a wonderful commodity to have, but I love to have my dollars always at work in the bank of AA neighborhoods. There are times to sell properties but if you do, what will you do with the cash? Will you have to invest somewhere else or will you spend your newfound cash?

Don't trip over the pennies to get at the dollars.

Fair-Market Value

Value is a nebulous concept that comes into play after you have inspected a property and are beginning to negotiate a deal. Fair market value is defined by *Barron's Dictionary of Real Estate Terms* as the theoretical highest price a buyer, willing, but not compelled to buy, would pay, and the lowest price a seller, willing, but not compelled to sell, would accept. Another definition of the market value of a building is the sum of money in which the presence of that structure adds to, or subtracts from, the value of the land it occupies, with the land being valued on the basis of its highest and best use.

As discussed in the previous chapters, there are any number of factors that affect value. Similarly, there are any number of values attached to a property. If you can isolate the various values associated with a property, you will have the added advantage of acquiring the real estate at a realistic price.

Buyers and sellers tend to approach real estate transactions at cross-purposes: Sellers often will be sentimental and ask for a handsome sum, while the buyer is looking at fair market value—or less. In my experience, most sellers have some degree of sentimental attachment to their real estate, which explains why they price it too high when they put it on the market. There is no absolute measure of how much a house will sell for because each property is unique and every buyer and seller brings different needs and objectives to the table.

One of the greatest gifts a person can have is the ability to correctly estimate the value of things. (Here, I am referring to their value, not their cost.). Whether you're looking at a vintage automobile, a rare manuscript, or a piece of investment real estate, you have to be able to correctly estimate value.

If you're not able to estimate value, you're going to be left out in the cold. You won't be able to live in the real world if, for instance, you can't correctly estimate the value of your time. If you work for free all the time, you could go broke, end up homeless, or at the very least, watch passively as your neighbor gets rich.

To reemphasize an important point, values are created and destroyed by the actions, attitudes, and thinking of people. So, if the majority of people think a piece of property is valuable, it is. And that's all that matters. Value is something in the mind. If a lot of people start thinking an area is undesirable, then real estate prices plummet.

Look at Germany. The biggest problem that the government has had in integrating East Germany and West Germany hasn't been the monetary system; it has been the attitudes and values of people and the way they behave and think about each other. Because the attitudes of people determine value, the value of real property as well as business activities in the eastern part of the country will remain low. It may take decades for people on the two different sides to get back on good terms and truly understand one another.

The following chart shows the values that may be established on a property at a given time. Values appear in the overall formula many times:

Property: a 50-year-old, 3,000-square-foot residence used for a rooming house on a lot zoned for multiple residential.

Land value (assumed vacant) $150,000
Construction cost $100/square foot
Replacement cost $300,000
Income yield $2,880/month
Fair market value $240,000

Although the property might only list for $240,000 (at fair market value), there are numerous values worth considering:

Whole property:

$450,000	Replacement cost value (land and improvements)
380,000	Replacement value
330,000	Physical value
310,000	Summation value
250,000	Comparison sales value
240,000	Fair Market value
220,000	Condemnation value
200,000	Income value
190,000	Cash value
180,000	Mortgage loan value
170,000	Forced sale value
120,000	Inheritance value
90,000	Historic cost
60,000	Assessed value

Construction only:

$300,000	Replacement cost
260,000	Replacement insurable value
230,000	Replacement value
180,000	Sound value
150,000	Sound insurable value
50,000	Book value
20,000	Salvage value

Land only:

$150,000	Vacant
130,000	Improved

Other values to consider:

Catastrophe value	Sentimental value
Going concern value	Liquidation value
Goodwill value	Nuisance value
Improvement value	Plottage value
Leasehold value	Rental value
Charity value	Leased fee value
Use value	

during the purchasing and financing of real estate, while projecting its long-term worth and value, and then at varying intervals during the ownership period, especially for refinancing and buying other properties. Assume the subject property is a two-story residence built in 1954 and currently being used as a rooming house on a lot zoned for multiple residential building.

When I was teaching real estate courses, I used this type of example to emphasize the different values that can be applied to a property at a given time. A real estate investor should be aware of the various values associated with the subject property. The most important thing about an appraisal is its purpose. You have to know what the problem is. If an appraiser doesn't know what the problem or need is, or the type of value to be determined in the appraisal, he or she could make an improper analysis and the result could be disastrous.

When buying a property, location is the most important factor. You can't change the land or the surrounding area, but you can always replace or modify the building to counteract physical deterioration and functional obsolescence, such as poor floor plan or outdated amenities. As a property ages, economic obsolescence—the loss of value from all causes outside the property itself—becomes far more significant than physical deterioration and functional obsolescence because it affects the value of real estate more dramatically.

Remodeling

The building, originally designed by famed architect Richard Neutra was constructed in 1938. It was ultra-modern for that period, with an open roof sun deck, extensive use of glass windows overlooking the ocean, an original porthole and mostly built-in furniture with rounded, finished walls. Even the beds were built-in, with storage drawers beneath. It was constructed as an apartment building, a legal nonconforming, six-unit structure, of which four units are rentals. There are several curved narrow steps to the second and third levels on each side of the building. Time, weather and the ocean air had taken its toll on the building.

Oceanfront property requires constant maintenance and upkeep; the salt air penetrates everything. So in 1998 and 1999, we embarked on a major remodel of the building, primarily the exterior and our two units. We decided to include an elevator within the structure, for our own use, which would serve all three levels. The city building department was most cooperative with the stipulation that the elevator had to be within the confines of the original structure and not as an outside elevator.

The cost of the hydraulic, two-passenger, two-door entry car to three levels cost around $50,000, including construction of the foundation and the 30-foot-high shaft. When the elevator arrived on a flatbed truck, it was a mass of hundreds of separate parts. It took about 10 days to build the car and assemble all the various parts so it was running in good order.

As previously mentioned, the building was constructed in 1938, so we were prepared for additional costs. When you remodel, you invariably run into unexpected snags. For example, major plumbing pipes may need re-routing to accommodate a new sliding bathroom door. When walls are demolished, a number of added problems may surface.

So be prepared and consider 25% or so for extra costs above an original estimate to cover any surprises that may be in store. Be sure to use a licensed and bonded contractor and ask for referrals and talk to former clients. Ask to see some of the contractor's work before you embark on any project.

New Construction

This can be much less costly than a remodel, since estimates are more precise and there aren't usually hidden surprises. Southern California Beach home prices skyrocketed in 2003, with a typical tear down in Malibu costing anything from $1.5 million and up.

The trend at the beach today is to buy a single lot 30 feet by 80 feet for around $3 million, tear it down and build a brand new home. This is a very typical scenario for the South Bay beach front property. Construction is generally more expensive for beachfront properties, particularly in Manhattan Beach and Hermosa Beach, due to the nature of the narrow lots, narrow alleyways and steep slopes in Manhattan Beach.

In these two particular cities, construction vehicles are often delayed and cannot gain access to the job site when they need to, due to overcrowded parking conditions and congestion in the narrow streets and alleys. Delays and difficulty maneuvering equipment, trash trucks and other large delivery vehicles all adds to the high cost of construction in such areas. Building in open areas is easier and less costly.

One of our beach properties is a single-family residence with a single apartment in the rear, plus a one-car garage-all on one story. The land, assuming that the buildings weren't on it, is worth about $167 per square foot-vacant lot value. The lot is 3,000 square feet, valued at $500,000. The front house is a four-bedroom, two-bath rental, and adjacent to the single garage is a studio apartment. The major problem in the city is a serious lack of parking. So we decided to lift up the rear apartment 15 feet from the ground. We built a platform underneath at 10 feet, and then the apartment was lowered down onto the platform. The former garage was converted into a bedroom. Now we have six parking spaces underneath this new one-bedroom apartment. This provided adequate parking for everyone, including the front house.

This solution utilizes the land to a greater extent than before the raising without taking up any more space. The rental income for the two properties has doubled from what it was before we started construction. We used a professional house moving company and building contractor to do the lift up. To be sure, we had to go through much red tape with the city to obtain the permits, but the effort was indeed worthwhile. We now refer to this property as our "tree house."

LOCATION, LOCATION, LOCATION

According to US government statistics, in 1963 when records were accumulated, the average American home had a fair market value of $18,000. In 1995, the average American family home was worth $135,000. The $117,000 difference from 1960 to 1995 is astronomical compared to inflation. To purchase a home in 1963 had to be the best investment that a family or individual could make.

In 1963 I bought a house near the oceanfront in Hermosa Beach for $18,000. According to these statistics my house today should be worth $135,000 based on the increase. It is interesting to note that today the house is worth $800,000. Think about it; if you were to put out $18,000 in 1963, today, you could have a property worth $800,000.

What is the difference between the average home price or the average home market value in 1996 and the property that I purchased? The difference is location. There is an added increment of value over and beyond the factors of inflation that have created this astronomical value in real estate.

This book demonstrates exactly what we have been talking about for years. There is an added increment of value over and beyond the market value of real estate due to location. This added value is attributed to the exterior influences surrounding the real estate, which creates value.

In 1963, it was obvious that there were dramatic activities occurring in the community where I purchased this house. There were large industrial plants hiring engineers who were looking to the future to develop the present modern economy. There was a possibility of tremendous growth in family income and the developers within the community had expanded their scope of development; they were improving their community image by building modern facilities, expanding the school districts, and shopping and retail centers to cope with the impending upward trend.

When you consider increase in market value of the average single-family residence in the United States from 1963 to 2003, remember that housing structures have deteriorated or depreciated due to physical, functional and economic obsolescence. However, the market values have increased dramatically.

Land does not depreciate in the same sense that buildings and other man-made improvements do, but the cost of preparing land to accept homes has gone up. Many people don't realize that when you buy a piece of property, you are truly buying the land. The land and its location is where the value is. You can take the house, remodel it, change it or tear it down and build a new house, but the land is a scarce item. As Will Rogers always said, "The best thing to do is to invest in land because they are not making any more of it."

Economic obsolescence, or depreciation, is caused by factors that you as an individual property owner have little or no control over. These include the condition of the economy, interest rates, increased taxes, water shortages, smog, traffic congestion, crime rates, plant closings, and so on. There is more money lost because of economic obsolescence than there is from physical deterioration and functional obsolescence put together.

I mention this so that you may begin to think like an appraiser. Just as an appraiser needs to know the problem or needs associated with a subject property, so you need to be aware of the pertinent facts surrounding your investment. If you buy real estate for the long term, you can afford to pay a little more, especially if that property has some special, unique value.

Before I purchased the property next door to the six-unit apartment building I live in, I determined that it possessed several values above and beyond fair market value that affected me personally. To begin with, the owner of the property was an absentee landlord who let a real estate broker or property manager rent the place out. As a result, they would rent to four guys, or to two guys and two girls in one house, just to keep the place occupied. It was an "animal house" year-round. When I moved in, I had to buy the building next door. It was either that or move inland. I didn't have any choice; it was an intolerable situation.

It took me a few years to acquire the property, but when I bought it, my problem was solved. Besides having control over the occupants, I could also collect the rent very easily. I've since painted the two buildings the same color scheme and have torn down the wall and made a common patio area. Because it was so ideal and easy for me to manage, I was willing to pay more for that property than I was for my original building, even though it was probably worth less.

That building is more valuable to me than it is to anybody. Considering all the added values, it was a purchase worth every penny. Not only was there nuisance value and rental value, there was also use value, improvement value, and even plottage value associated with that purchase because of the common patio area and similar design of the two buildings. Although I really couldn't afford to buy the place, I also couldn't afford not to. I just made up my mind that I had to do it and figured out a way.

The property is even more valuable today after we decided to demolish the two rear units in early 1999, leaving the two oceanfront units intact. We even considered lifting up the upper rear unit while converting the lower unit into a covered parking area. But the narrow alley prevented us from proceeding with this concept. It posed a potential hazard to neighboring properties, as huge cranes and equipment are required to raise a building. The risk was too enormous. So we demolished both units facing onto the alley and created a "million dollar" parking lot for six cars. In the long haul, this decision will pay for itself multifold.

Similarly, somebody can have a great interest in a wilderness cabin in Idaho, a property that is not going to particularly increase in value but that can still have an added increment of desirability and escape value to the person buying it.

The following is a list of the many attributes to consider in the analysis of a property before you make the final offer and purchase:

Physical Value

- Valuation of the land, independent of improvements
- Replacement cost of the improvements

- Depreciation of the improvements, based on age and physical condition; also, functional and economic obsolescence

Earning Value (Income)

- Capitalization of net income
- Speculation
- Goodwill value of an established location

Effect of Supply and Demand

- Number of similar properties recently sold
- Number of similar properties on the market
- Advantages of good building design and desirable arrangement
- Harmony with surrounding improvements
- Any known demand for similar properties
- Any evident scarcity of similar properties

Values That Exist in the Mind of the Buyer

- General appearance of land and improvements
- Advantages of good arrangement and design
- Harmony with surrounding improvements
- Peculiarities in design (advantages or detriments)
- Social advantages of the neighborhood

Suitability of Improvements to Land and Location

- Whether improvements are too large and costly or too small and cheap for the location and land
- Whether land might be used for something more profitable
- Apparent trend of neighborhood development and future possibilities
- Interior and exterior design

- Extent to which the area is developed and subject to change

I once gave my real estate students an interesting assignment; they were to make a projection of what they thought the fair market value of a certain single-family residence in West Los Angeles would be after 20 years. Most of them concluded the property would be torn down and overtaken by an industrial development or a high-rise office or apartment building. It wasn't. And yet that's the way most people think—that a property will reach a certain plateau, not go up any higher, and outlive its usefulness. What you have to do is make a comparison of like properties in similar areas. The best way to project what a property is going to be worth 20 years from now is to find an area that had similar characteristics 20 years previously and research what happened to it from the standpoint of growth.

When I was doing appraisal work, part of my job was to perform retrospective appraisals determining the market value of a property 20 or 30 years before. I once did an interesting appraisal of the Hamburger Realty Company estate at Eighth Street and Broadway in downtown Los Angeles, the site of the original May Co. department store. When the May Co. assumed the lease on the property, company executives wanted to build three stories higher.

Our job was to assess the market value of the Hamburger Estate asset as of July 1, 1913 to determine the amount of capital gains the Hamburgers would have to pay taxes on. The appraisal was prepared in 1960. Obviously, by that time, the building at Eighth and Broadway had been completely remodeled into a six-story department store. The Hamburger Estate owned the land, plus the first three floors of the building. We did the appraisal mainly by reading the classified sections of old newspapers and by looking up old grant deeds from the title company. Real estate appraising is not an exact science; facts and data are gathered and analyzed to form an opinion of value.

Appraisers use three basic methods of estimating fair market value: the cost approach, market approach, and income approach. The cost approach is based on the depreciated replacement cost of improvements, plus the market value of the site. The market approach determines value through the sales prices of similar recently sold properties. The income approach bases value on the property's anticipated future net income. The three different approaches provide a framework for evaluating different properties. Table 10.2 outlines the approaches.

The Cost Approach

Generally speaking, the cost approach is the weakest of the three approaches. Excepting new developments, how can you value a piece of land independent of the improvement? The improvement, or actual building, has a direct bearing on the value of the land. Since there is no measure in the market to use for comparisons, the only thing you can do is determine the depreciated replacement cost of the improvement. Sometimes the cost approach is the only method you can use if you are valuing a school, government building, church, or specialized industrial or commercial property.

The Market Approach

The market approach, generally employed by buyers and realtors for single-family residences, apartment complexes, commercial properties, and general purpose industrial properties, analyzes the property in relation to comparable sales that occur in the surrounding area. The only effective way of determining market value of single-family residences is by examining comparable sales. Generally, three comps will suffice. However, every piece of real estate is unique and heterogeneous. Consequently, there are no truly comparable sales or listings.

Because of this, the market approach requires adjustments for the land and building size, location, age, setting, and a host of other factors, including the unique circumstances and terms of sales that are comparable. However, with all the facts that go into a transaction, it's very difficult to know whether you are truly analyzing a sale that is comparable. The seller might have increased the price to get better terms or might have been motivated to sell for a lower price for personal reasons.

The Income Approach

The income approach derives an income stream from any type of property that yields a regular flow of money, such as an apartment building, hotel, office building, restaurant or business, shopping center, or leased industrial building. The question becomes, how much net income can you reasonably expect from your investment? The net income is then capitalized into value using a capitalization rate commensurate with market conditions.

TABLE 10.2
Estimating Fair Market Value Using the Three Approaches

Cost Approach	Market Approach	Income Approach
Property is divided into segments (land and construction); each segment is valued separately.	Analysis of comparable sales of whole properties.	Analysis of net income, proper capitalization rate, and method of processing income.

An analysis of market data is necessary to estimate the following factors reasonably:

Land value
Construction costs
All forms of
   depreciation
	Adjustments of comparable sales	Gross income
		Vacancy and collection
		   loss
		All expenses
		Capitalization rate
		Capitalization technique

Pitfalls	Pitfalls	Pitfalls
1. Estimating land value independent of construction.	1. Locating enough similar properties that have recently sold to indicate a value.	1. Estimating future gross income, vacancy allowance, and all recurring expenses.
2. Estimating new construction costs.	2. Adjusting amenities to make them comparable to the subject property.	2. Employing the proper capitalization technique.
3. Estimating accrued depreciation.	3. Adjusting sales for down payment and terms.	3. Determining method of net income capitalization.

Correlation of the three approaches and the final demand-analysis estimate is generally a matter of experience and judgment based on factual data.

The income approach is generally reliable when appraising large income-producing complexes, such as office buildings, shopping centers, and the like. The income approach is generally unreliable when appraising duplexes, triplexes, and small income-producing buildings.

The fundamental reason for using the three approaches is that they bracket value, leaving the appraiser to use his or her expertise and best judgment in correlating one final estimate of market value. In addition, a market demand analysis should be made to estimate present and future demand for the subject property. As a buyer, you want to pay fair-market value or less. But when you start to consider what a given property will do over the long haul and what it will be worth after twenty or so years, current values become much less important.

A person with foresight has to be sure not to overpay for a property, but at the same time not let a good opportunity slip away because the property is slightly overpriced. In my opinion, if you can get desirable terms, you can afford to pay more than market value.

In the final analysis, you should pay the present worth of contemplated future benefits, in which case you could be prepared to pay more than market value. If you are right in your analysis, it doesn't make any difference. In 1963, I bought a four-unit apartment building for $35,000. Suppose I had paid $100,000 for it. It still wouldn't have made any difference because it's worth $1.4 million today. The key is to be right in your analysis of a property's growth potential.

As we have seen, there is no way to make an exact forecast. The only thing you can be assured of is that if you buy in an area with growth potential, there will continue to be increases in land values because growth in a capitalistic economy cannot exist without inflation. You can also be assured that there will be dips in the economy, but the overall trend inevitably will be up. Think how empty the term "millionaire" is becoming. It now takes several million dollars cash, in the bank, to be on par with a simple millionaire of 30 years ago.

As mentioned elsewhere, it is very difficult to make decisions without adequate knowledge. I recommended you buy a big map of the subject area and keep track of every development affecting the market value. This methodical system has helped me enormously over the years.

Another important thing is to get expert advice from people you can count on. The only way you get this advice is by talking with people who are knowledgeable and have experience. But it doesn't have to cost a lot of money. When I started investing in real estate, I had just lost all of my money in the commodities market, so I couldn't afford to hire anybody. While speculating in commodities, I followed other people's advice. After losing all my money, I decided that if I was going to lose again, at least it would be my own doing, not somebody else's.

So instead of hiring a lawyer to write my contracts, I went to night school and learned from an attorney how to write them myself. I also took classes in accounting, plumbing, electrical work, property management, just about everything that was relevant to my business. When you start relying on professionals to do all of your work, you run out of money pretty fast. And you may not always get what you're looking for.

On the other hand, there are many ways of finding informed, intelligent answers and obtaining advice from professionals for next to nothing; you'd be surprised how many people will give cheap or free knowledge. A friend of mine who is a fellow investor is an expert on that. He attends an adult education class and waits until it's over before he approaches the instructor to ask a question. He rarely enrolls in the class, but the instructors never know because there are so many students there for just one night.

When I was teaching, I used to have my students bring in their questions, and I would do everything I could to research the answers for them. Knowledge is powerful, but I've never in my life hesitated to share my knowledge with anyone who asked. I never felt there was much that was really confidential. Everything I know I've learned from other people, so the least I can do is pass it on.

Someone who teaches will probably answer just about any question you ask because he's not teaching to make money, he's teaching to help people. In a school setting, instructors are more than willing to transmit their knowledge, which they learned from other people, to someone else. But in a business setting, there's a fee associated with giving advice.

The last thing in the world I would do is hire a bunch of consultants to advise me. Think about it—they don't necessarily know anything more about the subject than someone who is willing to do their own homework. And if something went wrong, what would they care, as long as you paid them their fee?

If you are going to be successful in anything, you have to make your own decisions, not rely on the thinking and actions of your attorney, accountant, or broker. If you need information or advice, there is nobody in the world who won't help you if you show a genuine interest. If you show honest concern, people will go out of their way to help you, unless you're talking about taking someone's commission away, which is rarely the case. Rather than hire people to advise you, why not take a class in real estate, appraising, or property management to help get you started in buying and investing?

When I wasn't teaching one of my own courses, I'd enroll in a class. You really must keep studying all the time just to stay on top of trends. Not only that, I love to listen to what other people have to say.

My mother used to tell me how important it was to listen. If you can do that, you'll not only know what you know, you'll also know what the other person knows.

*A*nother way to get good information is by attending all the round table discussions on real estate you can. There's always someone giving a talk who is willing to share ideas. I used to attend real estate investment and appraisal courses. You can even form a discussion group yourself. It only takes two or three people to get together for breakfast or lunch every few weeks to bounce ideas off each other. You never know. The results could be astounding. Will Rogers used to say he never met a man he didn't like. Well, I never met anybody I didn't get a good idea from.

Whenever I attend professional meetings for such groups as the Society of Real Estate Appraisers (SRA), National Association of Independent Fee Appraisers (NAIFA), Certified Business Brokers Association, Certified Commercial Investment Members (CCIM), and the like, I get very enthusiastic because the people who attend those meetings are knowledge-seekers who want to learn and hear somebody else's opinion. When I was president of the Southern California Chapter of the CCIM and the president of the Independent Fee Appraisers, Southern California Chapter, I would go around the room and have everybody share what they thought were good ideas and worthwhile experiences. The brokers, appraisers, and investors who attend these functions are the people who stay up to date with the facts, and they have some of the best ideas. Even if you only want to invest in real estate as a sideline, you can still become active as an associate member of a professional group.

The best thing you can do to develop an effective investment program is learn all you can, be willing to put yourself at some risk, use your own ingenuity, and make your decisions based on a thorough examination of the facts.

Look Before You Leap—Two Mistakes I Made

When I bought my first triplex in Huntington Beach, California, I was operating in a vacuum—I just didn't know it yet. I knew just enough to be dangerous, and it showed in my results. My plan was to have two units rented out and live in the other one so my tenants would be making my payments for me. Sounds good, doesn't it? Ever had that thought yourself?

It was good idea in formulation, but not in execution. I didn't know the neighborhood well—lots of high-density living, police cars every other night and domestic disturbances. There was lots of action, including tenants moving in and out.

Besides not picking a better neighborhood, the second mistake I made was that I didn't know how to manage my residents. They ran me ragged. I let them seize control so I ended up with several drug addicts and the repair costs sapped my bank account. I let it go into foreclosure when I almost stuck myself with a used hypodermic needle one tenant had left. After they'd moved out in the middle of the night and I was cleaning out the apartment, I reached into a debris pile in their garage and there it was—a cooking spoon and the needle. I was so disgusted, I wanted no more to do with real estate investing. I lost money and lost the building to foreclosure.

Years later, I started meeting people who had years of experience in real estate investing (like Dr. Schumacher) at different real estate clubs around the area. Slowly, I started buying in better areas and learned how to start the landlord-tenant relationship on the right foot.

Don't do it by yourself! Read books, go to seminars and interact with people who are where you want to be. Go to the Web sites in this book and find a club near you. Find other landlords in your neighborhood and ask them questions. If they won't talk to you, move on until you find one who will.

11

Time Your Investment
to Get a Boost
From the Economy

Almost everyone I talk to both in and out of real estate has a story about how they could have made millions if they only knew 10 or 20 years ago that property values were destined to skyrocket. This familiar tale is told countless times from coast-to-coast whenever real estate experiences a boom and properties realize heady price gains. But rather than acting on their impulses, the vast majority of investors and real estate onlookers sit by and enviously watch as others get rich and achieve financial security.

The right timing can enable you to buy low and in a few years' time see your property significantly appreciate in value. In 1982, during the height of the recession, the median selling price of a single-family home on the Palos Verdes Peninsula, a prime residential community in the South Bay area of Los Angeles, was $313,000. In 1989, the median price had more than doubled, to $665,000. Timing can indeed pay off. Today, the median price is close to $1 million. But the willingness to take some risk is equally important in deciding when to buy and how much to pay. Whatever you do, just be sure not to overextend yourself.

In a capitalistic economy, ups and downs—recessionary and inflationary spirals—are unavoidable. As an investor, you just have to hope that they're not too deep or too severe. But if you're looking at the long run, your experience, knowledge, and ability can compensate for the dips and act as a bulwark against financial ruin. Still, you have to foresee the changes ahead and put yourself in a position where you won't get knocked out of the box.

Most people don't understand enough about investing in real estate to buy at the right time. Real estate goes in cycles. There are fantastic buys during the height of a boom and there are some terrible buys at the beginning of a recession. In general, the best time to buy is during a lull when people are anxious and prepared to bargain. When there is a recession, the downturn doesn't affect all parts of the country in the same way. But when there is inflation, which occurs when the economy is in a growth mode, it tends to affect all parts of the country. Consequently, it is easier to find a bargain during a downturn than an inflationary period because during a downturn sellers in soft markets are willing to accept less than what the market had previously borne.

Recessionary conditions that cause soft markets are really the best time for able investors to buy real estate. The main reason is that slow sales result in a large inventory of available properties. And when there is a glut of listings, competition forces sellers to make concessions they might not otherwise make. In a down market, it is easier to make a deal because sellers are eager to bargain. Such concessions might include:

- Deferring mortgage payments
- Accepting better terms
- Carrying a second mortgage
- Accepting a short-term, interest-only note
- Improving the condition of the property
- Lowering the asking price

Of all the above variables, I would worry the least about price. I figure that if I'm buying the property in the right location, I can afford to pay market value if I've done my homework. We're looking at the value of property as a long-term investment, so we should not be overly concerned about what we pay for it. We're more concerned about its growth potential and buying on the way up.

It's fine to buy property when it's available and when you can buy it, but it's a bonus if you can get an added boost from the economy by having the right timing. There are all kinds of data available to determine the health of the economy—reports by the Commerce Department, from the Federal Reserve, the trends revealed by leading economic indicators, and so on. Based on the information available at the national, regional, and local levels, you have to determine in your own mind how the economy is going to respond.

If you read the papers, every time there's a downturn you'll notice that there's a lot of gloomy prognostications of how the market is going to collapse. Those of us who have lived through the Depression and have seen all the recessions that followed know that the market has never done that and there's no reason why it will. Despite limited setbacks, the economy has adhered to a strong growth pattern since World War II and will continue to grow in the future, spurring continued investment in real estate.

*H*ow do you know when the country is reaching the end *of a recession? Well, let me post another question. How do you recognize the end of a boom? Economists, the supposed gurus of free enterprise, are always divided on these important questions, and they're intelligent. The slowdown of the real estate market in the late 1980s, as well as the dotcom bubble bust of 2000, took a lot of people, including the industry experts, by surprise. In the final analysis, there is no exact formula for determining what is going to happen. Before the end of the Cold War, how could you have known that the Berlin Wall would collapse even six months before it did? In the summer of 1990, no one was able to predict that Iraq would invade Kuwait—not even the CIA! And the government didn't see the September 11, 2001 attacks on the Pentagon and World Trade Center coming either.*

And who would have forecast the severity of the recession of 2005 to 2010, wherein property prices declined forty percent in some areas?

Despite the unpredictable character of modern life, there still are some general rules to abide by when investing in real estate:

- Evaluate factors that affect economic strength and weakness. When you detect weakness, don't buy.
- If you detect signs of an upturn, start to invest. Acquire as much as possible—sacrifice today will be rewarded tomorrow—but don't spend money on land and improvements unless you can see a return in rent.
- When prices soar so high because of appreciation that you can't afford to buy any more, start putting money into fixing up the properties that you already own so you can ask for higher rents.

The best time that anybody can make a real estate investment is when you can see change, namely, when you can see change for the better. We live in a world of change and the more dramatic the changes are, the more golden the opportunities will be. Look at all the possibilities that opened up by the collapse of Communism in Eastern Europe and the former Soviet Union. But the more dramatic the change, the more risky it can be.

A comment about current conditions is in order here. When prices plunge in recessionary and soft markets, it is absolutely the best time to buy. In states like California, Nevada, Arizona and Florida, local economies have been particularly affected. Mortgage brokers, agents, escrow, contractors/developers and financial institutions that loan in the real estate industries laid off the thousands of workers they'd hired during the boom times. Prices can drop dramatically as foreclosures surge.

It's happened before. The real estate markets in the Upper Great Lake states such as Michigan, Illinois, Ohio and Indiana were severely affected in the 1970s and 1980s with the massive layoffs form Ford, General Motors and Chrysler.

The 1970s was an era marked by stagflation, which is a combination of stagnation that costs jobs and growth and inflation that wipe out the purchasing power of money, causing all prices to rise. California property prices doubled during that decade.

In 1971, President Nixon tried to keep inflation at bay by instituting wage and price controls that were widely applauded by a fair number of economists at the time. Inflation had been raging between 4% and 6% a year. Wages and prices were supposed to be frozen for only 90 days, but it lasted 1,000 days. The initial attempt to dampen inflation by calming inflationary expectations was a monumental failure.

Along with the Arab oil embargo, the controls only served to fire up inflation as the economy became even more dormant. In 1976, Jimmy Carter was elected and tried to jumpstart the economy by printing money and dramatically increasing government expenditures. That drove FHA interest rates to 17.5% and buying activity slowed in most areas. Even though equity would have increased by many thousands of dollars, nobody could qualify for the high interest rate loans.

Capital tax rates rose to 50% and ordinary income was taxed as high as 70%.

Following the Carter years, many regions of the country saw not much appreciation, but property rents doubled or tripled in high job-growth areas. Well-located investment property benefits during good times and bad.

It is important to keep a clear head because everybody around you will start losing theirs. Scary newspaper headlines will trumpet the end of the good times. Front-page stories will profile all the families who were put out of their houses by unscrupulous lenders and it is easy to get caught up in the hysteria.

Do you see any parallels to the past in what is happening around you today?

Generally speaking, changes are beneficial to real estate values if they are positive in nature.

Take the 13-story Fidelity Building, an old landmark in downtown Los Angeles on the corner of Fifth and Spring Streets. Around 1926, you could have purchased that building for about $2 million. But by 1932, with the Depression, most of the tenants who were occupying it had moved out. It was 65% vacant. Whoever held it at that time would have lost the building because they would not have been able to pay the taxes, insurance, or upkeep with such a terrible situation of office vacancies.

But if you had purchased that same building in 1944, you could have bought it for maybe $1 million with very little down because of all the vacancies. By 1946, after the war was over, the downtown business scene started booming and rents doubled and tripled. By 1948, the value of that property probably shot up to $5 million. I can only imagine what it's worth today.

These historical examples are instructive because they show how timing your investment to get a boost from the economy can be very advantageous. Inflation can make a foolhardy investor look like a wise man because he hopped on the bandwagon of ascending land values. But an investment made before or during a depression can make a wise man look like a fool, and there is nothing anyone can do about it.

If you had bought a property in 1945 at market value and experienced the economic growth of the late 1940s and 1950s, you wouldn't have had to know anything; you couldn't have missed. But if you had bought a property in 1928 and even paid below market value for it, there is no way you could have held on to it because of the Depression.

The only way you can know whether the time is right or not is by doing research. But even after you gather all the data, listen to all the lectures, and do all your homework, you have to go with your gut feeling of what you think is going to happen. To take advantage of what's going to happen, you have to make a decision to act. Most people are afraid to try. Yet, if you act on your knowledge rather than procrastinate, you won't be watching from the sidelines as others make their fortunes.

Imagine the investor who went to Austin, Texas in 1980 to buy a 72-unit apartment building for $10,000 a unit, or whatever the going rate was, with $50,000 or $100,000 down. If it was done right, when Austin's market heated up because of all the high-tech development that ensued, the property value and rents went with it. Today, if the prosperity continues over the next 20 years and the investor has a structured activity in which he/she just sticks to a pattern of making the payments and fixing and maintaining the building, he/she will be wealthy in 20 years. I think the best time to take a chance is when you're young, so if it doesn't work out you can start over again and not be set back for life.

Central to an effective strategy is determining the proper time to make an investment. The only difference between salad and garbage is timing. In the above example of the Fidelity Building, it wouldn't have made any difference how smart you were if you had bought that property before the Depression. You would have lost it because you couldn't have made the payments. But, if you had purchased it in 1945, it wouldn't have made any difference how informed or misinformed you were. As long as you were in the right position at the right time, you would have made a killing. This is an extreme example, but there are trends like this all the time during which you can get this extra push.

As the world economy becomes increasingly integrated, the United States has an historic opportunity to take advantage of this foreseeable global activity. And, I believe, the cities and communities that will be the main beneficiaries of this increased activity are those with information industries, high-technology centers, and business services that can provide what the new economy needs.

BEING IN THE RIGHT PLACE AT THE RIGHT TIME

I mentioned the advantages of buying during a recession. But, timing isn't everything. One of the cardinal rules of investing is not to overextend yourself. Provided that your area is going to have continued economic growth and you don't have any balloon payments (a large lump-sum final payment) to make, you can survive even through a downturn. With units that are not rentable, you may have to come up with innovative ways to find tenants.

When negotiating a real estate transaction, you're dealing with two individuals, so what the economy is like may not make all that much difference on a personal level. Pay attention to economic trends, but judge them in general terms.

In 1975, a friend of mine who was a schoolteacher wanted to buy a house. We found a single-family residence for her for $65,000. The owner said he wanted 10% down, or $6,500. So my friend got the money, and we made an offer for slightly less. We decided to make an offer with a set of harsh conditions and try to extract every concession we could. We wanted the owner to carry the second mortgage for 10 years for about three points below the going market rate with no interest payments for the first two years. We asked for the range, the refrigerator, the washer, dryer—all the appliances. From a buyer's point of view, it was perfect, but we knew the owner would have a negative first reaction.

So we put the offer in his mailbox, and I told my friend not to answer the phone for two days in order to let the seller think about the deal. At first, buyers are furious, then they're mad, then they look at their situation and realize they're not getting anybody else. After a few days he called and said, "Well, I don't know—I can't let you take my washer and dryer." That's what he was concerned about. He wasn't upset

*about the really important thing, the 30-year note with only
5% interest. We wound up buying that property for $61,000.
You just never know what the other person is thinking.*

Sometimes, real estate can become burdensome to the owner. If you can buy from a distressed seller, it's amazing what can happen. If, say, a couple owns some rental property in one area, and they live a distance away, and they're having trouble keeping the place up or keeping it rented, then that property has become a burden for them. A burden of that sort can easily become a bargain for you. Such timing may not have anything to do with the economy, but it is being at the right place at the right time nevertheless.

O ne time I was going to buy some property, a single-family residence in Sylmar, California, a community about 25 miles north of Los Angeles. The owner wanted $165,000 for it, but I didn't think it was worth that much, so I hired an appraiser, and he appraised the place at $100,000. I went to the owner and told him what I thought it was worth, but he was adamant and said, "No, I want to sell it for $165,000."

Sizing up my position, I said, "Okay, I'll give you $20,000 down if you agree to carry back a $145,000 first mortgage with no interest. All payments have to go toward principal." Miraculously, he agreed. Being an honest guy, I told him he was crazy because, in essence, he was selling it for the equivalent of about $75,000 with interest at 8% or 10%. He said, "No I'm not. That's what I want." Apparently, he owned the property free and clear. He probably wanted to tell his brother-in-law in New York that he got $165,000 for the place, but his brother-in-law wasn't going to ask him what the terms were. It just goes to show that everybody has a different way of looking at things.

Every property and every situation in real estate is unique. No two parcels are exactly alike, and no two buyers or sellers are exactly alike. You can never be sure of the attitudes, needs, and desires of people. What might be absolutely fantastic for one person might be entirely unacceptable for someone else. The only way to uncover the problems is to make an offer on the property. Then you begin to understand what the sellers want out of it, why they have to leave, where they're going, and what price they need to sell for.

Making an offer is the quickest way I know of getting to the heart of the problem, learning the seller's true motives, and negotiating the best possible deal for yourself. As we'll see in the next chapter, the terms of sale and the size of the down payment are far more important than the purchase price.

Personal Timing

*A*bout 20 years ago, I had some friends who were renting a duplex in West Los Angeles. They lived in the front unit and shared the premises with other tenants in the back unit. The owner, who wanted to sell the property, had listed it on the market for $75,000. My friends were afraid that if the place was sold, they would be forced to move. I told them, "You have to buy this place." They said they couldn't afford to. They had managed to save up a couple of thousand dollars, but the husband had just lost his job. But I said there was absolutely no way they could afford not to buy it.

With a little prodding, the wife ended up borrowing some money from her mother and they managed to do it. I helped them negotiate a deal and now they send me thank you notes every Christmas. Every year they write: "Thank you, thank you! You don't know what you did for us!" Now their place is worth three-quarters of a million dollars.

Whatever you do in this world is a risk, but some of these real estate deals are no more risky than things you do in your everyday life. If my friends in the above example hadn't taken that risk, they wouldn't have had a place to live in, let alone a solid investment, appreciating asset, and source of rental income. They would have had to find some other vehicle to put their kids through college and become financially secure.

12

Negotiate the Purchase as a Long-Term Investment

Great real estate deals are not found, they are created. Finding a good real estate investment is not a matter of luck; it's being able to act when you should. Once you have identified a neighborhood with growth potential, you can find a bargain that fits your needs. You may work six or nine months to find a good bargain, but all you have to do is find one good buy a year—if even that much. I believe that if I really put my mind to it, I could walk around the city block where I live and find a good bargain from someone who was anxious to sell.

Of course, what might be a bargain for me might not be a bargain for the guy next door. But there's probably somebody close by who wants to sell. And if you approach them in the right way, explain your position, and find a seller with the right circumstances, you can probably do very well.

You should always negotiate the terms of a transaction while considering your purchase to be a long-term investment. There are various factors to consider and strategies to employ before ever making an offer on a piece of property, including, most significantly, buying properties with maximum write-off potential and obtaining seller financing.

Seller-assisted financing is the most desirable situation when buying because it enables the buyer to customize the terms and conditions of the deal. For instance, if the seller agrees to "carry paper"—accepting partial payment in the form of a promissory note—you can insert a clause on the note that allows you to pay off the mortgage at the current fair market value of the note. This can result in a tremendous savings advantage if interest rates rise dramatically during the payment period.

A deed of trust, which is used in many states in lieu of a mortgage, refers to a negotiable note that is worth cash. The note is a written instrument that places a lien on real estate as security for the payment of a specified debt. In the contract offer to purchase, the buyer can write whatever terms he or she thinks the seller will agree to.

In addition, the offer should include clauses guaranteeing that the building is legally located on the subject parcel and that it does not encroach onto adjacent property. I once bought a property and wrote into the terms of the first mortgage the option of tearing down the building on the premises without affecting the value of the note.

Certain items are not permitted, however. For instance, the buyer isn't permitted to allow the property taxes or insurance to become delinquent, to underinsure the property, to let the property become completely run down, and so on. There is a whole series of guidelines in the trust deed or mortgage. If the borrower doesn't comply with these rules, including making the payments, the lender can call the note due and payable and initiate foreclosure proceedings. Even if you make the payments on time, the other requirements have to be complied with. When slumlords run into legal difficulties, it's more often because they haven't abided by health and safety rules, rather than the fact that they are behind in their payments.

As mentioned, when negotiating a real estate transaction, *the size of the down payment and terms of sale are far more important than the purchase price.* The asking price really doesn't matter that much as long as you know the area has substantial growth potential. Strive to negotiate a deal where you can live with the terms now, and grow more comfortable with them over a period of time. If the property is in the right location, eventually you won't worry about purchase price.

If, over a 40-year period, you have growth in an area that causes a property initially appraised at $100,000 to rise in value to $2 million, you can see how what you paid ceases to matter anymore. The important thing is to do your research to make sure that you've got the right location.

Availability of Financing

Most sales are dependent on desirable financing, on whether the buyer qualifies for a loan, and the terms of that loan. Check whether financing is available from a recognized institutional lender, a lender that is solid and secure, as opposed to a fly-by-night operation or an unreliable, "hard money" private lender. Hard money lenders generally finance problem

---

TABLE 12.1

How the Down Payment and Terms of Sale
Are More Important Than the Purchase Price

Example: A commercial property is on the market for:

$200,000

The gross annual income on a substantial lease is:

$ 16,000

The property is owned free and clear. The owner is in the high tax bracket and also is burdened with available cash that he is required to invest. The owner asks you to make an offer on the property based on the following:

Minimum price	$200,000
Minimum interest	8%
Maximum due date	9 years

Ideal Purchase
Here is the most ideal set of terms to offer:

- No down payment
- $200,000 first trust deed, carried by the owner for 9 years at 8 percent interest (a deferred mortgage loan)
- Interest to accumulate to principal and be due and payable in 9 years

The total balance due in 9 years would be:

$400,000

Undesirable purchase
A cash offer of:

$200,000

These are the two extremes. Now set the parameters for negotiation. Under the ideal purchase, you could collect substantial rents, watch property value appreciate, and in nine years refinance it and satisfy your debt to the previous owner.

---

properties by extracting high interest rates in exchange for assuming risk. Hard moneylenders typically offer short-term financing, which results in a balloon payment at the end of the financing term. Their loan processing fees are generally expensive as well.

Hard-money lenders can be very useful if you need to borrow money quickly and without hassle. All they care about is the equity; they want lots of security for the convenience they offer you. If you need to buy a property quickly, the deal won't last long or you don't have your financing in place yet, a hard-money loan may be your short-term solution.

You don't want to keep these loans a long time—refinance out of them or sell the property for profit.

If there are "clouds" in the title, such as unpaid real property taxes, unpaid street bonds, an IRS income tax lien against the property, construction liens, or money judgments against the owner, financing might be hard to come by. These disputes usually must be resolved before clear title can be given to the institutional lender or new purchaser. Sometimes, the mortgage can be paid in full but its satisfaction may not be recorded. All of these claims act as encumbrances that, if valid, affect or impair the owner's title, or evidence of free-and-clear ownership.

Financing Creates Value

It always happens that loans dry up during recessions. Likewise, financing loosens up when markets are hot. You have to take what the market gives you.

If financing is easy to get, it is likely that property will be expensive in a rising market and below-market deals may be hard to get. If the market is giving you expensive properties and banks are lending money, your job is to find discounted properties with all that easy-to-get financing. Use those bank loans to your advantage.

During recessions, when property values are declining, banks generally pull their horns in and tighten their guidelines. It is hard for them to lend to borrowers who may have lost their jobs or have credit issues or shrinking home equity. If you want to buy a property at a discount during these hard times, have the seller help you buy it. Sellers can carry back financing, take notes or provide you with installment sales if you can't get a bank loan.

Take What the Market Gives You

Here's what I did about taking what the market was giving me. I started buying bank foreclosures in the late 1990s because the lenders would finance the loans for me. It was called "expedited financing" in those days and boy, did I take advantage of it. Imagine that—a bank losing a house and giving me a loan when nobody else would. Those houses are worth much more today and the rents are up 30% to 50%.

Years later, after my houses increased in value, I took out lines of credit (second mortgages) to buy more houses that I purchased at substantial discounts because I used all cash from my line of credit. Loans were extremely easy to get in the early 2000s so I refinanced my new purchases and put a safe, 30-year fixed-rate loan on my formerly free and clear house. I used the proceeds to pay back my credit line. I had none of my own money in the deal.

In the latter part of the decade, banks were closing and not lending money. Bank foreclosures were proliferating. I now use my cash savings to pay all cash to buy bank foreclosures that are selling for 30% to 50% below their market highs.

When the market comes back, it will be time to possibly refinance those houses or let them ride free and clear. It all depends on what the market is giving me!

Obtain Proper Title

While obtaining financing, be sure that you have the proper title to the property. I once bought three lots, and a friend of mine bought a fourth lot adjacent to the three that I owned. We only paid a few hundred dollars apiece for them. But I decided to pull out some title insurance on my property anyway to protect myself from any loss sustained by defects that might be in the title. Title companies insure buyers against most claims to the title of the property.

About five years later, the California Department of Transportation started building a new freeway nearby and was looking for granite gravel. My hillside, which conveniently consisted of granite, was leveled free of charge in return for the granite. My friend had the same thing happen to his lot, but he didn't have clear title to the property. Later, when he decided to build on his land, the lender found a cloud in the title in the form of an unpaid judgment against the property, and the lender wouldn't make a construction loan until this cloud was removed. It cost my friend thousands and thousands to sue and go to court and finally get the right to do something with his property. The time, money and effort was spent needlessly by skipping the very important step of title search.

TITLE INSURANCE

When you buy a property, always get a policy of title insurance. I wouldn't touch a property otherwise, because I want to know what I'm buying. Are there any liens or encumbrances against it? Are there any easements of record or any assessments against the property that you don't know about which aren't covered by disclosure laws?

However, even with title insurance, you are not protected against every problem associated with a property. It only covers items of record, which may be different than actual problems. For instance, it doesn't protect the buyer of the property if the property is encroaching on the adjoining property or if there is a high voltage power line seven feet away from the property line.

Be sure to buy real estate in a comfortable way so that you don't have anything that will hurt you if you suffer a setback or decide to change careers, so it won't become a burden. It should be a pleasant experience, an asset you can enjoy and feel that you've got something that you really want and are proud to own.

How Financing Affects Market Value

As mentioned, *the size of the down payment and the terms of sale are far more important than the purchase price* in a real estate transaction. Most people never pay off their mortgage anyway, or if they do it will be after 20 or 30 years, so it's really not important how much you pay for a piece of real estate. What matters is how much you take out of your pocket each month to make your payment.

If a seller is concerned about the price, which most are, you can offer a higher price and still not have to pay any more or make a larger down payment. In the table below, notice how financing affects the purchase price.

If you can afford to buy a property at fair market value, you shouldn't hesitate if the terms are good and you know that the property will increase in value. The real estate investor does not buy merchandise (property) like other businesspeople. The retail price of land today may be its wholesale price in the future.

On the downside, if you make a purchase in the stagnant market, you run the risk of paying more for a property than its appreciation rate will justify. If this happens, you've made a mistake in your analysis. When you do your research, make sure you've got the right location. That's the basis of the whole thing.

Interest is deductible for tax purposes, so I don't argue too much about interest rates as long as they are fair. Interest rates can fluctuate due to economic pressures, which you can't foresee, so in an unstable market I try to get a fixed rate. Sometimes a property can only be bought with a variable or adjustable rate mortgage because the lender isn't offering fixed rate mortgages. If an adjustable rate mortgage is all you can find, make sure there is a cap on the rate to protect you from large increases. You have to remain somewhat flexible as far as interest rates are concerned, but drive a hard bargain wherever you can.

> *Say you buy a property and put 25% down, and the owner takes back a first mortgage equal to 75% of the selling price. Assume your loan has a 30-year term with a 9% interest rate. The note should stipulate that if the seller wanted to sell the note, the buyer has the first opportunity to buy it at current market value. This is a tremendous advantage because if interest rates rose to 12%, but you could still pay only 9% interest, that would represent a substantial discount.*

When negotiating, work out a payment program so that it fits into your need and financial position. If you can see that an acquisition wouldn't be a terrible burden on you, then it's probably a good idea to go ahead with it. As long as you can hold on to the property for a reasonable period of time, inflation will take you out of the woods. Down the line, you might be able to renegotiate for a better interest rate. Today's interest rates are tremendous—the best in 40 or 50 years—and lenders have been swamped with loan refinances.

The following example is used to justify the purchase price of an income property, in this case an older three-unit apartment building, or triplex, and may be used for other contemplated purchases.

TABLE 12.2
How Terms of Sale Can Affect the Sale Price

Example:

- Commercial property is listed for $230,000
- Seller will take a down payment of 40,000
- Seller will carry a first mortgage of.................................. 190,000
  15% interest per year, with the note to be amortized in full in 20 years.

Assume that the down payment of $40,000 does not change. The $2,500 per month payment on the note remains constant. If the interest rate is altered and the number of years to pay off the note is changed, the original principal sum on the first trust deed note, as well as the sales price, will change from $152,500 to $364,000 as follows:

Interest Rate (Percent)	Length of Loan (Years)	Monthly Payment	Sum of 1st Mortgage	Down Payment	Sales Price
12	5	$2,500	$112,500	$40,000	$152,500
18	10	2,500	139,000	40,000	179,000
15	10	2,500	155,000	40,000	195,000
18	20	2,500	161,000	40,000	201,000
18	30	2,500	166,000	40,000	206,000
18	40	2,500	166,500	40,000	206,500
12	10	2,500	174,000	40,000	214,000
15%	20 yrs.	2,500	190,000	40,000	230,000
9	10	2,500	197,000	40,000	237,000
15	30	2,500	197,500	40,000	237,500
15	40	2,500	199,000	40,000	239,000
12	15	2,500	208,000	40,000	248,000
12	20	2,500	227,000	40,000	267,000
12	30	2,500	243,000	40,000	283,000
9	20	2,500	278,000	40,000	318,000
9	30	2,500	310,000	40,000	350,000
9	40	2,500	324,000	40,000	364,000

TABLE 12.3

Justifying the Purchase Price of an Older Three-Unit (Triplex) Apartment Property

(A)	Purchase price		$ 200,000
	Allocation:	Land	50,000
		Improvements	150,000
		(Life = 27.5 years at 3.64%)	
(B)	Down payment		40,000
(C)	First mortgage at 13% (25-yr. term)		160,000
(D)	Annual mortgage payment	$1,861/mo. (× 12)	22,332
(E)	Annual gross rental income	$1,200/mo. (× 12)	14,400
(F)	Annual expenses (incl. real property taxes, insurance, utilities, repairs, maintenance), vacancy allowance, and collection loss		−5,400
(G)	Annual net income		9,000
(H)	Spendable income/out-of-pocket costs:		
	(G) Total net income		9,000
	(D) Annual mortgage payment		−22,332
	Annual loss		⟨13,332⟩
	Gains to be Derived from Purchase		
(I)	Equity buildup		22,332
	Mortgage interest ($160,000 × 13%)		−20,800
	Total interest		1,532
(J)	Annual appreciation (6% × 200,000)		+12,000
(K)	Tax benefits: Buyer's tax liability = 40%		
	Mortgage interest	$20,800	
	Depreciation	+ 5,460 ($150,000 × 3.64%)	
	Total	26,260	
		× 40% =	$ 10,504
(L)	Total gains from purchase		$24,036
(M)	Out-of-pocket cost to own property		−⟨13,532⟩
(N)	Net benefits derived per year		$ 10,504
	Net benefits of $10,504 per year (N) on a $40,000 outlay (B) represents a 26.3% return on investment.		

Because of the long-term gains of equity buildup and appreciation (estimated at 6% annually, assuming the property is located in an area with growth potential) combined with immediate tax benefits, the property has an annual yield of $24,036. Since out-of-pocket costs ("annual loss") to own the property are $13,332, the long-term net benefits are $10,504 per year, representing a 26.3% return on the investment in the form of a $40,000 down payment.

From an income standpoint, the property may continue to experience a negative cash flow for several years until increased rents eventually overtake the mortgage payments. Remember, though, that during this finite negative period, the property, if properly selected, will continue to appreciate and tax benefits can continue to be applied over the life of the loan and the improvements, thereby serving as a shelter.

THIRTY-TWO ITEMS TO CONSIDER BEFORE MAKING AN OFFER

Making an offer to purchase a property and writing a satisfactory agreement are paramount in the execution of successful real estate transactions. As a general rule, an offer should contain or consider the following:

1. How title should be taken by the buyer (joint tenants, community property, or tenancy in common).
2. The specific date and time when the offer from the buyer will expire.
3. The street address and precise lot dimensions of the subject property.
4. That the seller warrants the building(s) are located legally within the property lines.
5. That the seller warrants there are no encroachments on adjacent property.
6. That the seller warrants no other person has any right, title, or interest in the property other than what appears on the preliminary title report.
7. That the seller warrants there are no unrecorded liens against the property.
8. That the seller warrants there are no violations of building and safety laws, either pending or contemplated.
9. That the seller agrees to allow the buyer to obtain a permit of occupancy on the property. If there is any expense or corrective violations in connection with the permit, said expense shall be the total responsibility of the seller.

10. That the seller is not aware of any contemplated changes in zoning affecting the property.
11. That if the sale is contingent on a zoning change, the seller will cooperate by signing all necessary documents.
12. That the buyer shall have the privilege of approving the preliminary title report before the closing of the escrow or transaction.
13. That a termite report shall be submitted into the escrow or trust account and be dated after this agreement. And that the seller shall, at his expense, comply with all requirements of the termite report unless otherwise agreed to.
13A. If the property is located on a slope, make sure you get a geological inspection and/or a soil report.
14. If the buyer's funds come from a 1031 tax-deferred exchange transaction, the seller agrees to cooperate in furthering the exchange by signing all necessary documents, provided that the seller is not affected financially.
15. That the seller warrants the property is not located in any hazardous area, such as a flood zone, an earthquake fault, an area of earth movement, sinkhole areas, tornado or hurricane regions.
16. That the buyer has authority to approve all existing leases and verify all rents. And that the seller warrants no building areas were rented by giving any concessions of any kind. Seller warrants that all rents are accurate and correct as stated and that there were no free or reduced rents given.
17. If the buyer is assuming a promissory note or deed of trust (or mortgage) of record, buyer shall be given an exact copy of said documents for his inspection and approval before the close of the transaction. Seller warrants that terms of encumbrance are exactly as stated in the offer, and that there is no enforceable acceleration clause or due date or note or notes to be assumed.

18. That the buyer and/or his broker of representative shall have the authority to inspect the exterior and interior of the structure(s) and to approve the condition of the structure as well as the roofing, plumbing, heating, electrical, and the like, before the sale is consummated.

19. If buyer disapproves of any item or items, the escrow company or real estate attorney is instructed to return all funds to the buyer without further instructions or signature from seller.

20. Escrow or transaction officer is instructed to have all rent deposits prorated on the cash down payment and not on any trust deed(s) or mortgage(s).

21. If there are any monetary adjustments to be made, they shall be to seller's purchase money deed of trust.

22. Buyer may assume present insurance or take out a new policy at his option.

23. Seller shall pay all escrow charges in connection with the sale. All other charges shall be paid by the buyer and seller in the customary manner.

24. Buyer shall get possession of and be responsible for property after close of the transaction.

25. Seller warrants that all leases are in effect and have not been changed or modified. Seller further warrants that there are no defaults in leases, either by the lessor or the lessee.

26. Seller warrants that there is no filled ground, toxic waste, asbestos, or other hazardous materials on the premises.

27. Seller warrants that there are no loans or notes against the personal property involved.

28. Seller agrees to furnish buyer with a chattel mortgage report (pledge of personal property) at his expense. Seller agrees to list all personal property in detail that is to be included in the sale and provided a bill of sale to buyer. Buyer has authority to inspect all personal property before close of the transaction using said list and to verify the accuracy of said list.

29. If title cannot be delivered to buyer, no damage to buyer shall be incurred. Buyer shall be reimbursed for all funds deposited in escrow without further instructions or signature from seller.
30. Seller is to allow buyer two working days after close of the transaction to change over all utilities.
31. Seller is to deposit all keys to the property that are in seller's possession before close of the transaction.
32. Seller is to provide buyer with a list of all persons having keys to the property.

WHY PRICE IS NOT THE MOST IMPORTANT FACTOR

In the early 1970s, one of my students asked me about a house he and his family were considering purchasing. The house was priced at $375,000, which in those days was an astronomical sum of money, and still a high price today. He could only afford $340,000 so he was deficient by $35,000.

This young man had a wonderful job and a fine family. The family was most enthusiastic about this new house. They had looked at many other properties over a four-year period, and had not found anything else that came close to what they wanted. He expressed how happy and elated the family was about buying this house. But he could only afford $340,000 not the $375,000 asking price. Although, he was planning to advance even further with his career and make considerably more money, he was hesitant to make a deal and there was nothing he could do to persuade the owner of the property to reduce the sale price.

I talked to the young buyer for quite some time on two or three occasions and asked him how much he thought his time was worth. He said he didn't really know. He hadn't considered this. He was making close to $100,000 a year, which was a most substantial sum of money in 1973. I told him to think about how much his time and money was worth. I told him to forget about whether he was paying too much for the property. Go ahead and make the deal, because eventually, over a period of time, the real estate will enhance in value and will be worth three or four times what it is today. Then it really doesn't matter how much you paid for it.

With a higher-priced property you will have a higher tax basis, but if you can see your way to borrow the money or to negotiate a transaction where you would have a second trust deed that you would pay off in three to five or even six years, then you might buy the property for the full sale price and in time, the deal could work out superbly.

The family has stayed in touch with me for over 25 years. The (then) young man who had been my student said he remembered how wonderful it was to talk about his house purchase. Looking at his situation today, remember how ridiculous it was to argue over a $35,000 difference in price. Twenty-five years later, in 1997, the value of the house had increased to $900,000. Even during a recessionary period, the $900,000 was a very fair figure he could get if he decided to move.

His children have since grown up and are out on their own, enjoying life and success. One of the biggest things that contributed to their success was the fact that they grew up in such a wonderful community during their formative years. They were in close proximity to everything they needed—schools, theaters, parks, etc. They benefited immensely from their friends, neighbors and the surrounding community. It was a marvelous experience for them.

One of my students lives in San Clemente, which is an upper-end seaside community in Southern California. Prices there have always been high, even in a recession. He bought one house every few years and fed the negative cash flow out of his earnings from his job. He paid retail prices on every property.

Now, just ten years later, he brags that he has gotten rich paying retail in San Clemente!

13

Creative Financing

Creative financing is an umbrella term used to describe any financing arrangement made to acquire property other than a traditional mortgage from a lending institution. Creative financing deals typically involve multiple sources of credit, including sellers, investment partners and even real estate brokers, and usually depend on the seller's willingness to extend a loan to the buyer (or "carry paper") and become a junior lender. Although comparatively rare, creative financing deals become popular during periods of rapid appreciation when housing prices soar and buyers lack sufficient cash for a down payment or credit to obtain a loan. This happened in the early 1980s, when high interest rates and inflation resulted in real estate prices that were out of the reach of most first-time buyers. Creative financing is also used when the real estate market slows down and property-especially expensive property—becomes difficult to sell. In these conditions, sellers are much more likely to entertain a creative financing proposal than when the market is good.

Creative financing deals can take a variety of forms and are only limited by your knowledge, imagination and terms the seller will agree to. Once you find a house you like and agree on a price, the best you could do is tell the seller that you'll offer no money down, make no payments for 10 or maybe 20 years and, at the end of that time, pay off the mortgage in one lump sum. By then, appreciation should allow you to refinance the property so that you can easily cover the purchase price. Of course, no seller I've ever worked with would agree to such an offer. Nevertheless, individuals and other non-institutional lenders are free to take greater risks in their investments because there are fewer laws and regulations governing their activities. As a result, they may be willing to accept some form of deferred or interest-only payment plan or (more typically) a higher loan-to-value ratio than institutional lenders.

Creative financing deals more often involve loans from the seller, short-term balloon payment loans, so-called "wraparound" mortgages, assumable loans, sale-leasebacks, land contracts, and other alternative financing instruments. With real estate, the flexibility is tremendous, especially if you're not dealing with institutional lenders. If you're instead dealing directly with private parties, you can sometimes get them to agree to an arrangement that is very advantageous from the buyer's point of view. Since the most common type of creative real estate deal involves seller-assisted financing, it is very important to find a motivated seller. Before discussing seller-assisted financing in more detail, it may be useful to provide an overview of some of the more common creative financing instruments.

SOME COMMON CREATIVE FINANCING TERMS

A *balloon payment* loan is a short-term fixed-rate mortgage. It is similar to a conventional, long-term fixed rate mortgage in the sense that monthly payments are required, but different in the respect that the entire unpaid balance and accrued interest is due and payable on the loan at maturity-typically three to five years. As discussed below, sometimes you can negotiate with the seller to extend the life of the loan in return for an increasing adjustable interest rate. The monthly payment of most balloon loans are calculated as if the loan would not be fully paid until the end of a standard loan period, such as 15 or 30 years.

An *interest-only mortgage* is a balloon payment loan in which the monthly payments only cover the accrued interest. The unpaid balance of the loan, which remains constant and isn't paid down, is fully due and payable on an agreed-upon date. This is often one to five years after the consummation of the loan or upon some other event such as the receipt of the proceeds from the sale of another property.

A *tandem* or *piggyback mortgage* is usually used in residential income property financing where two lenders share in making a single loan. For example, one lender may supply 60% of the loan funds and a participating lender the other 25% of the funds. The originating lender holds 60% of an 85% loan and the participating lender (the piggyback investor) holds 25% of the loan. This is a form of junior mortgage financing, where the participating investor is subordinated to the originating lender. The purpose of piggyback loans is to provide a higher than normal "loan to value" loan.

A *wraparound mortgage* is also known as an "all inclusive trust deed" (or AITD). This financing device is used to legally combine an existing loan with a new loan when the buyer is having difficulty securing a conventional loan for the purchase. With a wraparound mortgage, the new loan is subject to the terms of the existing loans. The payments from the buyer to the seller are used first to pay the underlying loan or loans, with the balance going to the seller to recover the remaining equity. If the buyer and seller decide to use this financing technique, caution is advised. Most institutional loans contain "acceleration" or "alienation" provisions that prevent the transfer of the property to a new owner without lender approval. When exploring the possibility of a wraparound mortgage, sound professional advice is recommended.

An *assumable loan* or loan assumption occurs when a buyer pays the seller for part or all of the equity in a property and assumes the responsibility for payment of the existing loans. From this point on, the buyer makes the payments until the existing loans are paid in full or until the buyer refinances the property and secures a conventional loan. This financing technique is desirable in the sense that it saves buyers' and sellers' expenses, provided the buyer has sufficient funds to complete the transaction. The interest rate on older loans is often lower than the current loan market (except for today's market, where interest rates are at a 50-year low) and the remaining years of payment are reduced.

A *reverse annuity mortgage* (or RAM) is when the lender pays the borrower a fixed annuity based on a percentage of the value of the property. This form of creative financing may be used by elderly homeowners who have a low fixed income and who must move in order to utilize their equity. Under a reverse-annuity mortgage, the borrower is not required to repay the loan until a specified event such as sale of the property or death. At that time, the loan is paid back. In effect, a RAM enables a retired couple who owns their home free and clear to draw on the equity of their home. Instead of paying down their loan, they increase their loan balance each month. No cash payment of interest is involved, as the increase in the loan balance represents the cash advanced plus interest on the loan.

A *land contract* is sometimes used in real estate transactions when a buyer invests little or no cash in the purchase and is willing to let the owner retain legal title to the property for a given amount of time. The title is transferred after the buyer has paid a substantial amount of cash toward the seller's equity, if not all of it. In the meantime, the buyer obtains what is referred to as "equitable title," that is, a build-up of ownership in incremental fashion through payments on the loan principal and appreciation in the property's value. When the agreed amount is paid, the seller transfers legal title to the buyer, who then assumes the existing loan. Until that time, the principal loan payments, interest on the unpaid balance of the contract, and monthly tax and insurance payments are paid to the seller, who makes the monthly payments on the underlying trust deed. To insure the rights of the two parties involved, a title insurance company is often designate as trustee.

SELLER-ASSISTED FINANCING

When you buy a property, the most advantageous terms are to arrange for the seller to handle part of the financing by taking back or carrying a second, third, or fourth mortgage. Whereas the institutional lender determines the interest rate for the first mortgage, a second, third, or fourth mortgage is a negotiable instrument made between the buyer and the seller written with any terms they agree to. Second mortgages, which prolong the seller's liability on the property, are generally used when buyers don't have enough cash for the down payment. Most junior mortgages carried by sellers are short-term loans for periods of three to five years. However, some owners and builders take back long-term seconds that are completely amortized using a 15- or 20-year payback schedule.

Let's say you were buying a property for $100,000 and only had $10,000 for the down payment. The lender is willing to make a $70,000 mortgage loan, which leaves $20,000 difference. The seller, if cooperative, could allow you to accept the outstanding $20,000 in the form of a second mortgage, or second trust deed, which would be recorded on the property, terms to be announced. Depending on how bad the seller wanted out of the property, you might get interest—only for five years or something similar.

Sometimes brokers will agree to take their commission in the form of a third trust deed, which the buyer then pays off along with the other loans on the property. This situation may arise if the transaction involves a substantial commission and the buyer is just a little short of cash to close the deal. The broker may be willing to take some of the paper as a deferred commission, payable in monthly installments. If there is a lot of financing, the owner might be willing to take his profit in the form of a fourth or fifth trust deed. I once did an appraisal on a vacant parcel for which the owner had a sixth trust deed on the land! If the sellers are flexible, write the terms however you want, whatever they will agree to. Here, you have a certain amount of latitude. The one thing that isn't allowable is a note with no interest. The tax laws state that there has to be an interest rate assigned to the note. If you don't assign one, the IRS will assume the note bears interest at the going rate.

> *F*or another example, let's say you were looking at an income property worth $200,000. The owner is willing to accept a $5,000 down payment and take back a $195,000 first mortgage. But, instead of taking the first at $1,950 a month for 30 years at 10% interest, suppose he raises the price to $300,000 with no interest so that you only have to pay off the principal. The payments wouldn't be any less, but the owner of the property wouldn't be collecting any interest, so the principal would be treated in the form of capital gains, which is on 28% taxable, as opposed to interest, which is 100% taxable. If you buy a property that way, you might come out ahead tax-wise. If the seller agrees to carry the mortgage, the seller has to pay the interest. It's a buyer-seller issue.

Just as no two parcels are exactly alike, no two transactions are exactly alike because you never know what somebody else is thinking. And you can never really find out until you make an offer. If people are motivated to do things, it's amazing what will happen.

The more motivated the seller is, the more flexible the terms of the deal. A friend of mine bought a residence in 1982 at the height of the recession of the early 1980s. The seller was asking $400,000, so my friend gave him $100,000 down, and the seller agreed to carry a $300,000 note on the property with no interest, no principal, no payments, no nothing for five years. At the end of this time, my friend had to make a balloon payment, but with no interest attached to it. If interest were allowed to accumulate on the principal, the balance due would have been twice as much. Consequently, my friend was able to meet his obligation.

FINDING A MOTIVATED SELLER

To negotiate a fantastic deal, you need to find a motivated seller. Why do sellers become motivated? The reasons are varied: an illness or death in the family, an all-consuming lawsuit, job loss, divorce, another property that has been bought and is ready to move into, long vacant rental units, a property hat has been sitting on the market for an extended period without any takers, debts arising from a tax audit, or a small business that needs to be infused with much-needed cash. The greatest motivated sellers are those with a combination of reasons why they need to sell. Here are 10 more reasons why the owner of a piece of real estate might become a motivated seller:

1. The owner has allowed his property to deteriorate.
2. The property's rental income has dropped because the building has not been modified to keep up with the times.
3. The owners have inherited the property and can't manage it properly because no one wants to take responsibility.
4. The owners have inherited the property and are in a hurry to divide proceeds from the estate.
5. The owner is forced to sell to pay off personal debts.
6. The owners are absentee and do not keep abreast of actual rental or sale value.
7. The owner bought on speculation, became frustrated with a slow appreciation rate, and has decided to invest in another field, such as the stock market.
8. The owners are older and wish to liquidate their assets and take back the mortgage(s).
9. The owner needs to relocate because of a job transfer.
10. The owner is tired of the rat race and has decided to move to the Polynesian Islands.

---

11. The owner has gotten a divorce and needs to pay off his or her spouse.
12. The owner has lost his or her job, or has had his or her hours cut back.
13. A family member is renting the property and not paying the rent.

I once bought a house wherein the granddaughter was not paying her grandma the rent. She was taking advantage of the family situation because she knew that her grandmother would not evict her. It is hard on family harmony when you have to go to court with a family member.

So, instead of dispossessing her blood, she sold me the house and I evicted her. I got the house for 30% less than market value.

Sometimes, negotiating a transaction takes on the dimensions of a psychological battle. In the mid-1950s, a friend of mine wanted to buy a house. The sellers of the property, who were friends of his, were asking $25,000 for their residence. But he knew they were in the midst of a messy divorce, having real problems, and were about to be foreclosed upon.

So he called them up one day and said, "I want you to clear off the dining room table because I'm coming over to make an offer." He then went to the bank, took out $20,000 in $100 bills. Then he went to the seller's house and spread these 200 C-notes around the table. Even though the offer was $5,000 less than what they were asking—and that was a lot in those days—it didn't take much to convince them to accept.

NO-MONEY-DOWN TRANSACTIONS

I've made almost all of my real estate purchases with little or no money down. As a matter of fact, I don't think I've put more than $3,000 down on anything I've ever bought. I've done this by working with sellers. There is no way you can negotiate a good deal unless you find a person who is motivated and has a desire to sell. Finding motivated sellers is essential; the more motivated they are, the better the deal you can negotiate.

In 1964, I found a place where the seller wanted $20,000 down. I was really anxious to buy it, but I didn't have enough money for the down payment. So I kept talking to him and told him what the advantages were to taking a second mortgage, including monthly payments without any tenant problems, a higher interest rate than he could get from the bank, and the sale of the property, which he was anxious to accomplish because the market was dead.

After a while, he got tired of it. There weren't many buyers around in those days, plus you couldn't rent anything. It was driving him nuts. Eventually, I got him to take a third trust deed on the property so I would only have to pay $3,000 down. It worked out well, but we probably negotiated for nine months.

Another way to get around a large down payment is by putting a second mortgage on another piece of property in which the purchaser has equity, which the seller can accept as collateral—property pledged as security for a debt.

Say you are desperate to sell your $500,000 apartment building. The buyer could go to an institutional lender and find a loan for 80% of the property's market value, or $400,000. This leaves the buyer $100,000 that he has to come up with. Assume he doesn't have that kind of money, but that he has a valuable house somewhere. You can accept a $100,000 mortgage on his residence in lieu of cash payment and the lender will most likely agree to the deal because the apartment building the lender is loaning on will have a $100,000 equity cushion to protect the loan.

A "no money down" transaction is a form of seller-assisted financing. It basically entails taking equity in one piece of real estate and trading the paper on that equity to the seller in lieu of cash. No money down plans usually turn out to be schemes; the lender is defrauded when he is not informed that the seller—not the buyer—is really the person putting up the money for the down payment. Some banks still don't require this disclosure, but frequently some element of fraud is involved.

There are several drawbacks to no money down plans. First of all, you have to do them in an up market. Values have to be appreciating at a good clip. If there is a leveling off or if the market's dropping, no-money-down schemes are difficult. A lot of people try this who don't understand the problems and end up losing their shirts.

Another disadvantage to no money down transactions is that they typically result in a balloon payment of the principal balance at the end of the financing period. I think it is important to avoid balloon payments at all costs. I call

them "debt bombs" because they explode in your face at a
time when you least want them to.

With a balloon mortgage, you are compelled to refinance it at the will of the note rather than when you decide is the best time. That's constraining in itself. You might not be in a position to refinance when the note comes due or the market might be such that interest rates are at 20%, which could take all of your profit away from you.

If you do have a balloon payment, you always want an out. One escape clause that can be written in the note to postpone the satisfaction of a balloon payment may read:

> If the buyer is not able to pay off the loan in full
> when due, the loan will be extended for a period
> of time at a higher interest rate.

To illustrate how this would work, say you buy a property and the seller insists on a five-year due date for payment of the loan in full, and he gives you 10% interest. You could offer to pay 12% interest if he could extend the loan for one year, or 14% for two years, or 16% for three years. A 14% or 16% interest rate is still a lot cheaper than losing your investment. The market changes every three or four years anyway, so paying a slightly higher interest will buy you some crucial time to work on your investment and wait for property values to rise.

Most of the time, people who sell for no money down are desperate. Their property either is a dog or they are about to be foreclosed on. Several "no money down" gurus went broke when the real estate market started to flatten out. A few authors of "no money down" books even had to file bankruptcy because they weren't able to prove their chalkboard theories in the real world of profit and loss. They kept floating paper, but it never panned out for them in dollars and cents.

Getting an Infinite Yield on Your Money

We do no-money-down transactions all the time. They're the best way to buy real estate, but you have to watch out when you use this maximum-leverage strategy.

Because we had lines of credit from the bank that were secured by other property we owned, we were able to offer all cash on several houses we wanted. After we got these houses 20% to 30% below market value, we were able to turn around and get permanent financing from the bank. We then paid our credit line back; no money came out of our pockets.

No-money-down deals give very high yields. When you total up the package of benefits you get by owning property—appreciation, loan amortization, cash flow and tax benefits—you get an infinite yield.

What's an infinite yield, you ask? Since you have none of your own money in the deal, how can you calculate the return in your investment? You cannot. If you do enough of these no-money-down deals, you will be rich before you know it!

A DISCOUNT FOR THE BUYER

In the early 1980s, a relative of mine decided to buy a single-family residence and they asked me to handle the transaction. They found a beautiful house in an area that had potential economic growth and it appeared to me that it was a good long-term investment. The house had great usable value because it was ideally located near shopping centers and recreational facilities. The negotiated purchase price was $250,000, and the property was free and clear of any encumbrances. We agreed to put 50% down ($125,000) and the owner agreed to carry a first trust deed of $125,000, 6% interest, 30-year loan.

This sounded like an excellent idea, so we agreed to the purchase, but I insisted that the trust deed note state that if the purchasers of the property wished to pay off the trust deed note sooner than the due date, they had the privilege of paying it off at the then present fair market value of the note. Now, this is important to understand. This was written on the face of the note and thoroughly understood by both the buyer and the seller. At the time of the purchase, the interest rate was 6% on the mortgage and it was a 30-year loan.

The note stated that if the purchasers of the property wished to pay off the note in less time than the due date, which was 30 years, they had the privilege of paying it off at what the trust deed would sell for on the open market, assuming that a buyer of trust deeds or a bank or some other institution, or loan company would buy that note and pay cash for it. At that time, 6% was a low interest rate on a trust deed that had a 50% cash down on it, so there was some added equity built up since the time of purchase.

The house was rented for three years. In 1985, the purchasers were able to sell their home in a distant area and move to their new home. The rental period was satisfactory because the income off the single-family residence was more than adequate to make the payments on the loan as well as the taxes, insurance and maintenance on the property.

In 1985, the purchasers moved into the home and, after obtaining a sizable amount of money, they decided that they wished to pay off the first trust deed, which had a 6% interest rate. The going rate on single-family residences in the community where the subject property was located was about 9%, so in effect the purchasers had a 3% added increment of value in that trust deed and when it was exposed for sale on the open market, after advertising it in local newspapers, going to banks, mortgage companies, etc., we found that the very best that could be done on replacing the loan would be a 9% loan for a 30-year period. The fact that the existing loan was only at 6% interest made the mortgage subject to a discount. Through procedures that followed we were able to get the seller to agree to a 30% reduction in the payoff of the trust deed, which amounted to a little over $40,000.

The owners of the property had a tremendous advantage. If the purchasers had established the fair market value of the note and the seller said they wouldn't do it, even though it was written in the contract, the owners could have stopped payment on the note and would not have had to make monthly payments. If that had happened, the only recourse the sellers would have had would be to start foreclosure on the note or take it to arbitration or court.

So the purchasers were at a tremendous advantage. Instead of paying off $250,000 for the property, as originally stated, they paid the discounted price of around $210,000 for the property.

This is a good example of why anyone who buys trust deed notes, mortgages, etc., should read any clauses that affect the value of the property over and beyond what is generally the face amount. One should realize that today, if you are going to buy a piece of property, a suggestion of this kind could be worked in a second trust deed or even a first trust deed if it is a private owner handling the loan.

The Due-Date Escape Clause:
Why Every Second Trust Deed Should Have One

A number of years ago I purchased a duplex for very little down. There was an existing first mortgage on the property and the owner of the property took back a second mortgage. The owner decided on a two-year due date, which meant that at the end of two years, the second trust deed was due and payable. If the purchaser didn't have any money to pay off the second trust deed, he would probably have to refinance the first trust deed, meaning he would have to get enough from the refinancing to pay off the second.

Often, the economy does not increase satisfactorily to allow that to happen. When you don't have the money, the original owner—the seller—who holds the second trust deed can foreclose and take the property back.

To guard against foreclosure, if possible, do not get a two- or three-year due date. A five-year due date on any second trust deed is the best because two or three years is not long enough for a property to create any serious amount of appreciation where refinancing will help you get out of the second-trust-deed problem.

If you have a five-year due date on a second trust deed note that you are paying 8% interest on and you foresee some problems with the economy, you would do well to write a clause in the note during the purchase. The clause might read, "…after the five-year period, if the economy is not desirable or advantageous for refinancing of the first trust deed to pay off the second trust deed, Buyer or Trustor may have the privilege to extend the note for one more year with a 1% increase in interest rate." This would allow you to catch up with the refinance or then have an extension on the second trust deed. If the market is not desirable, then extend it each year by increasing the interest rate another point.

Once I made a transaction of this kind where the note was due and payable in five years and the interest rate was about 8%. After the five-year period, the economy was unsatisfactory to refinance the property, so I was allowed to extend the five years into another year, and extra percentage to 9%. The following year wasn't very good either, so I was able to go to 10%.

Finally, by the time I got to 11%, the economy was reasonably good and I was able to refinance the first trust deed to pay off the second. This is a very satisfactory method of avoiding a disaster.

I know of a real estate broker who recently purchased a piece of property by the beach. The down payment was about 10% and the owners took back a second trust deed with a three-year due date. She had quite a sizable existing first trust deed on the property.

Unfortunately, she made a gigantic mistake. She got hold of a sizable sum of money which she could have used to pay off the second trust deed. Instead, she remodeled the building using the cash and then tried to sell it. The property happened to be a single-family residence in a commercial zone. She wasn't able to refinance the first trust deed at any price because of the legal non-conforming use of the land. So by doing that she lost the property. The second trust deed was foreclosed upon and the owners got the property back and received a remodeled building in excellent condition.

It was a shame—you would think that a real estate broker would know better. At the very least, the broker should have known what the zoning was on the property she had purchased. The amount of the loss was very severe. When you buy real estate and you have a mortgage with a due date on it, there is no reason in the world why you cannot negotiate with the seller to have some kind of escape clause. If the seller is anxious to sell at all, he will do something and most people are not unreasonable. Most people do not sell their property with the idea that they are going to foreclose on it and in due course take it back.

Generally, when a property is sold and a second, third, or fourth trust deed (mortgage) is involved in the transaction, the seller hopes the purchaser will pay off the second trust deed in the designated time of the due date. Second trust deed holders are usually people who help to create transactions that are beneficial to all parties concerned.

HOW TO OWN A HOME FREE AND CLEAR... IN 15 YEARS OR SOONER

For the investor who wishes to purchase a home with little or no money down, owning the property free and clear might take less time than you think. At the end of 15 years, you could be in a position to pay off the mortgage and own a home without any payments or encumbrances.

To start with, find a neighborhood that has potential growth characteristics, where the value of the property has the potential to increase in market value. Then buy a single-family residence in this growing neighborhood for as small a down payment as possible. And also try to acquire the property next door so that you have two single-family residences adjacent to each other.

Preferably, purchase these properties in an area where you have residentially zoned lots that will permit at least two units on each property. You could move into one house and rent out the other. You could divide the other one, say with a room and bath and get $750 in rent. This would bring in enough money to make the mortgage payments on the loan. Such a mortgage should be for 30 years with fixed interest rates as low as possible.

By buying these properties in what we call an R2 residential zone you would be able to convert the house next door into a two unit or maybe into a large two bedroom, if you had three bedrooms and two baths. You could have the large house with two bedrooms and the other unit would be a single, apart from the house.

If you are also willing to subdivide the house you are living in, you would have a total of three rentals and, at the end of 15 years, you would have paid both properties down considerably due to consistent monthly payments. After 15 years, the second house would be ripe for sale and the proceeds from the sale of that house would be sufficient to pay off the mortgage on the first house that you own and are living in. This would allow you to have the property free and clear after 15 years. Normally, it would take 30 years to pay it off but it can be done sooner this way.

After 15 years, you would have a home that was free and clear of all encumbrances and you might have an additional sum of cash to reinvest or use to spend on a vacation. This strategy should be easy to follow because it is possible to find good bargains in built-up communities of major cities that have opportunities to grow in capital appreciation over a reasonable period of time. The key to the project is to select a set of properties that fit the criteria. Be sure the properties will support this opportunity.

Having two properties together eliminates any burdens of maintenance or keeping them rented; you are always close by to see that everything goes well. There is also another advantage. When you own the property next door, you have control over the kind of people who will live there. If they are disturbing you or your family by having a dog, being a nuisance, or making too much noise, you can evict them for not complying with your rental rules.

Another advantage that should be mentioned is that the house next door is considered an income-producing piece of real estate and, therefore, it will produce rental income. This income can be sheltered by depreciating the improvements on the property, thereby creating a tax shelter for the basic income. The property should be allocated a proportionate sum toward the value of the land and the improvements. The improvements can be depreciated over a 27 ½-year period for creating the tax shelter for the income. Also, the payments on the loan that are attributed to the interest are deductible for federal income tax purposes.

Other things, such as insurance, maintenance, upkeep and repairs on the property are also deductible, so it makes a good tax shelter towards the ownership of the property. When the property is sold, use the proceeds to pay off the home you are living in, thereby solving the problem of having a ,home free and clear in 15 years or sooner.

14

The Advantages of Using a Real Estate Broker

FREE EXPERTISE: THE FIRST ADVANTAGE OF USING A BROKER

The buy-and-hold strategy affirms the concept that you buy your property for the long term. However, if circumstances are such that you must sell, here are some suggestions. Selling your home in today's unsettled economy requires knowledge and experience. There are always a few competent people who can handle their own transaction, but the great majority of homeowners who wish to sell their property must rely on a real estate agent.

Although I myself am a real estate broker, I can't recall ever buying a property without another broker representing me. When a property is sold, the buyer doesn't pay the commission; the seller does. So it's in the buyer's best interest to have a real estate agent or broker, especially one who understands your way of thinking and will negotiate the purchase the way you want it to be negotiated.

So, how do you select a competent agent to represent you in the sale of your home? Most people put more time and effort into planning their summer vacation than they do in selecting the person to represent them in the sale of probably the most valuable physical asset they own. Thousands and thousands of dollars are at stake when the property is sold.

Probably the biggest mistake the homeowner makes when selecting an agent is that he or she usually lists the property with the first agent who gives a plausible sales pitch instead of analyzing the situation and selecting the most competent agent available to consummate their transaction.

Both brokers and sales agents must be licensed by the state in which they work. The main difference between an agent and broker is the amount of education and training required. Real estate agents must work under the auspices of a broker, while a broker may be independent, work out of an office, or manage his own office and employ other realtors. In the state of California, which is recognized for having a model real estate license law, brokers must complete several college-level courses before taking the licensing exam. To become a sales agent requires only one college-level course, although continuing education requirements must be satisfied for both brokers and sales agents.

You can never be too knowledgeable about real estate. Since realtors tend to specialize in certain areas, they are usually familiar with the local housing market, zoning laws, and tax rates, along with the reputation of school districts, and the location of churches, shopping centers, public utilities, and mass transit. They also know where to obtain financing and which lenders are active in the market.

For investors who are new to an area or new to buying real estate, a broker or agent may provide valuable assistance helping to locate the right property using the resources of the regional multiple listing service (MLS). An MLS report can provide a picture of what property is currently available and at what price, along with recent sales. Sometimes, properties for sale aren't advertised as such, or are in exclusive areas that only residents and Realtors with permits have access to. A competent broker would bring these so-called "pocket listings" to your attention.

A reputable real estate company conducts thorough research on a community, including market data and projections, and makes that information available to potential buyers. It's important to look at this information yourself, as a broker may not interpret the raw figures the way you would analyze them. A broker is generally looking for an immediate commission in buying and selling, whereas a real estate investor seeking an opportunity to buy a property for the long-term is more inclined to think in broader terms than buying today and selling in a year or two. As mentioned, sometimes a property that is overpriced and in a run-down neighborhood might have the great potential of being a gold mine 20 years from now. That might not be obvious to a broker who is dealing in terms of yesterday and today.

I believe it is important to find a broker or agent who is active in the community, who belongs to the local chamber of commerce, who participates in civic affairs, who attends professional meetings and seminars, who stays informed about the community—all to keep close tabs on emerging developments and discern what the trends are. As a buyer, that gives you an edge. If, for example, the city plans to widen a certain street and you learn about it ahead of time, you have the opportunity to contact the agency involved and find out the reason behind it. Buyers who know this type of information are able to make informed decisions.

If you discover the city is widening the street for a positive reason that is beneficial to the property you are considering, then that's a valuable piece of information worth knowing well in advance. I've noted that real estate values are created by people's actions, attitudes, and thinking. If you have a pulse on a community, you also have a pulse on its people's actions, attitudes and thinking. An informed broker can keep you in touch with the latest developments from an insider's point of view. If, on the other hand, you are oblivious to such important developments, you're more of an outsider. It can definitely pay to have a broker.

How do you find a good real estate broker who is cooperative and thinks along the same lines as you? In my opinion, the only way is to ask questions of people who are familiar with the local market and find out who is most active and informed in the area where you wish to participate. Locate a broker who belongs to civic groups and stays abreast of events that are happening regionally, statewide, and nationwide. The most important thing though, is to be able to communicate with him or her. If your broker is knowledgeable but isn't willing to communicate, you might as well forget it.

Financial Assistance

Besides helping find a suitable property, flexible real estate brokers and agents are sometimes willing to help buyers finance part of the deal by lending them their commission fee, typically 5% or 6% of the total price of the property. On a property worth $250,000, that's $12,500 or $15,000 toward the down payment, which averages about 20% of the purchase price or, in this case, $50,000.

A few years ago I wanted to buy some condominiums. So I found a broker and paid him a 3% commission for locating properties that were for sale for nothing down. He found two of them. Buyers usually don't pay any commissions, but sometimes it's worth your while. In this case, I was essentially paying him a finder's fee. He found two units for sale for nothing down. Their list price was $60,000. Today, they're probably worth $100,000.

In another instance, I purchased 26 condominiums in a complex through a broker who had connections to an institutional lender that was foreclosing on a number of units in the area and reselling them to interested investors. I felt that the condominiums were under priced and the terms were exceptional and decided to acquire a few of these properties through a broker.

The broker cooperated by informing me when any of these properties came up for sale for little or no money down. Since I am a real estate broker myself, I probably could have received a partial commission on each transaction. But to provide incentive to the broker I was working with, I offered him a full commission on each sale. At times, he really went out of his way for me.

Over several months, I bought six of these condominiums. At one point, four more were coming on the market, so my wife, somewhat tongue-in-cheek, said, "If we buy 10 of them, you ought to give us one free." The lender said he had never heard of such a thing. But he came back and offered to furnish one of our units if we bought four more. We accepted the offer, so the lender gave us several thousand dollars in cash to buy furniture.

This is important because the only way you can really make a good decision is when you know what the seller is thinking. Once you understand that, you can mold the deal to their needs and desires. You can't get that by talking directly. But a broker, because they're disinterested and detached, can ask the seller why he bought the property in the first place, why he wants to sell, and other important questions that can yield valuable information.

The broker usually presents the first offer. I always like to have my broker drop it off and let the seller consider it for a few days. Giving the seller a couple of days to think things over works out well because it allows them to get over their emotions.

If you were selling a new Cadillac and someone offered you $500 for it, your first response would probably be to get mad, but what you want to do is avoid what I call a "get mad" attitude. Many times people will say things they don't mean, and if they do, they won't back down. It's better that you don't say harsh things in the first place.

If you make an offer on a property, be sure this is what you really want to do. If the seller won't even make a counter offer, at least you will be informed as to what his or her thinking is. Be aware that when a broker is involved, sellers tend to raise their prices slightly higher because they factor in the broker's commission (again, 5% or 6% of the sales price) into their asking price.

Frequently, buyers make their offers subject to certain conditions, such as the plumbing and electricity being in good condition, a properly functioning heating and cooling system, no serious cracks in the walls or foundation, the mechanical equipment meets the present building code standards, no flood hazards exist, and so on. If the seller agrees and accepts your offer under these conditions, you then have the right to inspect the building using a building inspector. If you find anything there that is not to your satisfaction, you can cancel the deal. Using a third party, a broker, makes negating the offer a lot easier.

Synergy Effect

We discussed the importance of considering what type of investment to make and determining how it fits your needs, desires, personality, temperament, and available time. When looking for a real estate broker, find one who fits into that general framework—someone who understands your needs as well as your objective. If possible, find a broker who has the knowledge, personality, and ability to get along well with you and who understands what you're trying to do.

If you can find a broker who thinks along the same lines as you, it is possible to bounce ideas off each other and create a sort of synergy effect (where the combined effect is greater than the sum of each individual effort).

It stretches your mind and enables you to understand the problem better when you can explain it to someone else. The same problem appears completely different to different people. Having a good broker is the equivalent of having a good business partner; you might do five times better than if each of you were operating independently.

How do you place a value on real estate brokers? As a rule, if they can contribute more than you can by yourself, then they have value to you. If you can find a full-time broker who is in the field, studying the latest trends and developments, who keeps you informed on what's happening in real estate and allied business activities that affect real estate, then he or she is likely to be an enormous help.

Knowledge of the area is extremely important. Usually, brokers who have been in the neighborhood for a long period of time know and understand its problems much better than brokers new to the area.

If a person is devoting her professional life to real estate, she should be familiar with what's going on in the neighborhood, community, and surrounding area. She should also have a handle on what's going on at city hall, the public works department, and the school districts. Data from multiple listing services and realty boards are extremely important as well. But don't depend on your broker to do all of your work for you. I would rely on them to give you an indication of what is going on, but not a comprehensive analysis. You should do most of that research yourself.

My advice is to find a broker who isn't going to be embarrassed or chagrined if you make a ridiculous offer, because it might not be ridiculous to the seller. Once, when I first started investing in real estate, I thought about making an offer on a property in the Hollywood Hills. I figured it was worth $25,000. I asked my father what he thought it was worth and he said, "Why don't you ask the seller what he wants and we'll counter?" I asked the seller, but he said he wanted an offer first. I said, "You know more about the property than I do. You've lived here. You know the neighborhood." So he said, "Well, how about $22,000?" So we readjusted our sights to around $18,000.

Even though this offer was made informally, that is, verbally, it would have been a big mistake to start talking about more money than I needed to. Even so, I don't think you're really doing anything serious in real estate until you have an offer in writing. That's when the broker comes in. If I was wholeheartedly interested in making an offer on that Hollywood Hills property, I would have gone through a broker and put my bid in writing. As it turned out, I never did.

Disadvantages of Using a Broker

One of the chief disadvantages of using a broker is feeling pressured. Inasmuch as you have to be able to communicate with your realtor, it is important to have a certain chemistry. If you can't communicate openly, it makes the whole process very difficult. You need a broker who will keep you informed—about how the sellers are reacting to your offer, how important is it for them to sell, what kind of terms are they thinking of, and anything that might be wrong with the property that isn't obvious.

You also want to find a broker who doesn't talk too much! A lot of brokers will talk themselves right out of a deal. As noted above, when you're negotiating a deal, you don't want to tell the seller everything you know or are willing to concede up front. You want to know what they think first. I've known brokers who talk too much. And when that happens, they can ruin the deal for you.

The worst thing a broker can do is say, "The highest figure my buyer will pay is…" That's talking too much. You don't want to tell the seller how high you are willing go until you find out what he wants. Another example of "loudmouth syndrome" is: "This guy wants to buy the property because he needs it for a parking lot for his business next door." When the seller finds out who the purchaser is, the price can double.

When the Watergate Hotel (no relation to the well-known complex in Washington, D.C.) was built next door to my units in Hermosa Beach, a broker approached me and told me he had a buyer for my property. He said he would give me X number of dollars. I replied, "Oh, you will, huh?" He said, "Yeah, I've got a hot buyer." I told him to put it in writing. But he said, "No, I can't do that right now. The guy's going to New York but when he returns, I'll have him put it in writing." I asked if he really wanted to buy my property. He said, "Oh yeah," but it was obvious he represented the owner of the hotel next door who, no doubt, was worried that his ocean view would be ruined if I built a high rise.

So I told him I didn't want to sell it. After a while, we talked and he said, "I suppose you knew that the people next door wanted to buy your property." I said, "Of course I knew!" But I didn't tell him that I didn't want to sell because he went about it in the wrong way. If the owner of the property next door had said, "Look, I want to buy this place because I don't want to have my view ruined," I would have told him, "You are the first person I would sell it to." I'd even put it in writing. But I didn't like the way he tried to misrepresent the situation. Sometimes you have to be a little astute and read into what's going on.

Many brokers are big talkers but, when it comes down to it, they are less than imaginative. Once when the economy was down, a guy I knew put a single-family residence on the oceanfront up for sale. He advertised it and had a series of brokers working on trying to sell it but couldn't get anybody to look at it.

I went over and analyzed the situation and determined he was using the wrong approach. I told him to develop a profile of an ideal buyer. I figured it would be a husband and wife in their late sixties or early seventies who were quite wealthy, had three or four kids, and who were about to become grandparents. A couple in this situation would be ideally suited as buyers. They would derive tremendous use value from an oceanfront residence or vacation home and would have a terrific recreational facility—the beach—to attract their kids and grandkids to visit them.

After all, what good is a property when you have the money but can't do anything with it? This was a way to solve a family's problem. I told him to advertise in newspapers and publications in areas where people had a lot of money, such as Beverly Hills. So he went out and did just that and eventually found someone in a very similar position to the hypothetical couple I described. None of his brokers had thought of that idea.

It's hard to find a knowledgeable broker who really understands and is interested in what you're doing. If you find one, you don't want to let him or her get away. I think it's marvelous when you can develop a good rapport with your brokers. Good brokers, if they are willing to help you, are worth their weight in gold.

A lot of people are concerned about realtors, and for good reason. Many do give poor advice and mislead prospective buyers and sellers in order to close a sale. It's totally unethical, of course. You should know who you're dealing with. Not to cast too many aspersions on brokers, but there are a lot who really aren't fair with people.

They extract listings and, if something doesn't go exactly right, they'll file a lawsuit. Sometimes they'll find a bargain—for the buyers they're representing—and covertly bid against their own client when they come across a deal.

Often, disreputable brokers who just want to make a commission will exaggerate or not disclose all of the facts to make a property seem better than it is. Although many states now have disclosure laws that compel brokers to disclose the property's detrimental factors, not all realtors subscribe to a strict code of ethics, such as the one adopted by the National Association of Realtors. In a few worst-case scenarios, some unscrupulous realtors have been known to invest money on their clients' behalf and then skip town or declare bankruptcy.

I've never had to worry about brokers because I know as much as they do, if not more; as I mentioned, I am a broker. Moreover, I won't consider a real estate transaction unless I personally investigate it first. If my broker had a listing I was interested in, I would make it my business to know more about that listing than my broker by researching city records, talking to the neighbors, checking to see if there are any liens against the property, and obtaining a property profile from the title company. Most brokers don't do all this. They just take the listing and try to sell it.

I've never been surprised in a real estate deal. But then again, I don't think you can be too careful. I don't like to make snap judgments if they can be avoided, because if you give yourself enough time to think through all the ramifications of what will happen or won't happen, the right decision will usually present itself.

In the mid-1960s, a friend of mine asked if I would investigate a 25-unit-apartment building. My friend was very interested in buying it and wanted to know if he was getting a good bargain. The sellers gave me a price and told me the building was recently constructed. I visited the property and found not only that it had no vacancies, but that the rents were 20% higher than anything else in the neighborhood. Furthermore, I discovered that the contractor who built the place was also the seller.

I wondered why people would pay 20% more to rent in this building, even if it was new, than apartments elsewhere in the neighborhood. With a little more investigation, I learned that out of the 25 people occupying the apartments, 22 were on the owner's payroll. I did this by going around and talking to people. This telling fact had a tremendous bearing on my friend's decision to pay top dollar for this apartment building.

We wrote up an offer asking for the owner to guarantee that the rent roll would remain where it was or go higher for the next three years. The owner turned it down; he wouldn't even talk to us. I knew that as soon as he sold that building, the new owner was going to have a 75% vacancy rate and a lot of debt on his hands. I suppose the owner eventually sold it, but it wasn't to anybody I knew. I put in a couple of days analyzing the deal and probably saved my friend $100,000. This is an example of why you can never be too knowledgeable. When considering a major investment, you have to be cautious, thorough, and hire people who know what they are doing.

Do's and Don'ts to Consider When Buying Real Estate

1. Do put all terms and conditions of sale in writing.
2. Do record your deed immediately.
3. Do check property for easements or encroachments.
4. Do insist on a property inspection clause in the contract offer.
5. Do verify utility bills and tax bills.
6. Don't let the seller shop your offer around to get a better offer from other buyers—put a short-term due date on the offer.
7. Don't be influenced by phantom offers.
8. Don't ever give a deposit directly to the seller—make it out to the escrow company or bank.
9. Don't get caught in a re-zoning frenzy.
10. Don't sign a contract without proper legal advice.
11. Don't let buyers occupy the property before close of escrow (or final closing).
12. Don't allow the buyer to commence any labor or remodel work before close of escrow (or final closing).

Here are a few tips on how to select a competent broker or agent:

1. **Know your area.** It is essential that you select an agent who is thoroughly familiar with the real estate activity in the area where the home is located. An agent who is located 20 miles away from your property isn't likely to put out the effort to market your home as much as a local agent.

   The first step to finding a good agent is to gather as much information as possible about the active real estate agents in the vicinity of your home. Drive up and down the streets of your neighborhood looking for agent "for sale" signs, visit open houses and pick up data. Collect "for sale" flyers that come in the mail. Read local newspaper display and classified ads. Talk to your neighbors and friends. Check with the local realty board and visit escrow companies and ask for the names of active real estate brokers and agents.

   After you have studied the material gathered, you will no doubt come up with a list of the most active agents in your area.

2. **Interview at least three of the top agents on your list.** Ask questions pertaining specifically as to what the agent will do for you, the home seller, to obtain a qualified buyer and consummate a sale at a fair and reasonable price, commensurate with market conditions, within a reasonable period of time. Select an agent you can get along with and feel comfortable working with in answering your questions.

   Don't list your home with the agent who brashly tells you he can get the highest price for your property. That might be a ploy to get the listing. If you wish to have your home appear in the real estate multiple listing service (MLS), be sure that the agent you select has that capability.

3. **Be sure that the agent who lists your property is not the person who receives his commission from listings only.** Some agents are experts in listing property and they rely on other agents to make the sale. When there is a difficult real estate market where there are numerous houses for sale and few active buyers in the market, you want to list your property with an agent who is especially competent in handling and *closing* the transaction.

4. **Talk to other clients.** Before listing your property, ask the agent to allow you to talk to two or three of his most recent clients (within six months) and find out if the clients were satisfied with the results and if the agent did what he said he was going to do.

5. **Be sure the agent is knowledgeable about land development and community ordinances affecting the residence that you have for sale.**
   Remember that the *seller* is responsible for informing prospective purchasers of any detrimental factors that might affect the subject property and which might not ordinarily be disclosed. For instance, if the property is on a known earthquake fault, in a hazardous fire zone, land slide area, or flood zone, and this information is not disclosed to the purchasers at the time of sale, the seller can be liable for serious lawsuits if an undisclosed disaster occurs.
   A knowledgeable broker or agent should have the ability to gather information and disclose any potential problems to the buyer that might affect laws pertaining to disclosure. There are many potential physical defects in the construction of a residence that are often difficult to detect. Even though the seller might live on the property, he might not be aware of such things as cracks in the chimney, a poor foundation, major plumbing and electrical defects, inadequate heating, etc. A good agent should be able to recommend a knowledgeable

building inspector who can identify all of a property's potential defects even though the owner may not be aware of them. This could avoid serious lawsuits.

15

Parlay Your Initial Investment Without Overextending Yourself

When you become a property owner, it is important to decide exactly how much you can afford to pay out each month in bills and the type of cash flow you can live with. Unless you purchase an investment property with all cash, chances are you will have to absorb a negative cash flow for a while as the market catches up. During this period, it is important to maintain a long-term outlook and not overextend yourself.

Owning property is a means of forced savings. With this savings, or equity, it is possible to take money out of a property in the form of a second mortgage and use it for a down payment on another property. This is "parlaying" your initial investment. The key, as discussed, is to decide what level of debt you can live with comfortably. Some people are comfortable with considerable debt; others can't bear even a small amount.

Some people can live very comfortably with a lot of debt. They love it. They feel great about it. To them, it's a challenge rather than a burden. What one person may consider overextending financially could be a cakewalk to another person in the same income bracket. Assuming everything else is equal, the amount of debt a person can handle is a matter of mental attitude.

Strange as it may sound, some people are scared by money. I had a friend whose girlfriend inherited around $15,000 in 1980, a significant amount of money back then. It drove her crazy. She put the money in the bank, but it *bothered her there. She was afraid to leave it in the bank because she thought the bank was going to go broke, but she was also afraid to spend it. Finally, she went out and bought a car and that made her feel better. She was in debt again. She had been in debt all her life and that's what she was comfortable with.*

To my way of thinking, debt is a wonderful discipline. When you buy real estate and make payments on a mortgage, it's a means of forced savings, really. It's better than putting money in the bank because, as long as you make the right investment, you are putting money into an asset that is appreciating. Your money is working for you and you can control it. Since real estate obligations place you on a structured pattern toward an objective that investing will accomplish, you can stretch your income dramatically to pay off these loans.

Financial advisors recommend never spending more than three times your gross income when you buy your house. But if you make $50,000 a year, that's only $150,000, which isn't going to buy very much, at least in some areas.

As long as you can meet your obligations and not feel pinched, I wouldn't worry too much about debt. For virtually anyone who owns property, debt is a way of life. What you have to look at is how much your assets are appreciating.

At the most, your mortgage payments should be about one-third or 40% of your monthly income. If you are speculating and have a negative cash flow, then it's probably going to be greater. If you are prudent and frugal, you may be able to get away with paying 50 or even 60% of your monthly income, but it takes a lot of discipline to do that. If you're used to buying a new suit at a prestigious clothier every season, it will be difficult to keep that luxury.

When I started my real estate investment program, I made major sacrifices. At least 50% of my income went to pay off my loans. If I had any vacancies, it was disastrous, so I intentionally kept the rents low to minimize vacancies. After a few years, however, I started to raise the rents. If you buy in an area with growth potential where the property values are on an upward trend, it doesn't take too long before you start to get a pretty significant cash flow. The right purchase in an area of appreciating land values can bring lasting prosperity.

HOW I GOT STARTED

*I*n 1939, my mother and father decided to buy a property the family could use and enjoy together. This presented a great opportunity for my brother, Paul, and me to learn the elements of real estate investing firsthand. The subject property was a single-family residence that came with a two-car garage and an apartment over the garage. Both units were old but had not yet reached the point of functional obsolescence, so we could rent them without much trouble.

For this property, my parents paid $7,000 and put $500 down. Since the rental income from the two units covered our mortgage payments and the property carried itself without any appreciable out-of-pocket expenses, the land was easily worth the purchase price.

Over the next 25 years, my parents paid down the mortgage to zero while the land more than quadrupled in value. In 1964, my family and I acquired the property free and clear and were able to borrow enough money on it to build two beautiful new rental units. In 1980, this property was worth about $400,000. Today, its value has increased to $1 million.

When I started investing in real estate, I didn't have a dime. I had just lost all of my money trying to strike it rich in the commodities market, but I did have a good job as an appraiser. The first real estate investment I made on my own was in 1956, when I bought a four-unit apartment building in Hollywood for $20,000 with $1,000 down. At my job at Marshall and Stevens, the harder I worked, the more I could make. So I toiled with the objective of parlaying my initial purchases into a substantial estate.

In 1960, I bought the six-unit apartment building on The Strand in Hermosa Beach looking out over the ocean. I purchased this building for $85,000 with $3,000 down. Then I acquired the place next door, a four-unit, for $35,000 with

$5,000 down. The third property I bought, another four-unit apartment, took me months to negotiate. The seller wanted $20,000 down, but I only had $3,000. I finally got him down. My next purchase, a six-unit building, I bought for $5,000 down. With my fifth property, the broker took back the commission so I didn't have to put anything down. This was a two-unit.

From these initial investments, I have parlayed my holdings into a multi-million dollar estate that, in addition to these five oceanfront apartment buildings, includes seven single-family residences in the neighboring area and 30 condominiums in Orange County, California. The secret to an effective investment program is to buy in the right location, get the best terms possible, and accumulate equity against which you can borrow to make other investments. Sounds easy, doesn't it? It can be if you are patient and disciplined.

The seller of the first six-unit building I bought couldn't get rid of it fast enough. Even though he was asking an astronomical price back then, $85,000, I got it on terms that were so good, it didn't make any difference. As long as I could keep the place rented, the monthly payments were low enough that I could make them without too much difficulty. Plus I knew from my analysis of the area that over a long period of time, this place would more than pay for itself. And that's exactly what happened.

One of my favorite real estate sayings is: "What you owe today, you'll be worth tomorrow." By this I mean that with the right property in an area with assured growth, inflation and appreciation will eventually render the purchase price irrelevant. To illustrate this concept, consider the beach-front property I've owned since 1960, the six-unit apartment building in Hermosa Beach.

As you can see in table 15.1 on the following page, the amount I paid for this property is now inconsequential because of the degree to which the property has appreciated in value. The property, which yields a substantial positive cash flow, generates $150,000 gross income a year before taxes. I never would have been in this position had I passed on the opportunity to buy this veritable gold mine, even if it was "high priced" back then. The value since the time of purchase has risen more than 1,000%.

In my opinion, it is ridiculous to quibble over $5,000 or even $50,000 in the purchase price of a property. If you are buying for the long term, you know that the financial structure is such that you'll be able to hold on to it.

TABLE 15.1

Purchase Price, 1960		$85,000
Cost to renovate		nominal
Down payment		3,000
Loans:	First mortgage at 6.25%	45,000
	Second at 7%	32,000
	Third at 8%	5,000
Monthly payment on first loan, including taxes and insurance		600
Monthly payment on second loan		250
Monthly payment on third loan		100
Total monthly payments		950
(all loans were paid off in 1987)		
Present market value, 2000		2,500,000
Amount owed on loans		0
Gross annual rental income, 2000	($12,500 × 12)	150,000
Less expenses		
	Vacancy and credit loss	12,000
	Maintenance	30,000
	Loan payments	0
	Property taxes and insurance	18,000
	Utilities	5,500
Total expenses		$65,500
Net income		$84,500

The most important thing is to have a firm idea of what the property will be worth in 15 or 20 years. You have to be sure that you can foresee that growth.

It took seven years before the above property broke even. During that time, I probably lost about $500 a month, roughly 20% of my monthly income at the time. Today, that $500 would be equal to about $2,000 or $3,000 a month. But I had a good job and could afford to absorb some losses. Even if you have high monthly payments, you have to remember that with an income-generating real estate investment, you're going to receive income from your properties to help meet your obligations.

You can accumulate a substantial amount of debt as long as it is debt you can absorb. You can owe a creditor $10 million, but if you don't have to pay it back for 50 years, all you have to worry about in the short-term is the amount of your monthly payment. When you invest in real estate, you have to assume that the income from the property will increase as the value of the real estate goes up. You also have to realize that if you have any ability in your field or area of expertise, your salary will increase, too.

By 1965, I had accumulative debts on all my real estate equal to three-quarters of a million dollars, maybe more. I bought several of my original properties with multiple mortgages against them, but it wasn't the kind of debt that could hurt me because there weren't any balloon payments looming on the horizon, no "debt bombs" that were going to detonate at some point in the future. All of my loans were long term, so I didn't have to worry about coming up with a large sum of money in a short amount of time.

Investment Techniques

For the beginning investor, the first property, typically a house, is the most important. It establishes you as a substantial member of the community and makes it easier for you to borrow money since you can now use your property as collateral for a loan. Owning property enables you to build equity. If you have $100,000 equity in your house, you can create a $50,000 second mortgage and take that $50,000 to buy another property and use it as a down payment on one or more properties. Or you can borrow $50,000 from the bank and take it out and use it in other ways.

An ideal scenario is to buy a house in a growth area, make payments for five or six years, building a sizable equity, then take that equity to buy another property using your equity as a down payment. During this initial five-year period, assume that you will receive a promotion, increase your salary or business activity, and figure out a method for expanding your holdings.

If you intend to build an estate worth $10 million, you could start by buying a single-family residence for $150,000 with 20% down, or $30,000. Your monthly payments would be approximately $1,000. In the right location, that property could rise in value to $200,000—or more—over a five-year period. By this time, you will have accumulated a substantial amount of equity around $60,000—just by making your monthly mortgage payments.

Typically, lenders will make first mortgage loans equal to 80% of the property's current market value. In effect, your lending institution acts as your financial partner and checks your judgment. So, if your property is appraised at $200,000, you could take out a $160,000 loan. With that money, you could buy a duplex or small apartment building. It must be a good acquisition and you had better be able to live with the terms because in investing like this, you are not only building your assets, you are also increasing your debt.

*A*ssume an apartment building you are interested in purchasing costs $300,000 and you put $100,000 down. That leaves you with $200,000 in new debt and a new monthly payment of $2,000. Because of the new loan, your mortgage payments have increased from $1,000 a month to $3,000. However, your new property may only yield $1,500 rental income per month, so you have to decide whether you can hold on until you can raise the rents or whether that is too much negative cash flow for you to absorb. In pricey areas, very few properties will generate an immediate cash flow unless you put 100% down.

Another option would be to sell your first house, buy that apartment building, and move into one of the units like I did with my six-unit in Hermosa. If the seller is willing to carry a second mortgage, you can get a tax-deferred exchange to avoid paying taxes on capital gains, provided the total property is considered to be income producing. Under Section 1031 of the Internal Revenue Code, like-kind property used in a trade or business or held as an investment can be exchanged tax-free. The scenario described here is entirely plausible, but you can't sit around waiting for opportunities to come to you. Great real estate deals don't happen on their own; they are made.

Buying Your First Property

In my opinion, the first property you buy should be residential. A single-family residence with a unit in the back or a duplex would be ideal. After you buy a piece of property, you become more knowledgeable about real estate, you get to know the community better, and as a result of this you become more interested. You start to see the benefits for yourself firsthand and learn to relate these benefits to fit your particular need.

After you've bought your first property, you won't have as much trepidation. You become established and more informed as to where the trends are going in the community. Soon, you'll be able to buy a second property. When the house next door becomes available, you'll be in a position to take advantage of it.

Typically, the first purchase is not that terrific because you're coming into a community that you really don't know about even though you studied it. But after you've been there a while and see what's going on, you should get a feel for it. Your second acquisition should be a much better purchase as far as the price and terms are concerned. But even with the second property, you may have to carry it (i.e., manage a negative cash flow or a relatively high payment) for awhile as the market catches up.

There are literally thousands of possibilities, but what you need to do is establish yourself in the community. You should be an active part of the local area and know what's going on. When you've got a good reputation and get to know people and start talking to them, you can find out who is interested in selling and discuss with them the fact that you're in the market for another property. You might be able to work out a good deal that way. Who knows, the guy down the street may be willing to extend favorable terms because he knows you personally.

One of the single condominium units I purchased REO (real estate owned) in Orange County in 1986 for $50,000 is a good example of an ideal first investment that almost anyone currently paying monthly rent to live in an apartment could have afforded. The low $5,000 down payment would not take anyone with a good-paying job too long to come up with, and the $375 monthly mortgage (including taxes and insurance) plus the $110 homeowner's fee is actually cheaper than renting in many areas.

Purchase price, 1986	$50,000
Down payment	5,000
Loans: First mortgage at 8%	45,000
Monthly payment on first loan, including taxes and insurance	375
Homeowner's Fee	110
Total monthly payments	485
Present market value, 2000	$75,000

If, instead of inhabiting the above unit, you chose to rent it out for the going rate of $725 per month, the property would immediately begin to yield a positive cash flow, albeit a modest one, because the income generated by the property would exceed the total expenses.

Gross annual rental income, 2000 ($725 × 12)	$8,700
Less expenses:	
Vacancy and credit loss (5%)	360
Loan payments, homeowner's fee, Property taxes and insurance	6,500
Total expenses	$6,860
Net income	$1,840

Establishing Good Credit

One of the questions I am frequently asked is how someone can get their foot in the door and come up with enough money for their first down payment. There are a number of ways. You could save it, borrow from your relatives, or build up enough credit to get a loan from a bank. When you have good credit, banks are more likely to loan you money because you are perceived as a responsible individual.

When I bought my first place, I was unmarried and banks in those days generally thought anyone single was unreliable. But by the time I went back for my second loan, it was a lot easier because I had made all my payments on time and had established good credit.

In addition to becoming a substantial member of the community, owning real estate improves your credit rating. By definition, you're no longer a potential fly-by-night applicant. One of the best things you can get in this world is good credit. I've always had good credit and I've always paid my bills a couple of days ahead of time to establish and maintain good credit because credit is worth more than money.

Credit Scores

Lenders care very much how you have handled your credit in the past. They figure how that you have treated other creditors is how they will be treated.

The three credit bureaus—Experian, TransUnion and Equifax—rely upon the credit-scoring model developed by the Fair Isaac Company. The Fair Isaac credit scoring system gives lenders a pretty accurate idea of the chances of your defaulting on a loan. On a scale of 350 to 850, the model can accurately predict the odds of your defaulting. The higher your FICO score, the better the loan you get.

As a loan broker, I've seen many exceptions. For instance, I can get very good pricing for people with lower scores if there are other compensating factors. FICO scores are calculated from a lot of different credit data in your credit report. Of the hundreds of credit reports I see per year, here are the most common reasons why people have lower FICO scores. These are ranked in order of occurrence:

1. Recent credit card lates, mostly through carelessness.
2. Collection accounts wherein bill disputes are never resolved and the account holders get stubborn and refuse to pay.
3. Owing too much on credit cards.
4. The age of credit accounts is too young. Not enough long-term credit.
5. Closing credit accounts in the mistaken belief that it will help the credit score.
6. Tax liens.

7. Bankruptcies wherein not all accounts that were supposed to be cleared off the credit report were included.

When you apply for a loan, lenders will run all three credit reports. Of the three scores, they will take the middle one and use that to qualify you.

You should make sure that the information in your credit report is correct. Not only is your credit score based on this information, but lenders also review this information in making credit decisions. Review your credit report from each credit reporting agency at least once a year and especially before making a large purchase like a house or car. To request a copy, contact the credit reporting agencies directly:

- Equifax: (800) 685-1111, www.equifax.com
- Experian (formerly TRW): (888) 397-3742, www.experian.com
- TransUnion: (800) 888-4213, www.transunion.com

You should treat your credit report like gold and guard it closely. Your consumer credit history stays on your report for seven years and matters of public record (bankruptcies, foreclosures and judgments) last for 10 years. Lenders see it as an example of your financial character.

Bankruptcies and Foreclosures

Most loan programs require that bankruptcies and foreclosures be two to three years old to qualify for the good rates. I see way too many people take the easy way out and declare bankruptcy. Then, when they want to buy houses, they whine.

My first real estate venture did not end well. I had my first triplex end up in foreclosure. I did not know much about real estate investing or managing tenants. It took several years of diligent rehabbing of my credit to qualify to buy another property.

Compensating Factors

Almost all loans have some flexibility. Here is a short list of compensating factors that lenders will consider:

1. No debt or little debt
2. Excellent long-term credit
3. A large amount of liquid assets left after closing
4. A proven ability to save
5. Long-term job stability
6. Good potential for an increase in income
7. Working toward an advanced degree
8. A large down payment, low LTV loans
9. Little increase in housing expense—
   low payment shock

Here is where the skill and experience of your mortgage person comes into play. He or she should know very well what loan underwriters will accept and what they won't.

Often I can get my underwriters to waive many conditions because I give them a lot of business.

I used to give my students the following advice on how to build credit. Visit a bank and become acquainted with the people there, then try to get as large a personal loan as you can. Say you can get a $10,000 loan from the bank. Take that $10,000 and deposit that money into the bank across the street and make payments from that account to pay off your original $10,000 loan. When you have the $10,000 in the second bank, borrow another $10,000 to pay off the second loan. Do not spend any of this money. If you discipline yourself and keep doing this three or four times, you will build up a good credit rating.

Once you prove to banks and lenders that you are a good risk and will pay your obligations on time, you may then be able to borrow a little more money and come up with enough cash for a down payment on a piece of property. You may lose a few hundred dollars in interest payments, but that isn't important. The important thing is to establish good credit.

You can use credit cards for the same purpose, but targeting a real estate lender will enhance your standing where it counts the most. Using the above strategy, you may be able to build credibility and trust with a financial institution that could finance your first property. By proving that you can make your payments on time, the lender will view you as less of a risk and will deal with you on a more substantial basis.

The biggest hindrance for many people in their twenties, thirties, and even forties is how to possibly save enough money for the down payment. These are the same people who earn a good salary, but spend their money on an expensive apartment, a new car and dine out at fancy restaurants all the time. Their assumption is that they have established a certain spending level, earned a certain lifestyle, and don't have much money left over to save. They don't equate having any money in the bank with reducing their consumer spending. They don't realize that in order to get ahead, maybe they should sacrifice a little and drop their spending level.

Buying Your Second Property

It takes about a year to get a feeling for what a property can really do for you—whether it will show any short-term appreciation or income, and how long you're going to have a negative cash flow. After a period of five years, you should be able to take your first property, refinance it, and buy something else. Often, when you're in a good market, you can do it in less time.

*D*on't expect your property value to double in two years. You need to have a long-range perspective and forget about what it's worth today. Instead, you should be interested in what it's going to be worth 15 years from now. For some people it's better to become passive about investment property, let someone else manage it, and then come back to it in 10 years when you can see actual appreciation. I have some friends who buy investment property, hire a property manager, and then basically walk away. When they return, they invariably find that their purchase was worth their while.

A duplex is an ideal second investment because one vacancy can't eat up 100% of your monthly return. Usually, you can get more rent from two units than you can from a single-family residence of comparable value. As your family grows and your needs change, a duplex might also serve a personal need for you.

I would rather buy a four-unit because the risk is divided four ways instead of two. A vacancy in a four-unit isn't nearly as hard on your ability to make your monthly payments as a vacancy in a duplex or a single-family residence. Plus, if you raise the rents, you're raising them in all four units so your income increases faster. The ideal situation is to charge reasonably low rents in an exceptionally good location. My smallest unit on the beach rents for $750 a month. How long do you think it takes to find a new tenant? About a minute.

After paying off a four-unit apartment building I purchased in the early 1960s, I decided a few years ago to sell it for $1 million and make a tax-deferred exchange. This is a transaction in which a property is traded for the promise to provide a replacement of like-kind property or properties in the near future with tax on the gain deferred. With the profit I received from the sale, I was able to trade my single property for three houses and a condominium.

The above example demonstrates how accumulated equity can be used to parlay and expand your original investment. Years before I sold that apartment building, I had refinanced it for $360,000. With that money, I placed a $40,000 down payment on a $175,000 building. I was also able to acquire five different income-producing, tax-sheltering properties, which may in turn yield several more. Now that's a pyramid worth climbing.

Throughout this book, I've stressed that one of the great advantages to investing in real estate is its uniqueness. There are so many ways of doing things. With real estate, you have the opportunity to use your imagination and ability like no other investment.

About four years ago, I had a corner lot with four garages on it. I decided to tear that structure down and either sell the land or build something else. I wanted $150,000 for the lot, but nobody would take it. So I came up with an even better idea: to find somebody who was willing to build two condominiums on it at no cost to me.

*W*ith a little bit of effort, I found a contractor who was willing to build the two condos I wanted constructed. To find this builder, I put an ad in the paper, talked to people at the local building supplies stores, and put a sign on the lot. Eventually, a guy called me. The arrangement I made with him was to give him one of the units with all the mortgages on it, and I would take the other unit free and clear for giving him the parcel of the land. I told the guy before we started that I wanted the deal to be a complete success. I wanted him to make as much money as possible. There was enough for both of us. If he made a million dollars from the thing, I would be thrilled. The one option I reserved was the right to pick which unit I wanted when both were built.

The deal worked out great for both of us. He built his condo and sold it soon after completion for $350,000. In my arrangement, I didn't pay for anything, but I held on to my place. It has four bedrooms, three-and-one-half baths, and a sun deck which has a view from Catalina to Malibu. I would estimate that it's now worth about $700,000, and I can rent it for $3,500 a month. When I originally bought that lot in 1962, I paid $12,000 for it and put $1,500 down.

Where to Buy

Many first-time investors make the mistake of thinking that high-priced areas are the place to buy. They really aren't the best locations for somebody to start in. You have to find an area where there's the potential for growth and fight it for a few years until the upward trend takes you out of the woods. It's important to be realistic. If you're married and the baby needs a new pair of shoes, you want to travel around the world, and you're working at Sears, you're going to have a problem—even if you are the best vacuum salesperson this side of Chicago!

Since neighborhoods tend to go in cycles, there is always some place you can go that has already experienced phenomenal growth where you can look back and see where your position would have been 20 years ago. This type of exercise gives you incentive. It's a way of learning without doing. It's a way of visualizing how you can elevate yourself to the position you want to be in.

It's harder for people to buy property today than it was 30 years ago. To be sure, wages have not kept pace with housing costs. In 1973, the average 30-year-old could buy a typical house with 21% of his gross earnings going to mortgage payments. By 1984, he had to devote 33% of his income to make his mortgage payments. Today, that amount has increased to about 40%. In my opinion, buying a house is well worth the sacrifice because land is scarce. And if you think it's hard to own property now, just think about the next 10 or 20 years.

Everything is anticipated. You're never certain what your need will be even tomorrow. That's what's so exciting about life. No one is willing to take a chance if they don't think they will succeed. You must have some incentive and insurance, some motivating factor, that it's going to work out for you. Buy in an area with growth potential where you can afford the prices. As long as you can hold on to the property for the long haul, I can guarantee you're going to get rich.

I like to be close to my properties so I can see what's going on. When I first started acquiring real estate, I wouldn't buy anything that wasn't within walking or bicycle-riding distance. As mentioned before, I once owned a house in Hesperia, about 80 miles from Los Angeles where I couldn't communicate with the people. It got to the point where I didn't want to go up there no matter what the problem was. You have to be attuned to the community. I wouldn't buy a place in a location I wasn't familiar with just because I thought I was going to make some money on it, although a lot of speculators do. To succeed in the long run, you have to know the neighborhood to really understand what's going on.

Living With Negative Cash Flow

When you buy income property and experience a negative cash flow, you can take depreciation write-offs on the improvements (the actual building) for tax purposes. The IRS allows deductions for interest, repairs, and other expenses, which helps offset your losses at the end of the year.

You want to structure a real estate transaction so you have as low a negative cash flow as possible. Suppose you buy a property and the owner takes back a second mortgage. You want to do what you can with that second so you don't have to make any payments on it. Take advantage and try to write favorable terms on the second because the institutional lender won't allow you to alter the first.

When I was buying my first properties, I lived with a lot of negative cash flow. But, as I mentioned, I had a good job as an appraiser. So I worked hard and I made my payments. Even so, many times I didn't know where the money was going to come from to pay the taxes. I scraped the bottom of the barrel more than once.

It takes knowledge to accumulate real estate and the guts to put yourself on the line. You have to be disciplined and careful not to overextend yourself. But there is no way in the world you can succeed without taking a chance. It's like the turtle—he never gets anywhere if he's not willing to stick his neck out. You have to get out there and participate; otherwise it isn't going to work. A lot of people talk about what they *could have* done, but they aren't willing to put themselves at any risk to take advantage of what is within their reach.

16

Manage Your Investment for Maximum Yield and Satisfaction

You don't get rich by making money—you get rich by wisely managing the money you make. The truth in this statement becomes apparent when you consider that an improperly handled investment can lose as much money, if not more, as a properly handled investment can make. Therefore, it is in a real estate investor's best interest to keep property rented at competitive rates, see that good tenants are satisfied, and ensure that your property is well maintained.

A good manager will constantly study the market to see what the trends are, observe what the competition is doing, and then, when it makes sense, raise the rents conservatively. I always try to be a couple of dollars under the market so people are happy. As long as they're paying the rent, I treat my tenants as if they own the property and I do everything I can for them. Think about it: they're buying the real estate for me. What more could I ask for?

ON BEING A LANDLORD

Whenever something in one of my units breaks, I fix it as soon as possible because I don't want anybody to move. The most important thing you can do as a landlord is find a good tenant. Granted, a vacancy takes away profit

right off the top, but believe me, a vacancy is a pleasure com-
pared to a bad tenant.

If I can find a good tenant, I bend over backwards to
keep that person. I might even lower the rent if he had a
problem in his job or some other major crisis, just to keep
him. It costs time and money to find another tenant. If a
tenant leaves and you have to fix up the place, you lose a
month's rent by the time you can rent it out again. It can be
brutal, especially when you are just starting out.

A lot of good tenants have problems coming up with security deposits, plus the first and last month's rent. I always try to give them the benefit of the doubt. I require a security deposit equivalent to the last month's rent, but I'm willing to work with people to get it. If the tenants are credit-worthy, which you can determine through a credit check, I'll let them pay the security deposit over a three- or four-month period. I remember how tough it was for me when I was starting out, and I try to think about how other people might be in a tight situation.

Return on Investment

Because real estate is a "wasting asset"—the improvements, or building, eventually deteriorate and become obsolete—you should, for example, aim for more than the standard 10% return on your investment because you can use that return to invest in your next property. Theoretically, you could "recycle" that 10% return indefinitely.

There are three factors that make up the income stream, or flow of money, generated by a real estate investment: quantity, quality, and duration. Quantity is obviously important. Does the property generate $200 or $3,000 a month? The quality of that income, the certainty of receiving it, also has an impact on the value of that property. Do you have a non-cancelable lease with a large corporation or have you signed an agreement with the corner shoe store? Obviously, the income from the corporation is more secure than the money the shoe store will generate. Duration, the length of time the income stream from a particular property will last, is vital because it helps determine the financial viability of your investment.

Residential real estate is the best type of investment for the average person, in my opinion, because houses, duplexes, and apartment buildings maintain their economic viability for decades, if not centuries, while commercial properties become functionally and economically obsolete much sooner, owing to constant changes in the business community.

A single-family residence I purchased in 1963 for $16,000 demonstrates the long duration of residential investments. The subject property is a 1,500-square-foot house with a studio apartment on the side of a single-car garage. The property is zoned commercial, so it has a "mixed use." Mixed-use property is property zoned for a different use than the existing use. A commercial property on an industrial lot is another example of mixed use. Obviously, the original zoning was residential when the house was built. However, community influences over time acted to change the character of the area so that it is now more appropriate for commercial use. As a rule, it's difficult to find financing for mixed-use properties.

I put $1,000 down on this property and the owner took back the mortgage at 6% interest, or $95 a month. I've been very slow in paying it off. Today, because I have no due date on my loan, I continue to make my mortgage payment and collect the rent. I'm now getting $1,850 in monthly rent for the house and $650 for the apartment, which is $2,500 a month, or $30,000 a year. The property started to break even about four years after I bought it.

When I became interested in buying it, the owner lived in the city of Glendale, 30 or 40 miles away, and the tenant occupying the property said she didn't want me to come in because if I did, she knew I would buy the place and make her move. I said, "Well, will you at least let me stand in the doorway?" I could tell just by doing that that the beams on the floor were solid, which was all I wanted to know.

Although I didn't ask her to, the woman moved on her own volition at the end of the escrow. That gave me the incentive to upgrade the place a little. I remodeled the kitchen with replacement counters, cabinets, dishwasher, garbage disposal, range and oven, all from another house I had purchased, for $1,500. It made the place more inhabitable, so I could get slightly higher rent.

Common Interests

*P*eople are more tolerant of one another, and therefore more harmonious as tenants, when they have the same interests. When I was looking around for property to buy in Hollywood in the late 1960s, a lot of people were buying old apartment buildings and modifying them for cat owners. They'd install little pet doors, cat walks along the sides of the building, and backyards for them to run around in. It was a cat lover's dream, and a good idea because it attracted people with similar interests.

If you can alter the property to cater to common interests, that will help attract tenants, keep the place rented, and stabilize the vacancy rate. Common interests apply not only to pets, such as cats, dogs, or birds, but to kids, singles, or retirees. A condominium complex I am familiar with operates a nursery near the front entrance of the complex where parents can drop their kids off before work and pick them up afterward. It's an ideal arrangement for a single parent or a dual-income family. They don't usually have many vacancies.

I once owned an eight-unit apartment building in Los Angeles in the mid-Wilshire district. Whenever I rented an apartment there, I would ask the other tenants what they thought of the people I was renting to. I think it's important that I have a harmonious tenant mix like I do at the beach. I want everybody to be happy—after all, they're buying the place for me.

A friend of mine once looked at a property that had seven one-bedroom houses on it and a large, three-bedroom house at the end. The property was located near a hospital. I tried to talk him into buying the property and putting up fences to divide each one of these houses for privacy. My idea was to convert the large house into a day care center and rent the other houses to nurses with children. They could have taken their kids over to the big house when they left for work at the hospital. The owner of the big house could be a day care provider.

That would have been an interesting use of the property. The guy didn't do it and he really missed a great opportunity. It was a nice piece of land with improvements already on it and he could have bought it for about what the land was worth.

If landlords show a little concern about finding tenants who are compatible and work together with their tenants to maintain a desirable home and community, then things work out much better for everyone. Finding new renters who blend in with the existing arrangement in terms of their interests and attitudes shows a lot of concern for your existing tenants. In my buildings, I look for tenants who are compatible. If somebody moves in, I go around and introduce him or her to everybody else.

I make myself available if my tenants have any concerns or need something fixed. At the same time, I am sure to tell them that I don't want a lot of noise and people hanging around. If they just show concern for other people, then others will show concern back. If you establish guidelines that satisfy both you and your tenants, you will be able to create a desirable atmosphere.

Personal Sacrifice

Unless you are already independently wealthy, you have to be willing to sacrifice to make a real estate investment program work. When I first started buying income property, I never thought about buying myself a new stove or refrigerator if it was in disrepair, until all my tenants had one first. I needed their rental money to make my payments. Their comfort and satisfaction took precedence over mine.

When I started out, I lived in the cheapest apartment I owned and tried to spend money on my rental units before I spent it on myself. I tried to spend money in ways that made the rent come in. I wouldn't do anything frivolous to improve the condition of the property, but I would fix something right away if I could see that it would enhance the rental picture or make the tenants happy so they wouldn't move.

I used to do everything I could myself—put in tile floors, fix stopped-up plumbing, put in a new garbage disposal, whatever. I had no choice, really; I couldn't afford to do anything else. It costs a bundle to hire an accountant, property manager, plumber, electrician, and handyman. When first starting out, most people don't have that kind of money. Again, look at this as a business. As the president of a company, would you hire consultants you didn't need?

If you're doing all of this on a shoestring, you have to be careful with your finances. You can't always take draconian measures. When I started out, I wasn't married and didn't have much overhead. I had a good job, so I could work long hours to make a lot of money. Often, I burned the midnight oil until 3:00 or 4:00 a.m. doing extra appraisal work to pay off some bills, though I would have much preferred to go out to a square dance. But I knew what was more important and I was willing to sacrifice. Now, my sacrifices have paid off. But for a while it was an exercise in discipline, perspective, and dedication.

In the beach area where I live, tenants can move in and out rapidly on a seasonal basis. Renting in this type of environment takes more effort than it would in a more stable community. Yet I've had some tenants for years in large part because I keep the rents down. In addition, I bend over backwards for people whenever I can. As long as they don't hassle anybody, I tell them to act as if they own the place. No question about it.

When managing your investment for maximum yield and satisfaction, strive to work out an arrangement that is enjoyable and not burdensome. The way I see it, I've got a six-unit building that has already, and will again, make me a million dollars. That to me is more important than the sacrifices I've made because I have an objective. Sure, it's work. But there is no way in the world that you're going to make it if you don't put in the effort, no matter what you do.

SELECTING TENANTS

There are several ways to determine whether you have a good prospective tenant—through a credit check, recommendations, a personal interview, and talking to previous landlords. The best thing to do is talk to people where the prospective tenant lives. Get a conversation going with the neighbors. Tell them that you understand Charlie Brown is moving out and he owes you $100. You'll hear everything you ever wanted to know about him. The best way to find out about other people's business is when that person owes someone money. Also try contacting friends, associates, former employers—whomever they put down as a reference.

But be careful about landlords; sometimes they will tell you a really bad tenant is a great person because they want to get rid of him. If you talk to people and take these extra steps, it could be worth your while, because good ol' Charlie Brown could end up owing you a lot more than $100 if he's a bummer.

When I meet prospective tenants, I basically ask if they pay the rent on time, how much they were paying, whether they had any past evictions, and if they can afford what I'm asking. The important things as far as I'm concerned are whether they will keep the place clean, abide by the rules, and pay the rent. I'm not concerned with anything else, unless it is a situation, for instance, where a tenant is physically challenged and has difficulty getting into the place. I've modified several of my places by building ramps and decks to make them wheelchair-accessible.

I had a friend who told her applicants that she would contact them in two days if she was interested in renting to them. She would then go to their current place of residence, unannounced, ring the doorbell, invite herself in, walk around, and make a decision on the spot whether she would rent them her house or apartment. I think that was a brilliant idea, and I'm sure it saved her a lot of money. If you really want to know what the place is like, you might ask to use the restroom.

Remember, a vacancy is a pleasure compared to a bad tenant. I'd rather have an apartment vacant for a month or two than endure a bad tenant. It costs so much to get them out, they wreck the place, plus you're liable to lose good tenants who are already in the building.

Suppose someone rents an apartment, pays their first month's rent, and promises to pay the security deposit over a period of three months. Then they lose their job, but they don't tell you. So when the rent is due, you go there to collect it and they say they can't pay you right now, they'll have to pay you in a week. A week goes by and they say, "Oh, my dishwasher's broken and if you don't fix it, I won't pay." They might break a faucet or stuff a wad of toilet paper down the toilet. They maintain there are so many things wrong with the place that they don't want to pay rent. Since they refuse to pay rent, you decide to start eviction proceedings.

In many states, you start by filing a three-day notice to pay or quit followed by a 30-day notice to evict. The tenant has to answer the notice, and it could take another month or so to get on the court calendar. At this point, you are starting to lose money. Then, if you go to court and they can prove that you were negligent in maintaining your property, you are now in even worse shape because you are going to have to make the repairs, file eviction papers again, and then go back to court. If the judge rules in favor of the tenant, they're not going to move out, and you may not see any money for several more months!

I once had a problem with a property I owned that took almost an entire year to resolve. I lost a whole year's rent plus repair costs and legal expenses, probably $6,000, from that dispute. The tenants didn't keep the place clean, their dog dug up the yard, they had thrown trash all over the premises, destroyed the carpet, didn't pay their rent, and the other tenants were complaining. It was a living nightmare. After I finally got them out after a year, I had no choice but to replace the carpet, which was brand new when they moved in. It was brutal, absolutely brutal.

When I first rented to them, they seemed fine. Then, after a few months, we started having problems; they stopped paying their rent. I had a real estate agent taking care of the place. After these tenants stopped paying their rent, the agent went over and threatened them. Plus, the lawyer I had was disorganized; when the court issued the notice to remove these people, my attorney didn't receive the papers because he didn't provide a return envelope. I was on vacation at the time, so I wasn't there to handle it. It became a comedy of errors. This explains why I feel so strongly about good communication with my tenants.

When selecting tenants, the best thing to do is tell them up front what you expect. For instance, if you don't want any dogs or loud noise or any motorcycles in the front yard, make that known. It took me a long time to learn this. When I was new in real estate, I rented an apartment to a guy who rode a motorcycle. One day he decided to overhaul his bike, so he wheeled it inside the apartment and took it apart on the living room carpet!

Two weeks later I returned and found about 20 motorcycles parked all over the lawn. They were everywhere. It was terrible, so I tried to get rid of him. That type of thing can deteriorate a neighborhood and if you have good tenants, they won't put up with it—they'll move. If you're in a soft market with many vacancies in the area, you can lose a lot of good tenants over one lousy one. That can be devastating, especially if you're working on a thin margin.

When choosing tenants, try to get the best there is. Sometimes, you have to wait for the right tenant to come along, but when you find a good tenant, try to do everything you can to keep him or her. My mother was a master of keeping tenants. Within reason, she would do anything for them—offer a break on the rent, fix the place up, all kinds of things. And she'd always figure out the cheapest way to do it.

I prefer to rent to a person who fits the needs of the property. A single-family residence is ideal for a family. I think a one-bedroom apartment is great for a couple or a single person. My studio apartments are suitable for one or two working or retired people. My beach properties aren't suitable for families; they're too expensive, and they aren't laid out in a very accommodating manner. They're more suited for single professionals on their way up who plan to be a huge success. Table 16.1 is a list of tenant arrangements I believe are suitable for different apartment sizes.

TABLE 16.1
Suitable Tenant Arrangements for Different Apartment Sizes

Size of Rental	Tenant Arrangement
Single (Studio) Apartment	Single person, any age
One-Bedroom Apartment	Young couples, middle-aged single adults and couples, senior couples
Two-Bedroom Apartment	Couples, roommates, and small families
Three-Bedroom Apartment	Larger families

Credit Checks

In addition to asking questions, I always obtain a credit report from a prospective tenant. A credit report is both a history and evaluation of a person's capacity to repay debts. It lets you know if they have any outstanding lien or credit delinquencies, if they make their payments on time, or if they've ever been evicted from a rental. It's as good a sign as any that a prospective tenant is going to work out. The most important thing in a credit report is accurate information. A lot of people put down information that isn't accurate and this bogus data shows up rather authoritatively on their credit report.

As a landlord, you will encounter every kind of tenant with every type of problem there is. But it's extremely important to never, ever have a tenant submit his or her own credit report. I had a guy apply for one of my condominiums who worked for an automobile dealer that had access to TRW's (now Experian) credit reporting service. He was a crafty sort of fellow and found a way to insert his name onto other people's documents as they came in.

So when he applied, he said, "Here's my credit report so you won't have to go through all that hassle." The property manager at the complex accepted the report, which looked really good—almost too good to be true. Well, within two months, we started having a terrible time with this tenant. He drove a big limousine that he parked in the parking area, taking too many spaces which was against the rules. He wouldn't pay the rent and he was very noisy. He was a big liar, basically. We had to evict him.

With my condominiums, I have prospective tenants fill out a form and pay me $20 for the credit report in advance. On top of ensuring the veracity of the report, this method weeds out those applicants who aren't really interested. If someone pays and it doesn't work out, then they've lost the $20. If someone isn't willing to pay the fee, then you probably don't want him or her as a tenant anyway.

Rental Agreements

Most residential landlords use a standard rental agreement available through their local apartment owners association. Over the years, I have added several clauses to my rental agreement form to prevent routine problems that arise. Here is a facsimile of the rental agreement I use:

FIGURE 16.1

RENTAL AGREEMENT

__TENANT INFORMATION__   DATE: _____

Name _____   Home Phone: _____

Name _____   Employed By: _____

Name _____   Work Phone: _____

Present Address _____

__MONTH-TO-MONTH RENTAL AGREEMENT__

Address _____

Apartment is rented for $_____ per month. If tenant stays for a year, Rent will be increased $_____ each succeeding year due to inflation, increased costs of maintenance, taxes, utilities, etc. This provision of the Rental Agreement shall be continually in force with each succeeding tenant who occupies this rental unit.

Rent includes _____

Rent does not include _____

__SECURITY DEPOSIT__: Is refundable if tenant is not delinquent in rent, and if no damage occurs to the building and/or furnish-

Section 1950.5:   ings, and tenant leaves the premises clean. The total

Calif. Civil Code: security deposit will be $_____. Tenants may not, without owner's written consent, apply this security deposit to rent.

__OCCUPANCY__: Tenants acknowledge that they have examined the premises and found them to be in good and clean condition. Tenants agree to NOTIFY OWNER, IN WRITING, BY CERTIFIED MAIL (Return Receipt Requested), of ANY problems pertaining to the HABITABILITY of the PREMISES.

This apartment is rented to _____ person(s). No pets, no motorcycles ON OR NEAR PREMISES, no loud noises. If any additional occupants move into the apartment, then the manager has the right to request the tenants to move or adjust the rent. If Tenants are EVICTED, Tenants shall be responsible for ALL costs, including ATTORNEY FEES.

If ONE of the Tenants gives notice to move or if ONE or MORE Tenants VACATES WITHOUT GIVING NOTICE, this, in effect, GIVES NOTICE TO ALL OCCUPANTS in the Apartment that the premises ARE TO BE VACATED.

Rental starts on _____. Rent is due on _____ day of each month.

Upon signing this agreement, the Tenant(s) indicates full acceptance of all of the provisions, and further agrees that if Tenant does not inform manager, IN WRITING, at least 30 DAYS in advance of his/her intention to vacate the apartment, then the Tenant agrees to forfeit the deposit. This provision applies regardless of how long the tenant has occupied the apartment and the condition the apartment is left in. Upon receipt of written notice of Tenant's intention to move, the manager shall have the authority to show the apartment to prospective Tenants at reasonable hours. TENANTS MAY <u>NOT</u> SUB-LEASE APARTMENT FOR ANY REASON.

Amount paid by tenant as of
the date of this agreement: Signature(s)

First Month's Rent $_____   _____

Security Deposit $_____   _____

Total Paid This Date $_____   _____

Balance Due $_____   Date _____

Due Date   _____

Manager _____

Phone   _____

OWNER:
ADDRESS:

Occupancy Clause

With a rental agreement, you have the flexibility to stipulate whatever conditions you think are important and, of course, within the law. One item that I consider very important is my occupancy clause, which states: "Tenants acknowledge that they have examined the premises and found them to be in good and clean condition. Tenants agree to notify owner, in writing by certified mail (return receipt requested), of any problems pertaining to the habitability of the premises." Some landlords I know now take photographs of their units or videotape the apartment just before renting it out to protect themselves from bad tenants.

More often than not, I find that if a person can't pay the rent, they'll try to find something wrong with the apartment. They'll try to barter with you by saying, "I'll pay the rent if you fix this and that—" the ceiling or the window or the garbage disposal or whatever. If you file a notice of default to nullify the rental agreement, they'll counter by saying the reason they're not paying the rent is that the landlord won't make certain repairs.

If you appear in front of a judge without any documentation proving the habitability of the premises when the tenant moved in, the court might rule in favor of the tenant. But, if you have a signed agreement with an occupancy clause stating that this is the way you are going to operate or can provide other documentation, the judge will be more inclined to agree with you. Without this clause, it's your word against your tenant's. And you can't even get into an occupied apartment without the tenant's permission. Believe me, this statement is invaluable.

Other times, a tenant might not inform you about legitimate problems with an apartment, except when you start filing notices. Or they won't tell you because it's something they did. Hence, the second line in my occupancy clauses states: "Tenants agree to notify owner, in writing by certified mail (return receipt requested), of any problems pertaining to the habitability of the premises." This legally obligates my tenants to inform me of any problems formally and to have proof that they sent the letter.

Nobody ever does, of course. In all my time buying and managing property, I've only had one tenant who ever sent me a certified letter saying there was a mark on the wall and a little crack on the window. He didn't particularly want me to fix it, he just wanted me to know about it. I was glad he did.

Security-Deposit Clause

Another important item on the rental agreement is the security deposit clause. I try to get a security deposit equivalent to one month's rent. And I stipulate in the agreement that the security deposit cannot be used for the last month's rent. When a tenant moves out, you have two weeks to decide whether to send back all of the security deposit or withhold money for repairs and cleaning expenses beyond normal wear and tear.

Rent-Control Clause

In my agreement, I also have a clause that protects me in the event of rent control. Essentially, it states that if a tenant stays for a year, rent will be increased a certain amount each succeeding year because of inflation, increased costs of maintenance, taxes, utilities, and the like. I don't ever enforce it, but it lets people know before they come in that I reserve the right to raise rents to a certain level annually, although I am not that eager to raise rents when I have good tenants. Depending on the exact wording of a proposed rent control ordinance, this clause may or may not hold up. But I will say this, I have a better chance of raising the rent and getting away with it than if I didn't have this clause.

Keeping Tenants Satisfied

A contractor who was finishing up a remodel job for me a little while ago said, "Gee, you are going to have an awful time with your new tenant, he thinks he owns the place. He's telling everyone what to do, and he's real bossy." I told the contractor that I want him to think he owns the place. As long as he's paying the rent, and as long as he is taking pride in the place and keeps it clean and sees that nobody is stealing anything, he can go and tell the world that he owns it. I don't care. I own the deed. It doesn't hurt me.

To some extent I do feel that the tenants own the property as long as they're paying the rent because they're buying the property for me. Hence, I try to treat my tenants right. One way I do this is by not raising the rents. Why squeeze your tenants like a lemon? Keep your rents reasonable. I think you should keep the rents about 10% lower than similar properties so you get a good tenant who stays for a while; it's cheaper in the long run. It's important to be aware of what's going on in the market, but I generally only raise the rents when people move out.

One of my beachfront properties, a lower unit, 1,000-square-foot place with two bedrooms and an oceanfront patio right on the beach rents for $2,500 a month. The upper unit, which is the same size and has an ocean-front view and a sun deck, currently rents for $3,000 a month. I started renting the upper unit out about 14 years ago for $1,500 to a woman who never caused me any problems. Everybody got along with her, and I never raised the rent on that unit until she moved out.

Treat your tenants as equals, as you would like to have them treat you. Anybody who knows what they are doing can break a lease—they could just walk away, and then you have a problem on your hands. But, if you keep your tenants satisfied, they'll pay their rent on time and give you a guaranteed cash flow. I don't charge fees for late rent payments. I should, but I don't. I think it's terrible to extract blood. Besides, it would only create negative feelings.

On the other hand, you can't get too friendly with your tenants; they might take advantage of the situation. But, if you are fair, you'd be surprised how many people they'll send to you. If you treat a tenant nicely, after he moves out, you might get a friend of his as a referral and often he's a really good tenant, too.

Investigate the tenants to whom you rent and pick people whom you like and could get along with. Ideally, the person who owns the property should collect the money. Of course, you can hire someone to do it, but when you're starting out, you probably won't be able to afford to do this. And, if you own a large complex, some people will try to take advantage of you.

*A*s I mentioned before, my mother was extra bright when *it came to real estate. She never lost a tenant. I never in my life knew somebody who knew how to keep tenants so satisfied. She did whatever it took to keep the tenants happy. She always said it was cheaper in the long run to be accommodating. We used to have some property in Taft, California. One tenant lived in a house we owned there for 20 years, and another one for 18 years.*

I remember looking at my mother's tenant list once. There wasn't one tenant who had been in a house she managed for less than 11 years! She would do everything to keep her tenants. If someone would call up and say, "Well, we're thinking about moving," my mother would say, "Oh, don't do that.

Do you want a new roof? We'll have the house painted." Or, sometimes she'd say, "I'll reduce the rent." She knew what to do and it paid off because she didn't want to drive all the way up there to take care of vacancies.

Pets

If a tenant has a dog, I ask for a $250 pet deposit on top of the normal security deposit. Animals can ruin the carpet and scratch the walls. They may dig up the backyard and chew up the doors. But the worst thing is the smell. The stench they sometimes leave behind can be brutal.

My brother once owned a building in the north end of Hermosa Beach and rented to a tenant who had an ocelot, a wildcat similar in appearance but smaller than a leopard. The odor that it left behind was awful! We had to tear all the carpet out, paint the place, use disinfectants, even replace some of the floorboards. Even after we did that you could still smell traces of it.

I think it is fair to allow pets in places where they will be treated well. I don't think it's fair to keep a dog in a one-bedroom apartment where it sits in the dark barking all day while everybody is at work. On the other hand, I don't think it's unrealistic to allow a dog if you have a two-bedroom house with a yard in the back, since that's ideal for a dog. I don't mind cats (except ocelots).

Managing Your Investments

If you own real estate, it's important to manage your investments as you would manage a business. When I started accumulating multiple properties, I set up a little room where I kept my documents and files. I made sure to pay my bills on the first and fifteen of every month. Nowadays, my wife Margaret helps manage our properties out of a bedroom we have converted into an office. We make about 180 payments a month to utility companies, institutional lenders, and other creditors, and I always pay them ahead of time.

*W**ith repairs, every time someone does a job for me, I always pay him on the spot, immediately after the job is done. Whether the plumber, the carpenter, or the electrician comes down to work on a building, they all know to knock on my door afterwards to pick up their check. This way, if I want them to do something for me in a hurry, I know I can count on them. If they have to decide between two jobs, they're going to come to me first because they know they're going to get their money. I get better service than most people do, especially in times when people aren't paying promptly. When I call one of my repairmen on the phone, they're here in 20 minutes. And I know they won't overcharge me because they don't want to lose my business.*

To keep your affairs organized, it helps to have a separate room for an office. I keep at least one file for each property. I have another three-ring binder where I keep all correspondence, leases, and rental agreements.

At the end of the year, I add up the tallies for tax purposes and income reporting. I never made my bookkeeping system into a big deal, although now there are computerized accounting programs that streamline this whole process. I figure the best way to do it is to make it as simple as possible.

I also keep a folder (actually a photo album) of five-by-seven cards for tenant records—who to contact in an emergency, where they work, when they moved in, what they're paying, things like that. It also lists repairmen. I also keep a list of all bills from my properties. Finally, I maintain a separate notebook of all my properties, their current market values, their tract map parcel numbers, the dates the escrows closed, the purchase price, recording document, square footage, the escrow (or final closing) number, type of property, zoning designation, and estimated value.

Some people like to collect stamps or play volleyball on the beach. But for me, real estate is a sort of hobby. If you have another job, as I did when I started my investment program, you have to feel that real estate is a hobby. Otherwise, you might not enjoy it, and eventually you might get burned out. I really love the business, and I think that you have to enjoy it to be successful at it.

Managing Property

When you purchase properties, buy them close together if possible so they will be easier to take care of. When I started, my time was very valuable because I was working a steady job in addition to renting and maintaining my properties. When you start in real estate, you, too may not be able to afford to pay someone else to perform the maintenance and upkeep. Even so, you have to figure that your time is worth something and plan accordingly.

A person can hold down a full-time job and manage a four-unit building without any trouble. But in my opinion, it's much easier to buy five single-family residences that are close together than to buy a large apartment building. Once you get over 10 or so units, it becomes quite involved. In Los Angeles, apartment buildings with more than 16 units or more in one complex require an on-site property manager to handle rent collection, maintenance and repairs, and bookkeeping. The larger the complex is, the more variables are involved. If you own a 50-unit apartment building and you have an on-site manager, there are lots of ways a conniving person could take you to the cleaners, and you have to be aware of that. It is a business, after all.

With condominiums and townhouses, the homeowner's association takes care of most outside maintenance and assists with renting. Inside repairs are generally simple because the units have a uniform building design. But with a custom duplex or unique single-family residence, maintenance and upkeep can get complicated.

We have introduced a semi-annual safety and maintenance form in an effort to keep abreast of repairs at all our properties. It is wiser to fix problems before they get worse, but often tenants are reluctant to report problems for fear the landlord might raise the rent. Tenants are encouraged to inform the landlord of any dripping faucets, to check smoke detector batteries, report heating, lighting, electrical and plumbing problems, etc. The form should be filled out, signed, dated and returned as soon as possible to the Property Manager.

A complete list of forms pertaining to all your real estate needs is available on the Internet at www.nolo.com.

Semiannual Safety and Maintenance Update

Please complete the following checklist and note any safety or maintenance problems in your unit or on the premises.

Please describe the specific problems and the rooms or areas involved. Here are some examples of the types of things we want to know about: garage roof leaks, excessive mildew in rear bedroom closet, fuses blow out frequently, door lock sticks, water comes out too hot in shower, exhaust fan above stove doesn't work, smoke alarm malfunctions, peeling paint, and mice in basement. Please point out any potential safety and security problems in the neighborhood and anything you consider a serious nuisance.

Please indicate the approximate date when you first noticed the problem and list any other recommendations or suggestions for improvement.

Please return this form with this month's rent check. Thank you.—The Management

Name: _____

Address: _____

_____

Please indicate (and explain below) problems with:

[ ]   Floors and floor coverings _____

[ ]   Walls and ceilings _____

[ ]   Windows, screens, and doors _____

[ ]   Window coverings (drapes, miniblinds, etc.) _____

[ ]   Electrical system and light fixtures _____

[ ]   Plumbing (sinks, bathtub, shower, or toilet) _____

[ ]   Heating or air conditioning system _____

[ ]   Major appliances (stove, oven, dishwasher, refrigerator) _____

[ ]   Basement or attic _____

[ ]   Locks or security system _____

[ ]   Smoke detector _____

[ ]   Fireplace _____

[ ]   Cupboards, cabinets, and closets _____

[ ]   Furnishings (table, bed, mirrors, chairs) _____

[ ]   Laundry facilities _____

[ ]   Elevator _____

[ ]   Stairs and handrails_____

[ ]   Hallway, lobby, and common areas _____

[ ] Garage _____

[ ] Patio, terrace, or deck _____

[ ] Lawn, fences, and grounds _____

[ ] Pool and recreational facilities _____

[ ] Roof, exterior walls, and other structural elements _____

[ ] Driveway and sidewalks _____

[ ] Neighborhood _____

[ ] Nuisances _____

[ ] Other _____

Specifics of problems: _ _____

_____

_____

_____

_____

_____

Other comments: _____

_____

_____

_____

_____

_____

Tenant _____   Date _____

- -

FOR MANAGEMENT USE

Action/Response: _____

_____

_____

_____

Landlord/Manager _____   Date _____

(Reprinted with permission from the publisher, Nolo, © 2009,
from *Every Landlord's Legal Guide,* which can be found on www.nolo.com.)

*W*ith people moving in and out of our units I currently own and manage, some more frequently than others, it's virtually impossible to keep every unit rented 100% of the time. Today, that isn't a burden. I can afford a vacant apartment for a month or two and it won't hurt me. But when you're counting on the rent to make your payments, it's a different story. You have to be really diligent when you first start out because every nickel counts.

Say you own six units, and two of your six tenants aren't paying rent, or they write checks that don't clear. That can be a real challenge. Some landlords insist on cashier's checks. When times were tight and I received bounced checks, I'd ask my tenant when he got paid. When payday came around, I would be the first person there to collect the money. Other times I would accept postdated checks.

Handling Vacancies

In one condominium complex I own 27 studio apartments. During difficult rental periods, there are always one or two vacant. Whenever I have a vacancy, I put some of these $50 flyers on the doors of my current tenants and manage to find new tenants fast.

$50 $50

You can receive $50.00 for helping us find a satisfactory tenant to occupy our vacant Costa Mesa studio condominiums, located directly adjacent to the South Coast Plaza mall.

Just call . . . (714) 555-1234 or (310) 555-1234 and register your prospective tenant. Certain conditions apply.

Thank you. David T. Schumacher, Owner

$50 $50

When I bought the six-unit apartment building I live in, the entire building was vacant. The entire neighborhood was characterized by vacancies. The person who owned the property before me couldn't handle it. When I moved in, I got the names and addresses of all the real estate brokers in the area and had cards printed up. The cards stated that if the broker contacted me, registered his or her name, and referred to me a tenant, I would give him or her 25% of the first month's rent. I mailed these cards out until I got every one of my units filled.

A good manager will study the market constantly to see what the trends are, note what the competition is doing, and then raise his rents conservatively. I have found that it takes about a year to feel comfortable with a property in terms of finding good tenants, making necessary repairs, and setting the right rents. As mentioned, I always try to be a few dollars under the market so that people are happy. It works out well.

Here is another flyer I use to rent my studio apartments. I place these five-by-seven cards on bulletin boards, at the market, in laundromats, or wherever prospective tenants might congregate. The units I own there turn over fast, but with these cards and the help of the on-site property manager, I usually have no problem renting them out.

FOR RENT

LARGE STUDIO APARTMENT

$_____ per month

FABULOUS LOCATION
Walk to South Coast Plaza Shopping Center, supermarket, restaurants, medical facilities, etc.

SECURITY GROUNDS
Park-like setting, locked gates, swimming pools, jacuzzi, tennis courts, exercise rooms, laundry facilities.

APARTMENT UNIT FEATURES:

500 square feet (approx.)
Enclosed patio with sliding glass door
On-site parking for two cars
Laid carpet, drapes, range, refrigerator
Dishwasher, wall heater, air conditioner
Pulldown queen-size Murphy bed
Built-in nightstand, desk, breakfast bar
Mirrored wardrobe closets

CALL TODAY FOR A WALK-THROUGH APPOINTMENT!

(310) 555-1234

Common Mistakes

Many landlords make costly mistakes that cause no end of aggravation. Common mistakes I've seen include inadequate oversight, sloppy book-keeping, failing to run credit checks on prospective tenants, and holding grudges. Some property owners get annoyed if they are called by tenants to repair things. They explode if they receive a check that bounces or, at two o'clock in the morning, a renter calls because a water line breaks and there's water running all over the floor.

No matter what you do, you're going to be disappointed. People aren't going to show up or pay you when you want them to. They're going to trash the place and break things. You can't let these kind of things anger you because you'll lose sight of the objective. It's hard when tenants move out and you discover that they have ransacked the place. You just have to say to yourself, "Well, I have their security deposit and this property is really going to be worth something in twenty years." I admit it though, sometimes it's not easy to do.

Some of the biggest mistakes I've seen landlords make in terms of managing their investments is getting mad at tenants for no good reason, or being too nit-picky. Why be overly concerned about whether a tenant ruined the screen door or spilled grape juice on the carpet? This kind of aggravation is trivial when you think about it. I don't have a real affection for the buildings. If something is damaged, I can get it fixed. If somebody breaks the window, I'm not going to lose any sleep over it.

If a tenant calls me up with a mechanical problem, such as a backed-up sink or power outage, I get somebody out to fix it as soon as possible. I don't think you can expect to receive the rent on time if you wait two weeks to fix a clogged toilet. That's not being fair with people.

If you have a few good tenants and you establish a rapport with them, they'll keep you informed about everything going on at your units. I love being informed about my apartments, I really do. I don't mind being con-tacted. It's lots of fun. When people start to tell me what to do, how to run my business, I get fired up. I enjoy interacting with the tenants; I get a big kick out of it. When a problem arises, the most important thing you can do as a landlord is listen to what your tenants have to say. When you listen, it calms people down. You can avoid a lot of problems that way.

When I taught night school, I got into a lot of challenging conversa-tions. I thrived off that exchange and rhetoric. I loved it. Somebody else might have gone through the roof. Your personality has a lot to do with the type of landlord you are.

An adventure is defined as an unusual and suspenseful experience. If you enjoy spontaneous excitement, the problems you sometimes encounter as a property owner can make being a landlord adventurous and interesting.

One time a police officer knocked on my door at 2:00 a.m. and said, "You own the place, don't you?" I said, "Yes." He said, "Well, you have a flood out there." Some guy had apparently taken a sledgehammer in the wee hours of a Sunday morning and had broken my water spigot. It was shooting across the boardwalk. I said, "Oh my gosh, what am I going to do?" And the officer said, "You have two choices—either you call a plumber at triple time or you turn the water off."

I called my plumber, but he was in Lake Tahoe. So, mindful of the costs, I turned the water off and wrote a note to all the tenants saying we couldn't get anybody out to fix the problem until Monday. People were screaming, they couldn't take a shower, wash their dishes, or flush the toilets. It was pandemonium at first, but when the tenants realized what had happened, they calmed down and accepted the situation in good spirit. The goodwill that I had always extended to my tenants came back tenfold that day.

Another time, I got a call one night about 8:00 p.m. from a county health inspector who said he had found some hazardous waste in the trash bin of one of my beach properties. The inspector said he was going to have to cordon off the area and call a hazardous waste removal team. The inspector had received a call from one of my tenants who, when taking out her trash, noticed a bunch of hypodermic needles in a box that had fallen open. So the health department came down and made a big scene.

When I got down there, he told me that I had to get rid of this hazard right away. I told him I would talk to a tenant of mine who works for the hospital. But he was adamant. He said, "Nobody's touching this. We've got to get a hazardous team out here." He handed me a list of five companies that handle hazardous materials and told me to call. Finally, I got a hold of a guy in Long Beach who said he would come out for $2,500, but it had to be cash or a cashier's check. I said, "It's nine o'clock p.m., what do you expect me to do?"

So I told the health inspector that I thought he was being absolutely unreasonable. Then, I gathered up some bicycle chains and chained the container so nobody could get into it. In the morning I called up the waste disposal company that owned the bin, and they got their hazardous materials team to come out with their gloves and protective gear to remove this little box of needles. I had to pay them $650 to do it.

By taking pictures of the box and looking at it closely, they discovered that it had originated from a plastic surgeon in Los Angeles. Apparently, the doctor or someone from her office had dumped it into my trash bin. Since the origin of the syringes could be traced back to his particular doctor, the waste disposal company took her to court and the judge ordered her to pay my $650 back. I found out later that it was the health inspector's first case and that he wanted to make a big deal out of it to make himself look good.

If the tenant who originally spotted the problem had just called me, I could have taken care of it by chaining up the trash container and having the fire department pick it up the next day—they do that kind of work all the time. This whole incident was much ado about nothing, really. But it was kind of exciting, too. It was a challenging problem to solve, and I got to meet a few people. How you react to potential landlord problems like this is a matter of mental attitude.

Inadequate Oversight

If you agree to rent a two-bedroom apartment to two single guys, you want to make sure that it doesn't become a crash pad for a fraternity house. Most cities have ordinances limiting the number of occupants per unit. I'm tolerant of most situations, but I do care if renters disturb other tenants or infringe on their neighbors' rights. The minute they do, they're going to hear from me.

> *I used to have a tenant who blared his stereo out of his window onto the beach. I told him he had an inferiority complex, and he did this to attract attention; I could think of no other reason why he would do this. I told him that if he had a charming personality, he could attract girls some other way. We talked about it for awhile and came to the conclusion that he should see a therapist, which he did, and it worked out—he didn't play his stereo loudly anymore.*

I like my tenants to be considerate and respect other people's wishes. That's the way I would act if I was renting, and I expect them to be the same way.

Hasty Move-Ins

When renting to a prospective tenant, you don't want to have them sign a rental agreement today and have them move in later that afternoon or the morning after. Even if you've interviewed friends and former neighbors, you may not know why they're so anxious to get in, or where they were kicked out from. Usually, people are more willing to give their previous landlord notice and go apartment hunting at least a few weeks in advance of their move date.

If, on the other hand, a renter gives notice in the morning and moves out in the afternoon, they might do the same thing to you—without even telling you. In some states, the law stipulates that tenants must give two weeks' notice before they vacate. But what are you going to do if they don't—hire a private detective to track them down? You can't get blood out of a turnip. One of the things you can do is demand a cashier's check when a new tenant moves in. As a rule, I never accept an out-of-state check.

Sloppy Bookkeeping

Most people don't like bookkeeping, but without an orderly system, you won't be able to keep track of who's paying the rent on time, who's late, who's coming and going, and who your renters are. Many times you may have two or three people sharing an apartment, and each pays their rent separately. It can get really complicated, especially when some of the checks start bouncing.

Even if you only regard real estate as a sideline activity, you still need to be very careful to keep accurate records. With sloppy bookkeeping, you can lose track of things. A friend of mine once owned a 20-unit apartment building, which his wife would not have anything to do with. She refused to collect the rent, even if a tenant brought it by. She would say, "I'm sorry, that's not my department. Bring it back tomorrow when my husband's here." They probably lost a few month's rent just because of that.

Holding Grudges

If you're bothered by quirks, nuances, and relatively minor things, then you're not going to be able to keep tenants for any length of time. My mother, the super landlord, never held a grudge against anybody. If something happened she didn't like, she had a way of dismissing it from her mind. She didn't believe in gossip, either; she felt that if you didn't have something good to say about someone, then you shouldn't say it. It's very easy to find fault in people; we can look in the mirror and find fault in ourselves. Nobody is perfect.

If you hold people in low esteem on account of their failings, that attitude will certainly be reflected onto your interaction with tenants because they're anything but perfect. It doesn't work to get into grudge matches as a landlord because if you irritate your tenants, and they annoy you, everyone is going to be unhappy. Life's too short for that kind of aggravation. Happiness is a journey, not a destination. The journey should be filled with rich and rewarding experiences, rather than pet peeves, grudges, and other things that make people upset.

Both of my parents were positive thinkers. They always looked at the bright side of what was going on. For me, things always work out better when I think about the good side of a situation. If you look at the bright side, it's easier to adjust to life's setbacks. And most things do have a bright side.

EVICTIONS

In almost 50 years of renting houses and apartments, I've developed a method of ejecting tenants that could help people tremendously. I sometimes offer problem tenants money to leave; dismiss the back rent if they move out immediately; or help them find an apartment at a more reasonable price to expedite their departure.

When I bought my first six-unit apartment building by the beach, I rented out the penthouse suite to a couple who wrote me a check that bounced. I kept after them. But one night about two weeks after they moved in, they decided to move out. I figured they left about 2:00 a.m. because I couldn't hear them, and none of the neighbors saw them leave. They took my barbecue. I should have called the police, but I felt sorry for them. I knew they were in worse shape than I was. I figured that in a few days I would forget them and have someone else to worry about, but they would carry their problems with them and probably suffer for the rest of their lives. I generally don't file judgments against current and former tenants and go after them for back rent. Most of the time, you can't collect anyway. If they couldn't pay you when they lived in your place, why should they be able to pay you now?

*O*ne of my tenants in a beach apartment couldn't pay his rent and knew that he had to pay or leave, but couldn't adjust to the fact that he had to move out. He ended up living in his car for six months. That was much worse than anything I could have ever done to him. I could have sued him and maybe taken his car away from him, putting him on the street, but what good would that have done?

Another tenant who couldn't (or wouldn't) pay his rent stayed until the moment the sheriff came and told him he couldn't go back in. Then he wanted to cut some kind of deal with me. Lots of times people just don't want to accept reality. We all have problems. Life is just that way. So I don't view someone who doesn't pay his rent as a vindictive person who is hateful toward me. I see it more as that person's problems playing themselves out on a financial level.

Many people bite off more than they can chew. For them, life is just one darned problem after another. It's sad, really. But as long as their delinquency doesn't hurt me and as long as I can absorb the extra expense, I'm not going to raise a major fuss over it. I figure there's enough in the world to go around for everybody. I really feel sorry for people who get into circumstances like that. Then I say to myself, "Well, maybe I made a mistake by accepting them as tenants in the first place."

When it comes to evicting tenants, there are important differences between residential and commercial properties. Residential property is someone's home. There's a different feeling about it than a commercial property. There is an emotional or sentimental attachment to shelter, whereas commercial real estate is a business and you deal with people like you would with any other type of business. One of the difficulties associated with buying residential real estate is not realizing the humanity that comes into play.

When you're dealing with a family living in a residence, they might have a baby and haven't been able to sleep for two nights. You have to be sympathetic and understanding toward that, even if they are late on their rent. Commercial property is a horse of a different color. If someone doesn't pay their rent, you kick them out, no questions asked; it's more cold-blooded. I would be more inclined to let a person who told me their problems, slide along with the rent in a residential setting than in a commercial arrangement. I wouldn't want somebody to kick me out of my house, but I would understand if I was running a business and wasn't meeting my obligations and got evicted. That said, it does become necessary at times to initiate eviction proceedings against delinquent tenants.

17

Make the System Work to Your Benefit Through Refinancing and the Tax-Deferred Exchange

REFINANCING

After the crash of the stock market in 1929 and the Great Depression that ensued, the financial industry was virtually crippled. These two events rocked money markets all over the world. Prior to the Depression, the typical homebuyer with adequate credit would take out a short-term loan from a bank. The loan was usually interest-only. At the end of the financing term, the bank would renew the loan, enabling the borrower to defer payment of the principal balance almost indefinitely.

When the Depression came, banks could no longer afford to extend these one- or two-year "rollover" loans, so many properties were foreclosed because property owners could not come up with the cash required to meet their obligations. After congressional legislation restructured the Federal Reserve Bank, lending institutions were allowed to place amortized mortgages on real estate, on which borrowers could make payments of both interest and principal over 15 to 30 years.

Because amortized mortgages prevented serious financial hardships created by the one- and two-year mortgages, building became a boom industry in America. The new method of debt satisfaction allowed investors to accumulate huge debt loads without painful consequences as long as the payments were met. Refinancing of equities soon became a prudent way to take out cash for these investments.

Refinancing basically involves paying off an old loan with a new loan and getting a new, preferably lower, interest rate. Refinancing works best when property values appreciate, because you can take out a new loan for up to 80% of the current appraised value. So, if you bought a place for $100,000, and its market value had doubled to $200,000, you would be able to refinance for up to $160,000. That $60,000 above and beyond the purchase price is yours to do what you want with, although there might be some tax liability.

Property owners refinance their property for various reasons. They may need the money for a down payment on another property, for an addition or remodel of their current home, to sustain their small business, or to finance their children's college education. Some owners refinance their property every few years while some may never refinance. If the value of the property keeps going up, refinancing is advantageous. It's better than having money in the bank, really, because when your real estate increases in value it allows you to draw out a percentage for other uses.

When a better interest rate is available, there are financial advantages to refinancing your mortgage. It generally becomes advantageous to refinance long-term loans when interest rates fall two points below the fixed rate of the original loan. A new loan with an interest rate three points lower than your original loan would be fabulous. You can save real money in a deal like that.

Other times, refinancing is done for a specific, personal reason. A friend of ours refinanced his condominium once to take a vacation. He was paying 18% on his new loan, but for him, it was a question of going or not going. Luckily for him, interest loans are deductible.

When you refinance a mortgage, you can often gain access to cash which you otherwise couldn't use. I know a woman who, by refinancing her first mortgage, was able to take out a $1 million loan on her property, which she had purchased for $20,000 in the early 1960s. Of course, she might have been subject to paying tax on the loan, depending on what she did with the money.

Usually, refinancing a first mortgage will enable you to get better terms, including a lower interest rate and a longer duration loan. With junior liens, such as second, third, or fourth mortgages, the risk involved generally demands a higher interest rate and shorter due date on the loan.

In 1965, I acquired a four-unit building for $45,000. Today, the four units produce $6,000 a month in rental income, or $72,000 a year. My monthly mortgage payment, *however, is only $350 a month. In 1985, 20 years after I bought it, that property was worth about $500,000. Today, it's worth over $1 million. I know for a fact that the people I bought it from thought I would refinance the place and pay them off.*

I still have about $15,000 outstanding on the mortgage, but I receive $6,000 a month in income from the property, so worrying about paying off the loan is a moot point. At only $350 a month with 6% interest, I have no need to pay it off. Although today I could get 6% from a bank, for many years this was not the case. And for $15,000, where else could I find this type of write-off?

When I first started buying real estate, most of my loans had a 6% to 6.5% interest rate. Once, I had a 5.5% rate. Over the years, interest rates have fluctuated dramatically. During the recession of the early 1980s, interest rates peaked at around 20%. Mortgage rates, currently around 4.5% for adjustable mortgages and around 6% for fixed-rate loans, are at their lowest levels since the 1970s, so many property owners who still have high interest rates are refinancing.

Unless I had some solid reason for refinancing, such as an incredibly guaranteed rate, I would refrain from doing so because refinancing usually results in a higher payment. The publisher of the local newspaper refinances his property regularly to get cash for his business. That's marvelous. But I think it's better if you have low interest loans to try to pay the loans down and work with the income from rents rather than borrowing on the property and creating heavy debt. I've had second, third, and fourth mortgages, but I've only refinanced a property once.

If you have to rely on refinancing a property in a certain amount of time to pay off your loan or to make a balloon payment, you might not be able to do it unless something dramatic happens to real estate prices—inflation, appreciation, or you enhance value through your own improvement efforts, such as remodeling or rebuilding. Again, you have to be in a growth area so that the property goes up in value.

An example of how refinancing can benefit an investor was demonstrated to me recently. An intrepid friend of mine owned a residence and four separate houses within a short walking distance. He understood the area completely and had studied it, knowing that the values would increase over a period of time because there was tremendous growth potential. He would refinance one house every fourth year and thus have one refinancing project every year. By doing this, he was able to pick up close to $50,000 each year in cash to spend on other investments.

> *O ne of the main advantages to refinancing is that you can take out a loan for more than the original mortgage or purchase price. Say you purchased a property five years ago for $200,000 and took out a $120,000 loan. Now you want to refinance because the value has risen to $320,000. So you visit your lender and obtain a loan for $220,000. Since the tax laws change periodically, consult your tax accountant for the latest tax information before making a financial decision.*

The drawback of refinancing to get a lower interest rate is that it costs money to go through the process. When lenders agree to refinance a loan, they charge a few points in transaction costs, so refinancing may cost some money. In order to tap the equity in a property, some owners would rather put another lien on their real estate than refinance the first mortgage. In general, if you have favorable terms, it's not a good idea to disturb the first mortgage but rather to take out a second. If you can't get a second from a conventional lender, you might decide to take out a second mortgage from a "hard money" lender—a private lender who gets funds from private parties and loans it for individual properties.

As mentioned, hard money lenders demand a higher rate of interest than institutional lenders because they assume more risk and don't have to comply with regulations as strict as those governing lenders who deal with public funds. Hard money lenders usually require a balloon payment as well. I would avoid a hard moneylender if at all possible. They generally charge higher interest rates and more points.

TAX-DEFERRED EXCHANGE

Although never selling is my rule of thumb for successful real estate investing, there are rare instances when selling after an extended period of ownership is advantageous, particularly when a tax-deferred exchange can be made. Under Section 1031 of the Internal Revenue Code, like-kind property used in a trade or business or held as an investment can be "exchanged" tax-free. The tax system, through the tax-deferred exchange, encourages sellers to buy similar properties of equal or greater value by making their profits tax exempt.

Many residential income property owners choose to make an exchange when, after owning a piece of real estate for over the 27½-year depreciation period, they can no longer take a tax write-off because the paper value of the building for tax purposes has reached zero.

After owning a four-unit apartment building for 25 years and seeing its real value soar from $45,000 to $1 million (while its paper value dropped to nothing because of depreciation), I decided to sell it and make a tax-deferred exchange. With the profit I received from the sale, I traded my one small apartment complex for three houses and a condominium.

The old property, although worth a great deal, was only yielding a 5% annual return. Because the depreciation period had expired, it was in my best interest to exchange other properties I could take depreciation on. By selling one property and buying four others, I increased my assets without paying taxes on capital gains. If you buy enough property, the depreciation you can take will offset the taxable income you receive. It works out so you don't have to pay as much tax.

If you bought a property in a mediocre location with a huge structure on it, a higher dollar value might be allocated for the improvements, on the actual building, than for the land. For tax purposes, you make an allocation of the depreciable assets compared to the non-depreciable assets. Depreciable assets include the building, utilities, underground plumbing, sidewalks, fixtures, contents, everything except the vacant land, which isn't depreciable.

The higher the building-to-land ratio, the more depreciation you can take. For this reason, I decided to buy apartment buildings on the oceanfront rather than single-family residences; with apartments, you can allocate more value to the buildings.

The most desirable thing is to find a property that is over-built, for instance, a multi-unit, legal, nonconforming apartment building you can't replace with a building of similar density because of city downzoning. By buying the nonconforming building, you get a better depreciation write-off because you can allocate more for the building than the land. In some instances, it is wiser to put money into improving a legal nonconforming building than investing in a teardown property or new development.

Industrial and commercial buildings have a longer depreciation period than residential dwellings. But an advantage to buying an apartment building is that you can take many of the things that aren't considered construction items and put them in a separate category of furnishings and equipment. Furnishings and appliances such as carpets, drapes, refrigerators, drop-in ranges, window air conditioners, portable heaters, swag lamp fixtures, gardening equipment, and pool and patio equipment can all be valued and depreciated over a short-term period.

For tax assessment purposes, I always segregate the purchase price into the land, the improvements, and the furnishings, appliances and equipment. Say you paid $100,000 for a property, $90,000 for the real estate (including land and improvements) and $10,000 for the equipment that came with the building. For tax assessment purposes, that $10,000 for equipment should not be assessed with the building; it should be a separate category.

I do this to achieve a lower assessed value. If you start at a lower base, your taxes are going to be lower. The mistake accountants make at the time of acquisition is taking the assessed value of the land and improvements for depreciation instead of going to the site and studying the problem. When most county assessors establish property values for tax purposes, they distinguish between land and improvements but they don't isolate the equipment value. It's important to be honest with everything you do. But if you know your facts and what to do, you can save some money here and there. If you own real estate, it's important to manage your investments as you would manage a business.

*W*hen you buy real property, the allocation for improvements is depreciable over a 27½-year period. As the value of the physical building depreciates, some of the net income is sheltered for tax purposes. It's a loss, but a paper loss. Actually, the building will probably appreciate in value if the market goes up.

In the above example, say the land was allocated at $20,000, the improvements at $70,000, and the personal property at $10,000. Assuming you can take $10,000 off the value of the building improvements attributable to depreciation over a few years, your basis will then be $60,000. At the end of the fourth year, you decide to spend $20,000 on an addition.

Your basis then rises to $80,000 on the improvements, plus $20,000 on the land, plus whatever amount you have *not depreciated on the personal property, for a total of, say, $105,000. Now, assume you trade up for a like property for an equal or greater value. You wouldn't have to pay any federal income tax on it; you simply exchange the basis to the new property and continue on. If you sold the property outright, you would have to pay the depreciation you took back. This is called recapture. When you trade up, you change your basis—the purchase price less the depreciation taken on the improvements and the personal property, plus any added monies you put into the property.*

A tax-deferred exchange is a way of extending your wealth and achieving your goal. It's not a tax-free exchange. Rather, you're deferring your payment of taxes until such time that you're through with all of your exchanges. In a tax-deferred exchange, you sell your property and put the profits into an accommodator account. You can then take the money from the sale and purchase another like-kind property of equal or greater value.

The IRS looks at tax-deferred exchange as if you were extending your first investment onto the next property as it increases in value. Suppose you own a duplex worth $100,000, which has a $60,000 loan against it and $40,000 in equity. If you trade that duplex for a $200,000 triplex or four-family apartment building, you're trading your equity into a new property. As long as you keep extending your investment and the price goes up, there's no tax to pay or recapture of depreciation. But if you make the exchange and have to put in some of your own personal property to make the payment—cash, or collateral like rare coins, jewelry, cars, or anything of value that isn't considered like-kind property—that's added cash, which you as the seller will have to pay tax on.

Suppose further that you have $60,000 in equity in a duplex worth $100,000, which you trade for a $200,000 duplex that the seller only has $40,000 equity in. You're assuming his $160,000 loan. But if you have $60,000 equity to trade, he has to give you $20,000 cash (known as boot) to make the deal. That's money the buyer has to pay taxes on.

Although I have used it, the tax-deferred exchange was never much of a consideration for me because I never planned to sell the property I bought. If you pick the right piece of real estate in a good location, you want to retain the property for the long-term, not exchange it for something else. The best time to make an exchange is when you want to buy something better or consolidate your properties.

When you are involved in making any kind of real estate exchange, it is essential that you consult a competent tax attorney and accountant to be sure that you are complying with the current rules and regulations of the IRS. Tax laws change rapidly and rules that are applicable today might be drastically different tomorrow. It is therefore important to stay current and make adjustments that reflect changes in the tax laws.

18

Protecting Your Investment and Accomplishing Your Financial Objective

There is a natural human instinct to protect one's family, home, and personal belongings against threats and disasters of all kinds. One of the reasons that casualty insurance companies have been so successful in past generations is that they have played on the fears of people and stressed how a loss would affect their lives. Casualty insurance is a business based on fear.

Some close friends of our family never carried any insurance, except on their automobile. They had no life insurance, health insurance, or fire insurance. Since they owned their residence free and clear, they were not required to carry fire insurance on their home. If they had a mortgage on the property, the lender would have insisted on adequate fire loss protection. This family insured themselves by having sufficient revenues in the bank, plus other debt-free income property.

The husband lived to be 89 years old and his wife died at the age of 87. Neither of them ever spent a night in a hospital, and they seldom went to the doctor. I often thought about how much money they saved by not paying insurance premiums (during their lifetime).

On the other hand, my father and his business partner had about every kind of insurance imaginable. In later years, when my father became ill, the insurance company refused to pay for his medical bills a few months into his illness. When I complained to the office of the Insurance Commissioner, the insurance company promptly canceled his policy. Wasn't my father fortunate to have investment real estate with sufficient income so that the loss of his insurance policy was unimportant?

Fire Losses

A fire insurance policy is very difficult for a layperson to thoroughly understand. Fortunately for the insurance company, the policy does not require strict interpretation until a loss occurs. All reputable institutional lenders require adequate fire insurance on real property improvements if a real estate mortgage is in force. The insurance policy may be written to cover the replacement cost of the building. The difference is in how the costs are calculated.

Replacement cost is defined as the cost to replace a structure with one having utility equivalent to the subject structure but built with modern materials according to current standards, design, and layout. Depreciated replacement cost is defined as replacement cost, less accrued depreciation based on age, use, and condition. Another method of calculation used by insurers is reproduction cost, or the cost of reproducing the subject structure with one that is an exact replica in quality of workmanship, design, and layout.

Most fire insurance policies are written using the replacement cost method (the loss in value of a structure due to any cause) in dollar amounts. As an investor, it is very important for you to be fully aware of the type of insurance you are carrying, how your assets will be calculated in the event of a loss, and if your policy carries adequate protection.

When I worked for Marshall and Stevens, one of my responsibilities was to appraise real and personal property for fire insurance purposes. With real property, my job was to write a report describing in great detail the physical structure of the building and all of the components, including the foundation, frame, floors, ceilings, exterior walls, interior layout and design, plumbing, electrical, heating, air conditioning, fire protection, roofing, and exterior features such as porches, balconies, and fire escapes. I would also list in detail the attendant personal property, including carpets, drapes, kitchen appliances, lobby furnishings, and other types of portable equipment necessary and pertinent to the operation of the building. Each component was priced showing replacement cost and depreciated replacement cost. In addition, the furniture and equipment was priced showing present and replacement value.

The benefits of a fire insurance appraisal to the investor are enormous. The most important benefit is that a fire loss is virtually settled before the fire happens. The appraiser is an unbiased, third party who has described in detail and placed a value on each of the characteristics of the construction and personal property in sufficient detail to support the property owner's claim of loss. It should be pointed out that it is the policyholder's responsibility to provide the insurance company with a proof of loss statement listing the value of all items affected by the fire.

With a replacement cost appraisal in hand, the proof of loss settlement is, in effect, prepared in advance by a competent, disinterested third party who is qualified to testify in court on the validity of his or her appraisal report.

Under certain circumstances, this report could be invaluable. Years ago, one of the appraisers working in our company prepared an appraisal of the construction and equipment of an industrial building for fire insurance. The industrial plant's main process was metal plating. About two years after the appraisal was completed, there was a tremendous explosion in the plant, blowing the building and equipment into oblivion. The explosion was so severe, it catapulted chunks of concrete in the air, hitting buildings one and two blocks away from the scene of the accident.

As I recall, a number of people perished in the explosion. Afterward, there was nothing left; only some parts of the concrete foundation from the building could be seen around the deep hole created by the blast. The only copy of the appraisal report prepared two years earlier was in our office. The other two copies were tucked away in the company's fireproof safe. No trace of the safe could be found anywhere.

The copy of the original appraisal report that we had in our office became essentially priceless. Criminal charges were filed against the owner. Lawsuits were filed by homeowners and commercial property owners in the surrounding neighborhood whose buildings suffered damage in the explosion. People affected by the disaster were up in arms. It was a terrible tragedy.

The property owners used the appraisal report to construct on paper exactly what activities were performed on-site, what type of equipment was used, and what condition the items were in before the loss. Using that as a basis, the owners proved that they were not negligent in maintaining the plant premises and operating the business. I was later informed by a reliable source that the insurance company had no recourse but to pay up in full. I bet it cost them millions.

If no surviving appraisal had existed after the explosion, the final outcome for the property owners would have been altogether different. A fire loss or any kind of catastrophe can be devastating. I periodically check my property for hazards, such as an accumulation of junk in basements, attics, garages, and storage areas. Also, it is extremely important to have working smoke detectors installed as well as fire extinguishers and garden hoses.

O ne of my buildings had an outdoor fire escape with a drop ladder to the street. A few years ago, one of the large trucks that pick up trash in the area hit the fire escape and bent the ladder, rendering it useless in the event of a fire. I wrote several letters to the trash company explaining how the bent ladder posed a safety hazard to my tenants and asking them to repair the damage. After nine months of getting nowhere with letters, phone calls, and personal interviews, I figured out what to do.

The trash company collected trash from five of my buildings. So when the bills came in, I held them for two months. Then I made out the checks for the five accounts but did not sign them. I sent the unsigned checks to the trash company, along with a letter again explaining the fire escape problem and how disturbed I was about it. I told them if they wanted the checks signed, they should bring them along when they came to repair the fire escape. They sent a repairman within two weeks and performed the repairs to my satisfaction.

Most insurance policies covering investment-type properties are written with a co-insurance clause in the policy rather than as a stipulated amount. A stipulated amount policy is one where the value of the improvements are specifically stated in the policy for a given period of time. With this type of insurance, the policyholder usually pays a higher premium than for carrying coinsurance.

Over 90% of all the fire losses throughout the United States are partial (not total) loss claims. The insurance industry realized many years ago that if you owned a commercial building that would cost $150,000 to replace but only insured it for $50,000, the odds were nine out of ten your $50,000 policy would cover any damage resulting from a partial loss. The odds would be in your favor of having the building restored, provided the insurance company paid for the loss. You can see from this example how an insurer could lose valuable premiums by not having buildings insured to full value.

The insurance companies concluded this was not good for business and decided to correct it by issuing co-insurance policies. For a reduced premium rate, the insured policyholder with a coinsurance policy agrees to insure his building for the full value. If a coinsurance policy is in force and a fire occurs, and it is determined that the building is underinsured, the policyholder becomes a coinsurer and must make up a portion of the loss.

For example, say you own a commercial property. The market value is $400,000. The land is estimated to be worth $200,000 and the building, or improvements, to be worth $200,000. Through negligence or an oversight, you only have the building insured for $100,000. If a fire occurs, causing $50,000 damage to the building, the insurance company will penalize you 50% for not having adequate coverage under the terms of the policy.

Firestorms

The Southern California firestorms of October 2003 were just horrendous. These firestorms lasted about 10 days, burning some 750,000 acres and destroying over 1,500 homes and structures. The landscape was completely destroyed in parts of Orange County, the San Bernardino mountains, parts of Ventura County and north of San Diego. After the fires came the rains and the added danger of mudslides in these same rural areas. Thousands of people live in these areas where fires occurred, and many lost their homes and everything they owned. Many wooden fences, instead of concrete walls, helped to kindle these fires. One or two structural steel homes survived the ordeal.

People will continue to reside in these areas, sometimes rebuilding more than once in a lifetime because they enjoy the environment away from the hustle, bustle and smog of large cities and towns. But it takes a lot to settle all the claims—time, energy, estimating and accounting with special agencies and countless people involved. Many of the properties that were destroyed were probably substandard, because building codes have changed dramatically over the last 30 to 40 years. New codes have been enforced and it may have been difficult for many people to settle their claims.

The importance of location cannot be emphasized enough when you are purchasing real estate on hillsides, in rural areas surrounded by heavy brush and trees. Buyers should be especially cautious when purchasing in rural areas. Vegetation should be cleared close to the buildings and for at least 50 feet away from any structure. Roofing materials should be noncombustible. It is a wise policy to take photographs of your property and personal items and keep these records somewhere in a secure place away from the residence. Victims also have to be wary of people posing as contractors in the wake of such disasters. Sadly, "sharks" are always ready to attack and feed on the emotions of the victims.

When a Fire Loss Can Be Advantageous

Sometimes a fire "loss" can actually be profitable. A widow I knew once inherited property on a valuable corner lot in downtown Los Angeles. She leased the building to a commercial tenant on a fixed rental of $1,500 a month for 30 years. The tenant paid all expenses, including real property taxes, insurance, and maintenance. The fair market value of this burdensomely leased property was $225,000. Astutely, *the property owner had the building appraised for fire insurance by a qualified appraiser. The insurance company stipulated the full value at $185,000.*

About two and a half years later, while the widow was on vacation in Europe, the building burned down. Happily, it was a complete loss. She came home, collected her $185,000 from the insurance company and sold the vacant land to a parking lot operator for $200,000. She ended up with $385,000, all cash, for a property that a few years before had been worth only $225,000. The land then was no longer burdened by the building and could be put to better use.

Contingent Liability

If an investor owns a property in an area where its construction does not comply with the present zoning laws, the investor must be sure to carry special coverage to protect against contingent liability. Contingent liability insurance covers situations where, if a structure is partially destroyed to the point where the city or county won't permit reconstruction to its original use, the insurance company will consider the structure a total loss.

If a fire loss occurs and the company's adjuster and the insured cannot agree on a settlement, the case usually goes to arbitration. In this event, the insurance company selects a representative and the insured selects his own representative. The two representatives then meet and mutually select a third person. The three people become the arbitration board. After hearing all of the evidence, two out of the three arbitrators agree on a settlement.

A number of years ago, I represented the owner of a restaurant in arbitration after a serious fire damaged his kitchen. The insurance company offered the insured $20,000 to settle his claim. During this period of my appraisal career, I appraised many of the fine restaurants along La Cienega Boulevard in Los Angeles. I was very familiar with kitchens, so the first thing I did was to draw a floor plan of the burned-out kitchen with the ashes from the fire. With the help of the employees, I was able to plot the location and sizes of all the equipment in the area before the loss.

We were then able to determine all of the items on the

countertops, racks, and shelves that were necessary to oper-
ate the business. During the course of my analysis, I was
able to discern the extent of fire damage to the building.
When the case went to arbitration, I represented the prop-
erty owner and, with all of the factual data at hand, agreed
on a settlement in excess of four times the original offer from
the insurance company. If you ever have a need for someone
to represent you in a fire loss settlement, be sure to get a
person who understands the problem and has experience in
that type of case.

Hurricanes

Technically, a hurricane is an atmospheric disturbance characterized by masses of air rotating around a low pressure center with heavy rains and wind reaching beyond 75 miles per hour. Hurricanes that affect coastal areas of the United States generate their wind velocity in the Pacific Ocean, Atlantic Ocean, the Gulf of Mexico, or the Caribbean Sea. During the early and mid-1900s, hurricanes created devastation without warning to coastal communities, killing scores of people and destroying almost everything in their paths.

Since the onset of the space age, satellites have traced weather patterns, enabling scientists to predict the course of hurricanes well in advance, thus allowing evacuation plans to go into effect, saving money and lives and protecting property. Today's improved construction standards take into consideration hazards from high-velocity winds and severe rainstorms.

Obviously, for the investor, it is best not to purchase property in the path of hurricanes. Before you purchase a property, study the history of the area to determine what has happened in the past. Remember, history often repeats itself, especially where nature is concerned.

Accomplishing Your Objective

Henry Ford, John D. Rockefeller, Andrew Carnegie, and Thomas Alva Edison all rose from poverty to become great innovators, catalysts who helped spark our nation's tremendous economic growth in the late nineteenth and early twentieth centuries. Each of these industrial giants is credited with setting and accomplishing monumental goals during their distinguished careers. These men must have taken countless risks before achieving great success. And their willingness to do so paid tremendous dividends when combined with perseverance and commitment.

We can apply the experiences of these towering figures in American history to long-term real estate investment. The importance of developing the qualities that helped make them successful, namely patience and dedication to a task or objective cannot be overemphasized.

When you buy real estate, a strong sense of what you hope to achieve through investing is paramount. As with a college education, you should know what's involved and what kind of return you expect to get from the efforts you put into it. You never want owning real estate to become a burden; you want it to be a pleasant experience, something you can always be proud of and enjoy.

As realtors are so fond of saying, location is everything. You'll always make money if you buy the cheapest property in the best location, but you'll always lose money if you buy the most expensive property in a lousy location. Most importantly, you must identify an area that has economic growth potential.

Everything we do in life is a risk. I don't care what you do. Walking out the front door is a risk. Putting your money in the bank is a risk. Speculating in the stock market is a risk. But the odds of investing in real estate the way I have outlined are a great deal better than the odds of winning the lottery.

The thing you should never do is overextend yourself. You have to take a chance, but you have to take a chance that's in your favor. The risk you take should be commensurate with the return, but taking a risk doesn't mean putting everything on the line.

American financier and statesman Bernard Baruch used to say that a guy is rich if he has a dollar more than he needs. In real estate, success comes to those who make smart decisions, are willing to take a certain amount of risk, and have lots of patience.

I felt like I was starting to accomplish my objective of increasing my net worth through real estate after I had acquired five buildings on the oceanfront, which was about five years after I started my real estate investment program. I felt that I was on the road to financial success. It probably took me a few more years to realize my first significant positive cash flow, however, at that point, I felt I was accomplishing something. I was building an estate, creating some wealth. That gave me incentive to continue investing.

When I first started, I bought everything I could with the money I had. I knew that after prices went out of sight, I would not be able to afford to buy any more and would have to concentrate on improving my existing properties. Some people hold a ceremony where they burn their paid-off mortgage. Whenever I pay off debt, I immediately think about new possibilities. It frees me up to start thinking about making other investments. Opportunities do not come in real estate if you stop buying.

Patience Is a Virtue

A lot of people are easily upset because they can't see the end result when they embark on a project. But you can't think about real estate that way. If you own an apartment building, you may have to deal with a negative cash flow until the area improves. But it is important to maintain a positive attitude. There are always people who have a negative outlook rather than a positive way of seeing things. They hate getting up in the morning to go to work, they don't like their community, their city council, the way their kids are treating them, the smog, the congestion, the way Congress is acting.

My reply is: Change your attitude. There is no other solution. My mother had this way of only remembering the good things in life. She used to tell me it was too much trouble to remember all the terrible things, probably because there was so much of them. She regarded all the bad little things, especially gossip, as so much trivia that didn't do any good for anybody. The worst thing you can do is worry about things you have no control over. That will destroy you more than anything. If you can do something about the things that bother you, great, take action. Otherwise, why dwell on them?

With real estate, you've got to find property that fits your need, attitude, desire, and personality. If it isn't for you, don't meddle with it; it probably isn't worth fighting. I don't know too many people who would have bought in Hermosa Beach when I did in the early 1960s, when motorcycle gangs used to blare up and down the main street and rumble down the alleyway. Sometimes, they would stop outside my door at 3:00 a.m., open up the throttle, and rev their motors, driving me crazy.

Yet thousands of people who lived in this area during the 1940s and 1950s who sold their property in the 1960s wished they hadn't. That goes for so many areas across the country. I had a friend who owned a house on The Strand *in Hermosa Beach who tried to sell it in 1972 for $60,000. He did everything he could: advertised it, sat on it, and told people about it. Finally, he found a buyer. Today, that house is worth around $3 million. I talk to him all the time. Now he regrets selling. He said he needed the money at the time to help his kids, but his kids are in worse shape now than they were before.*

In real estate, you shouldn't sell just because the market is good. You have to look beyond the short term. I know if my friend had The Strand property now, he could borrow $1.5 million on it without any problem, as long as he had the income to support the loan. It's not easy to distinguish between today's reality and what a property will be worth 20 or 30 years from now, but this is the way you should start thinking about real estate.

A single mom I knew once wanted to sell her house. I told her that if she sold that house, she would never have another one; she would always be renting. No matter what her difficulties were, I told her she should hang on to it. She was divorced, living on her own. The fact that she didn't have enough income to qualify for a housing loan would have prevented her from buying another property. But I'm sure a broker came along a few years later and persuaded her otherwise.

Selling is tempting. It endows you with a bundle of cash to pay off your bills, buy a new Ferrari, yacht, RV, or whatever. But you're really in worse shape when you sell property for that reason. I always hate to see that happen to families because it's always so hard for the kids. They have to move into a rented apartment or house and never experience from their parents the stability and security that ownership provides.

If you locate a true growth area, prices will rise rather dramatically, so if you sell today for $120,000 and over a few years prices increase to $265,000, you're going to have a hard time qualifying for a new loan, unless you've hit a jackpot in the meantime. Rents will rise in proportion to land values, so it's much better to hold on to property than sell.

When I moved to Hermosa Beach, every Halloween there were hundreds and hundreds of kids who walked up and down The Strand. It was fantastic. Last year, there wasn't one trick-or-treater. The spiraling price of real estate has taken young families out of the market. It's sad, really. But it's also a firm indication of what the trends are in the community.

I'm amazed at the number of people who come up to me and say, "The price of that lot over there is $1 million. How can that possibly go up? How can it get any higher? That place used to sell for $20,000." And I say to them, "It hasn't even started to go up yet. You're dreaming. You're talking about five-cent beer." Do you think the real estate market will ever revert to former levels, that housing prices will start going down instead of up? That's like saying the horse and buggy will one day replace the automobile. Prices may fluctuate from time to time, but I don't foresee any drastic downturn.

For genuine perspective, you should travel to other parts of the world, if you ever have the opportunity, and see what houses are selling for in major metropolitan areas. Try pricing real estate in central Tokyo, where a three-bedroom house sells for about $12 million or more. There isn't any major city in the world in a desirable area where the prices aren't out of sight: London, Paris, Tokyo, Hong Kong, Geneva.

In the United States, look at Houston, Dallas, Phoenix, Seattle, or Portland compared to Los Angeles or New York. Prices are rising in these areas, but I'd have to have a reason to go to one of these cities and invest. If you have studied the community and are correct in your analysis and buy real estate for the long haul following the principles of the buy-and-hold strategy, you're going to get rich. I know you are.

Out-of-Area Investing

The aforementioned high-growth regions will continue to be great areas in which to invest far into the twenty-first century. People in this country will continue to move south and west from the Rust Belt to the booming Sun Belt in search of jobs and opportunity.

But if you don't live in these areas, watch out. You won't be there to make sure they rent to the right people, see if workmen show up on time or notice changes in the economic/political climate that will affect the long-term viability of your investment.

I've had mixed success with having out-of-area property managers watch my houses, collect the rents and manage the relationships with the tenants they put in there. Some property managers have even stolen from me.

If you are bound and determined to invest in an area not close by, the best way to do it is to have a partner who is on the ground and familiar with the neighborhood. Work out a deal with him wherein he gets part of the upside and some of the cash flow. This partner should manage the property and have an equity interest in the real estate. A partner with an ownership interest is more likely to:

1. Take care of the property
2. Put in tenants who will not tear up the property
3. Make sure the rents get paid on time since they are part of his income
4. Be on the alert for any adverse changes in the area

In short, if he screws up, he hurts himself.

The Impact of the National Debt on Long-Term Real Estate Investing, Interest Rates and Other Considerations

It is important to talk about these rapidly changing times; it is even more vital to talk about the government's handling of small business-people such as us—long-term buy-and-hold investors. We are affected by the vagaries of the economy on all levels. Every layer of government, from the federal tax code down to a local city council's decision to grant a zoning variance, affects your real estate. Your assets are fixed in place; every bureaucratic decision can have a lasting impact.

The ballooning national debt is heading towards $13 trillion and higher, which might seem like a large number to owe our debtors both foreign and domestic. A trillion here, a trillion there—as someone famous once said, soon you are talking about real money.

Historically, America's budget deficit has averaged about 6% to 7% of our gross domestic product (GDP). During WWII, the GDP/deficit level was closer to 14%. We had to take on massive debt to pay for the war, which was promptly paid back to the 85 million Americans who financed the war effort.

Our budget deficit in 2010 now averages 13% of GDP. That's not good. It's not so much what you owe; it's more about how are you going to pay it back and when. If our deficit-to-GDP ratio stays above the historical norm, the government can only finance the shortage in four ways:

1. Raise taxes to increase government revenue
2. Borrow more from the credit markets
3. Print more money and inflate the currency
4. Stimulate growth so there is more economic activity to tax

Each scenario requires a different strategy. As long-term real estate investors, we are affected and there are things to do to ameliorate the impact.

When Taxes Go Up

First off, as a small business owner you get write-offs—anything that has to do with the maintenance, management, acquisition and holding of your real estate can be deducted off your tax returns. The deductions of depreciation include travel to your properties, magazines, property interest, taxes, buying and selling expenses. Of course, check with your tax professional and see how this affects your individual situation.

I don't mind paying taxes, but it can get ridiculous. One time I had the city of San Bernardino impose a fee of a hundred dollars a year per property for a business license. Per property? Seems a bit onerous.

The county also charged me a hundred dollars a year to inspect my properties, to make sure the neighborhoods did not deteriorate. A fee here, a fee there and pretty soon you are talking about real money. These fee increases get passed on to the renters. Tax increases are ultimately inflationary as costs always get passed on down to your consumer—the renter.

But when you *own*, it's a lot different. Some say that real estate is the last great tax deduction for the common man, and I agree. There is nothing like being able to shield other income through the favorable tax treatment the IRS code gives us.

Too Much Debt

The United States is by far the world's biggest debtor. It is the big indebted gorilla in the room that everybody dances around. Nobody knows how long the US can continue taking on copious amounts of debt before Uncle Sam will have to raise interest rates. Higher interest rates are inflationary, devalue the currency and can spiral out of control. Rents rise and property values increase during times of inflation—at least, most of the time. It is supposed to work where inflation brings growth and jobs, and as the economy recedes there is job loss.

Too much debt can exacerbate inflation with a whole bunch of unintended consequences. Job losses coupled with high interest rates are stagflationary. The late 1970s was the last time this happened, and it was tough on real estate investors. Financing was hard to raise and rents were falling, as were property values.

Location remains of paramount importance. If people all around you are losing their jobs, buy-and-hold investors will suffer lower rents and vacancies. That is why I buy only in areas of high demand; well-located properties close to freeways and work centers rent first and stay full the most during hard times.

The wise real estate investor fixes the cost of his debt and doesn't take on too much of it. Out of the many bank loans I have taken on, all but two are fixed for 30 years. In rising interest rate times, fixing the cost of your debt is wise.

Too Much Money

The M1 money supply grew by about 120% in 2008. In response to the financial meltdown in that year, the Federal Reserve Bank reported that the money supply went up by a factor of 12 after 50 years of nominal 5 to 12% growth in our money supply.

Basically, that's a lot of money sloshing around, and it will kill the value of the US dollar if the Federal Reserve Bank doesn't remove all those dollars from circulation. A devalued currency is never good for the real estate investor. It makes foreign goods—cars, electronics, clothes and machinery—more expensive, leaving the renter less money to pay rent.

The economy suffers when foreigners don't invest their money over here. If our currency suffers and becomes unstable, then investors lose money because they have to cash out of their investments in cheaper dollars.

You hope the government sees this long-term devaluation of the US dollar as not good for anybody.

The best protection is having your properties in desirable locations close to where jobs cluster. Areas that have been economically vibrant in the past should remain so.

Stimulating Economic Growth

This is a win-win for the real estate investor. More jobs mean more people moving to the area, more renters, and rent increases. Rents go up in areas of economic vibrancy, especially where attractive rental properties are scarce.

Most of my renters work in or own small businesses. By some measures, 120 million Americans work for companies employing less than 100 people.

Tax revenues the US government receives have increased since 1980, when we had a $5-trillion GDP. Small firms have contributed 80% of all job growth since 1969, and they pay taxes. Wouldn't the best way to overcome economic stagnation be to stimulate small businesses?

I love Southern California's history of small business creation, which is one of the chief reasons why I invest there. From 2000 to 2006, by some estimates 95% of all job creation in areas where I own property came from small businesses.

Summary

I hope you see that the attitudes of the powers that be have direct effects on how your real estate does. Higher taxes drive inflation. The higher cost of doing business gets passed on to your consumer, the renter. Some inflation is good, but spiraling-out-of-control inflation destroys jobs and makes small-business creation difficult.

Buy-and-hold investors can become targets for municipalities starved for tax revenue. If that local government is not business friendly, then the real estate investor suffers from job scarcity. Where will your renters work?

But in the end, you will win when you buy well-located property in high-demand areas. The appreciation you get will be amazing. Cash flow will do nothing but go up. As the area in which you invest prospers, so will you.

19

The Alameda Corridor and Its Future Impact on California and the Nation

After 20 years of planning and five years of construction, the 20 mile railroad, which opened in April 2002, has and will continue to significantly affect both Southern California and the nation for decades to come.

During the late 1800s early 1900s, New York became one of the greatest cities in the world due primarily to trade and the sudden influx of ships into New York harbor. New York became the hub of the world mainly due to commerce from Europe. As trade increased, many cities in the eastern and southern Unites States became very prominent, especially cities of the New England States and Louisiana Territory. As the development of America spread westward, trade became larger and larger and boomed into tremendous activity. As a result, real estate flourished in New York. The George Washington Bridge was built and skyscrapers towered toward the heavens.

The cost of living there has always been more expensive than on the West Coast, but the West Coast will have its turn. The Pacific Rim countries are much larger and more dramatic than what Europe was at the turn of the century. Trade will be so monumental and the economy will be unparalleled compared to what happened on the Eastern Seaboard. This will have a dramatic effect on real estate. Unless the density requirements are changed by local authorities, we will not see high-rise structures along the West Coast in the same density as the East Coast.

These ports of Long Beach and Los Angeles are the largest and second-largest ports in the country; combined they are the fifth-largest port complex in the world.

The Alameda Corridor is already playing a major role in this gigantic trade influx. This new railroad connects the transcontinental rail yards near downtown Los Angeles to the ports of Los Angeles and Long Beach along Alameda Street via a series of bridges, street improvements, underpasses and overpasses. The corridor passes through Wilmington, Rancho

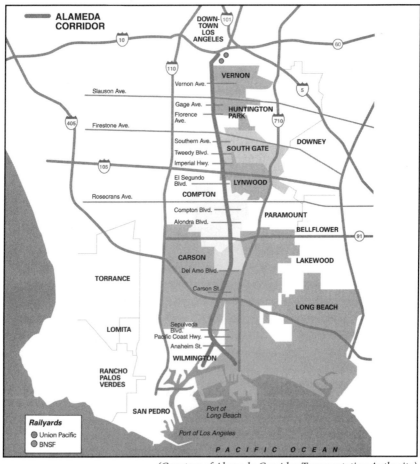

(Courtesy of Alameda Corridor Transportation Authority)

Dominguez, Carson, Compton, Lynwood, South Gate, Huntington Park and Vernon. It accommodates rail traffic for both the Burlington Northern Santa Fe Railway and Union Pacific Railroads, utilizing three rail tracks. Approximately 90 miles of rail branch has been consolidated into one high-speed 20-mile corridor.

The signature Mid-Corridor section trench is approximately 50 feet wide and 31 feet deep and makes up 10 miles of the 20-mile Alameda Corridor. This below grade section required the construction of approximately 27,000 cast-in-drilled-hole piles 36 and 48 inches in diameter, 30 new bridges and over 900,000 cubic yards of concrete for trench walls, retaining walls, and miscellaneous construction. Rail traffic descends into the underground section just north of the SR91 freeway and travels parallel to Alameda Street, where it returns to street grade near 25th Street in Los Angeles. This shift of rail traffic from street grade to below street level has significantly increased public safety by decreasing traffic congestion.

(Courtesy of Alameda Corridor Transportation Authority)

The mid-corridor facilitates rail traffic at average speeds of 30 to 40 mph, compared to 10 to 15 miles per hour on traditional at-grade branch lines. Cargo and containers leaving the ports now reach downtown Los Angeles in approximately 45 minutes, compared to two hours prior to completion of the project.

Funding came from loans, payments and grants through the US Department of Transportation, Port of Los Angeles, Port of Long Beach and from Los Angeles County Metropolitan Transportation Authority. These amounts totaled approximately $1.55 billion. Another $130 million was drawn upon from other sources. A large share of the funding was provided by $1.16 billion in revenue bonds that are to be paid back over 35 years with railroad user fees.

In order to tap into the $1.16 billion in bonds, officials had to understand the value of the work. This is where the authority- Alameda Corridor, had to get creative.

> The conventional multi-contract strategy left the governing board in a dilemma, as construction costs would not be known for almost two years while waiting for project design and public bid solicitations. This is when a different construction process was evaluated.

The decision to utilize the design-build process was made easier as the project value was guaranteed at the outset where construction could start before the final design on the entire project was complete. Risk for cost over-runs, schedule difficulties and overall excess construction costs was passed down to the selected design-build contractor. But the final result was an on time, on budget, completed project.

As with all projects of this magnitude, there were some 289 parcels of land acquired for about $55 million by negotiation or eminent domain during the acquisition of the Alameda Corridor Right of Way. Eminent domain is when the public has a right to use private land for a public purpose, regardless of what the property owner may think. After the land parcels were acquired, the Alameda Corridor Authority decided which buildings would remain for public use and which would be demolished. Property owners were justly compensated. For example, if a county or city decides to widen a street, they have the right of eminent domain whereby they can acquire property and compensate the property owner at fair market value. The same was true for construction of the Alameda Corridor project. If the property owner is dissatisfied with the Appraisal, the acquiring authority does everything in its power to settle amicably with the property owner. In the event a settlement is not reached, then the Court decides the value.

(Courtesy of Alameda Corridor Transportation Authority)

The Los Angeles and Long Beach harbors are now the fifth-busiest port complex in the world after Hong Kong, Singapore and some Chinese ports.

It is anticipated that $88 billion in annual regional economic activity will be generated, making southern California a leader in international trade. Already, approximately one-fourth of all cargo entering the USA by sea arrives through the ports of Los Angeles and Long Beach. One person out of every 15 in Southern California is connected—through their work or otherwise—to international trade. By 2020, Los Angeles and Long Beach harbors will handle an estimated 36 million containers of ocean freight annually, over three times today's volumes. Prior to the construction of the Alameda Corridor, approximately 35 trains traveled along Alameda Street daily. This corridor can now accommodate over 150 trains per day. The development of the corridor is monumental and should have a positive impact on real estate values both in southern California and other affected regions. Over 10,000 new jobs were created during construction. Approximately 3,000 manufacturing, service and transportation jobs were generated to supply materials and equipment to the construction project.

> Other positive results from this project completion is the tremendous reduction in train emissions by about 28%, reduction of noise pollution by about 90%, and a greater-than-80% reduction in vehicles and trucks idling at railroad crossings.

The corridor has greatly enhanced the surrounding areas with new landscaping, the planting of many new trees, and the installation of new street lighting, generally enhancing the neighborhoods along the corridor.

Local authorities can only go in an upward direction as a result of the construction and continued container traffic through the area. To understand the impact that the Alameda Corridor had on the local economy, you have to understand the status of the local economy prior to the development of this large-scale project. The communities affected by the corridor were mixed industrial, commercial and residential areas with high unemployment rates. The Alameda Corridor project developed programs to utilize the local businesses and workforce, promoting economic growth and community development.

Knowledge of a proposed major project such as the Alameda Corridor is particularly beneficial to the real estate investor who has the opportunity to acquire real estate in and around such a project. This is where knowledgeable investors can gain significant financial gains. Be sure to read newspapers, check with local building departments and listen to the news so you can be ahead of the trend. If you think real estate values are high now, just imagine what prices of industrial, commercial and residential real estate will be like 20 years from now! The economic impact of the Alameda Corridor will be phenomenal. This is exactly the type of infrastructure that can give an area growth potential.

Update on the Alameda Corridor

The super rail-line system designed to move cargo from the ports inland and reduce truck traffic on local freeways reached a milestone recently, according to ProgressiveRailroading.com.

In 2008, the Alameda Corridor marked a six-digit milestone. The Los-Angeles-area intermodal corridor logged the one-hundred-thousandth train to use the high-speed freight-rail expressway since it opened in April 2002. The 20-mile corridor connects the ports of LA and Long Beach with downtown LA railyards and the national rail system. The Alameda Corridor Transportation Authority owns and governs the corridor, which includes a 10-mile, below-ground and triple-tracked mid-corridor trench shared by BNSF Railway Co. and Union Pacific Railroad via trackage rights.

Construction of the Schuyler Helm Bridge, beginning in October 2010, will replace an older, seismically deficient bridge over Cerritos Channel with a fixed-span bridge and add an elevated, four-lane highway that will bypass three congested intersections and five railroad crossings. The Helm Bridge is an essential service link for trucks between Terminal Island and the mainland.

An additional 5% to 8% of port-related trucks will be kept off area freeways and arterial streets and out of residential areas.

Southern California real estate values will benefit from the jobs this project will produce in the construction, trade and transportation, and import/export industries.

20

BONUS CHAPTER: Locating Your Investment for Success

We have talked about the economic backdrop wherein you place your real estate investment. It is wise to address the coming economies that will build wealth far into the twenty-first century.

Where should you buy in the twenty-first century? And within those hot cities, where will the entrepreneurs locate? What specific neighborhoods will do best?

Cities That Will Build Wealth Far Into the Twenty-First Century

I've always believed that demographics are destiny; you want to go where people are moving. For the last 30 years, Americans have been moving from the northern parts of the country to the South and the West. From the Rust Belt to the Sun Belt, Americans have been moving in great numbers. Here are the cities that are poised for monumental growth in the West:

1. Phoenix, AZ
2. Charlotte, NC
3. Raleigh-Durham-Chapel Hill, NC
4. Las Vegas, NV
5. Austin-San Marcos, TX

6. Memphis, TN
7. Nashville, TN
8. Austin-San Marcos, TX
9. San Antonio, TX

I own properties in some of the above areas. They are out of my geographic area, so it is not easy to manage them, but the robustness of the local economies has offset this substantial disadvantage.

In my area of Southern California, we have been growing for a long time. The area has become congested and very car-centric. With gasoline prices staying high and mass transit becoming more important to city planners, interest is growing in maglev trains—magnetically propelled trains that run along a monorail at up to 200 miles per hour. They will become incorporated in the infrastructures of more cities. DLA Piper, the nation's largest law firm, has agreed to help raise $20 billion for the Orangeline Development Authority. The project will connect Orange County and LA County through Cerritos, Downey, Bellflower, Paramount and other cities. So, neighborhoods that are close to the transit stops will be more valuable.

Also, the Port of Long Beach is considering a five-mile maglev link between the docks
and a West Long Beach railyard to move shipping containers and bulk cargo.

Electric trucks will be tried, too. Union Pacific plans an experiment with electric trucks at a site near the ports of LA and Long Beach.

The Best Neighborhoods of the Twenty-First Century

I really think that the more urban the neighborhood where your investment property is located, the better it will do. The closer your property is to the job centers and the freeways, the better you serve your ultimate customer—the tenant.

Be close to the twenty-first century's newest job centers in your town. Whole new industries are being created now. Buy your property close by to these job-creating areas if you can. If you get the chance to have your investment grow with the new jobs of the twenty-first century, how good is that?

No Boondock Areas

I think boondock properties located far outside of town, and the brand-new ex-urban areas where builders have erected housing, will take a long time for the commercial infrastructure to catch up. Renters must drive a long way to get to work, so well-located properties that are close by will remain in high demand.

Example: Victorville, California, is located in the high desert and is a long drive to the robust economy of the Inland Empire counties of Riverside and San Bernardino. Most residents commute a long way to work. When I had a vacancy during this last real estate downturn, I got a lot of calls from high-desert residents who would pay more rent just to be closer to work.

These long commute areas will always be harder to rent, will not get as much rent and will be the last to appreciate when the economy gets hot.

Smart Neighborhoods

Tenants want their kids to grow in an economy that is remaking itself. Whole new industries that require higher levels of education are being created—high tech, nanotech and biotech. Good neighborhoods near these job creators will become expensive and in high demand. Scarce and scarcity is what economics is all about, right?

Green energy is hot. Electricity production will be the leading green technology, the next big thing. Why is that important? The world's largest solar farm is being planned in California. The 80-MW San Joaquin Valley Customer Choice Solar Farm, which will be located near Fresno, will, at 640 acres, be 17 times the size of the current US title holder, the 4.6-MW Springerville Generating Station near Tucson, Arizona. It will also be approximately 7 times larger than the world's biggest existing plant and twice the size of the largest planned farm, both in Germany.

The Mojave Desert in Southern California will have a huge solar farm near Calico. There will be 34,000 solar dishes, each 40 feet high and 38 feet wide on 8,230 acres of the Mojave Desert.

The rush to develop alternative fuels will be the story of this century. In San Diego, jobs will be produced in an area nicknamed Biotech Beach. They are making biofuel out of pond scum. A growing community of investors and inventors believe that algae holds the potential to produce an affordable biofuel.

The mayor of San Diego said, "It's a critical industry, and it's kind of exploded. There's a long pattern of huge companies being spawned out of [UC San Diego] and our other research centers, and it's going to create a tremendous number of jobs." These are just some of changes will affect the nationwide.

Education Is of Paramount Importance

Good school districts are ever more important. Tenants want their kids to grow in an economy that is remaking itself. Whole new industries that require higher levels of education are being created—high tech, nanotech, and biotech.

Smart neighborhoods will be in high demand. For example, Irvine, California, where a lot of engineers live, has few vacancies. There is demand for housing there as well in Southern California's Inland Empire. The Rancho Cucamonga/Fontana area rents faster than the rest of the surrounding neighborhoods because of the Etiwanda School District.

The last time I had a vacancy there, I had parents climbing all over themselves to apply. One applicant said she would stay in a drafty barn in the middle of a field if it meant she could keep her kid in that school district, which has a long heritage of high school scores, above-average athletic programs and dedicated teachers. I am surprised that those houses don't go for more.

What Future Tenants Want

I have found that the more tenants feel like real homeowners, the longer they stay and the happier they are. Usually, well-located, pride-of-ownership neighborhoods are worth more, cost more and grow more in value. In the long term, the extra cost is worth it.

Think like a tenant: They want the same things you do. Who would not want a good job, to live where they feel safe and to raise their kids in a good school district? Their quality of life is enhanced by spending time around like-minded friends in the community and walking tree-lined streets in a peaceful, stable atmosphere. In short, the best neighborhoods of the twenty-first century will be like today's, only more energy efficient to ease the cost and more dependent on the commercial infrastructure to cut down on travel times and work in the new industries of the twenty-first century.

Ride the Multiplier Effect

All these new industries that create the high-paying jobs of the twenty-first century will have a multiplier effect.

In a study done for the auto industry, the US Chamber of Commerce estimates that a business with 100 manufacturing jobs will produce:

- 34.42 other manufacturing jobs
- 34.42 wholesale and/or retail jobs
- 45.89 service jobs

Total jobs created amounts to 236!

For every new employee created, they will need plumbers, maids, mechanics, home-improvement providers and the like to support him or her. Many of these service people will want to rent in areas close by and, ultimately, live in them. If you buy in these cheaper neighborhoods where the cash flow is better, your wealth creation will be monumental.

A Challenge for You

Buying and holding rental property in these neighborhoods of the future means your investment will grow with the economy. It has always been known that neighborhoods matter, but in the neighborhood of the future it will make a difference in new and powerful ways.

No matter what city you live in, you can find these hot spots of economic growth. Your job is to locate these beehives of prosperity and then buy next to them and hold for the long haul. The story of the twenty-first century will be one of unparalleled economic growth, much of it in industries that are not here yet.

That will be the story of the next hundred years. The only question is, how will you write your story?

21

Schumacher's Real Estate Axioms

- Manage your investments as you would manage a business.
- Some people are scared to have money.
- Man's greatest wealth is to live adequately with a contented mind.
- You don't get rich by making money. You get rich by wisely managing the money you make.
- If you're smart enough to have some money, you're smart enough to use it wisely.
- Attitude: the magic word.
- There's only one positive guarantee of security: a life term in Leavenworth maximum security prison.
- You can't move people out of the slums until you get the slums out of the people.
- When real estate is involved in a transaction, have it in writing.
- Enthusiasm makes the job easier.
- If you give a man money, he'll spend it in a day; if you teach him about real estate, he'll make money for a lifetime.
- The more you learn, the more you can earn.
- Everybody has a right to their opinion, but to make a good decision, you have to get your facts straight. Don't confuse an opinion with a fact.

- Not taking a risk may be the biggest risk of all.
- Debt is a wonderful discipline.
- Many people are afraid of the unknown. (It's mostly like the known, it just hasn't happened yet.)
- A grudge is better off dismissed.
- You want a location where people need, want, and have to be.
- A vacancy is a pleasure compared to a bad tenant.
- The old myth, "a new house is better than an old house" is not always true due to bad workmanship.
- Investing in real estate can be like a trip through the looking glass with Alice in Wonderland; if you don't know where you are going, it doesn't matter which way you turn.
- A sure way to fail is to do nothing.
- Experience is a better teacher than advice.
- Bogus advice has always been around. But advice that is bogus for one person might be good for someone else.
- You can only learn to do by doing.
- I never met anybody I didn't get a good idea from.
- Desire attracts opportunity, fear attracts failures.
- Great real estate deals are not found. They are created.
- Always correct mistakes as soon as possible.
- Finding a good real estate investment is only half the job; acting on it is the other half.
- Have a positive attitude when confronted with negative conditions.
- Opportunities do not come in real estate if you stop participating.
- Scarcity is what economics is all about.
- All you have to do is find one good bargain a year.
- If you think education is expensive, try ignorance.
- You can be rest assured that values will increase—a capitalistic economy is based on inflation.
- Today's market value of a piece of land is the present worth of future anticipated benefits.
- Don't make snap judgments if they can be avoided.
- To be successful in anything, you have to make the decisions—not your broker, attorney, or tax adviser.

- You have to like real estate or it's going to be a burden.
- If you can tell good advice from bad advice, you don't need any advice.
- When making a purchase, it's more important to consider economic obsolescence rather than functional obsolescence.
- If you can put up with tenants, you can make money.
- Get the best terms possible but don't miss a good deal by haggling over a few dollars.
- You must have a positive attitude when owning real estate.
- There's always a price at which a property is worth purchasing.
- For the right property, you can afford to pay top dollar.
- You don't learn anything when you are talking.
- The real estate investor does not buy his or her merchandise (property) like other businesspeople. The retail price of land today is its wholesale price in the future.
- Repetition is the mother of learning.
- There's no way in the world you can succeed without taking a chance. A turtle never gets anywhere until it sticks its neck out.
- Scores of books have been written on how to sell property, but the most important aspect of real estate is how to buy.
- There can be profit in confusion, depending on who is confused.
- A good buy will sell itself.
- The down payment and terms of sale are more important than the purchase price.
- Knowledge plus experience create results.
- Don't ever buy a piece of real estate without knowing the subject property's growth potential. Ask yourself what it will be worth in 20 years.
- Spend time studying neighborhood trends.
- We wish you a merry Christmas and an affordable New Year!
- Think back 20 years—"…if only I had held on to that property!"

- Nobody plans to fail, they just fail to plan.
- If you think it's hard to buy property now, just wait 10 or 20 years.
- Think and take plenty of time, before you ever spend a dime.
- The dips in the 20-year cycle are what take you for a ride, but the only way to get rich is to hold on for the long haul.
- "Luck" is when preparation meets opportunity.
- Don't get caught up in the trivial or let short-term adversities get you down.
- If you have an opportunity, take it; if you don't, create one.
- Residential property, including houses, apartments, and condominiums, is the smartest investment for the average investor because everyone knows something about housing.
- If you want to see the rainbow you must first endure the rain.
- Today's best investment is the single-family residence.
- When demand is high, severe restrictions from the city, such as zoning changes, will increase the value of existing property.
- In a densely populated area, downzoning a land parcel will help eliminate rental competition. That's why some of the best real estate buys are legal non-conforming buildings.
- Be sure not to buy a 22-unit motel when a Holiday Inn is being built two blocks down the street.
- If you can't afford to buy a large apartment building, buy a few smaller buildings in a clustered area that are easy to manage.
- Avoid the loss of income by performing a periodic rental analysis. Keep up with what is happening in the market and adjust the rents accordingly.
- You can never be too knowledgeable.
- Read the morning paper. Pay attention to news. Governmental actions, defense contracts, and economic conditions all affect real estate values.

- Keep abreast of how legislation in your city, county, state, and region will affect your real estate.
- Evaluate factors that affect economic strength and weakness. When you detect weakness, don't buy.
- If you can detect signs of an upturn, start to invest. Acquire as much as possible.
- When prices go so high you can no longer afford to buy, start putting money into fixing up your existing properties.
- You should look at real estate as a vehicle to accomplish an objective; a place to live, a source of retirement income, a tax shelter, or an estate to leave behind to your kids.
- Your objectives must be realistic and suit your abilities, interests, personality, and finances.
- You're bound to make money if you buy the least expensive property in the best location.
- Location is everything. When you buy property, you want to get a sweeping view, not a view of the sweepings!
- "Quality" is a key word in acquiring real estate; quality of the neighborhood, the construction, and the condition of the building.
- Don't be afraid of debt; what you owe today you'll be worth tomorrow.
- Buy real estate to fill a need.
- Treat your tenants as if they own the place; by paying the rent, they are buying the property for you.
- If you have a good tenant, do everything you can to keep him or her; it costs too much to rehabilitate wear and tear caused by people constantly moving in and out.
- Try to stay out of potential rent-control areas.
- An ideal location to get started is in an area with growth potential that has hit bottom and can't go anywhere but up.
- Sometimes it's cheaper to keep a tenant at a lower rent than to lose money on a vacancy and repairs.
- An economic depression can make a fool look like a wise man and a wise man look like a fool.

- The only difference between salad and garbage is timing.
- Wherever possible, enhance a property's value by rehabilitating it to a higher and better use.
- Save money by using your know-how to fix up and maintain your property.
- Don't spend money on property unless you can see the return in rent or better tenants.
- When you first start out, do all the work yourself to make as much profit as possible.
- Keep good records for cost control.
- Increase the value of your property by buying and improving the place next door, around the corner, and across the street.
- Most people don't know how to invest for the future. If you buy real estate in growth areas and let it ripen, no more decisions are necessary—just patience.
- Good credit is essential. Pay your bills two days before they are due. Always pay the plumber and the electrician on the spot.
- Never overextend yourself. If you are not able to control your finances, you are not able to control your destiny.
- The sooner you realize that there is no easy way to get rich, the better off you are going to be.
- Consult a competent real estate attorney and accountant on all important matters.
- You can sum up success in real estate in one word: Perseverance. If you don't make it the tenth time, try the eleventh.

Appendix A

The Appraisal Process
of a Single-Family Residence

This appendix contains a narrative single-family residential appraisal report outline. This format and outline is intended to be a guide to assist in understanding what an appraisal should contain and how the data and information may be presented to the client.

Single-Family Residential Appraisal
Report Outline
(Title Page)

Fair Market Value Appraisal
Of A Single-Family Residence

For
(Name of Client)

Located at
(Address of Property)

Value Estimated
As Of
(Date of Value)

Appraised By
(Name and Address
of Appraiser)

(Letter of Transmittal)

Appraiser's Name
and Address
Date (letter was written)

Client's Name
and Address

Gentlemen:

In accord with your request, I have prepared a fair market value appraisal of the fee ownership in land and Improvements of a single-family residence located at

(Address of Property)*

Based on the data and conclusions set forth in the detailed report of _____ pages and exhibits which follow, in my opinion, the fair market value of the subject property as of (date of value estimate) is in the sum of:

_____ Thousand Dollars

Descriptions of the property appraised, together with explanation of appraisal procedures used, are set forth in this report.

The opinion as to value expressed in this appraisal is contingent upon the limiting conditions as set forth as the beginning of this appraisal report.

Respectfully submitted,
(Signature of Appraiser)

*Use legal description if street address does not properly identify the property.

APPRAISAL TABLE OF CONTENTS

Summary of Important Facts and Conclusions

Statement of Limiting Conditions

Photograph of Subject Property

Site Plan

Construction Floor Plan

Identification of the Property

Purpose of the Appraisal

Definition of Fair Market Value

Approaches Considered in Valuing the Property
    Cost Approach
    Market Approach
    Income Approach

Date of Value Estimate

Property Rights Appraised

Trends Affecting Value of Subject Property
    Nation
    Region
    Metropolitan Area
    Community
    Neighborhood

Land or Site Data
    Legal Description
    Zoning

Restrictions

Easements

Highest and Best Use

Real Property Tax Date
    Assessed Values
    Tax Rate
    Current Real Property Taxes
    Trend of Future Taxes

Physical Factors Affecting Site
    Frontage
    Shape
    Area
    Topography and Soil Conditions
    Landscaping
    Available Utilities

Relationship of Site to Surrounding Area
    Corner Influence
    Rear or Side Alley Influence
    Detrimental Influences
    Advantageous Influences
    Street

Description of the Construction
    Residence
    Garage
    Yard Improvements
    Discussions of Construction

Cost Approach
    Land Value
    Land Sales Analysis
    Discussion of Land Sales
    Correlation of Land Values
    Land Value Estimate

Construction Value
    Replacement Cost
    Depreciation
        Physical Deterioration
        Functional Obsolescence
        Economic Obsolescence

Cost Approach Value Estimate

Market Data Approach
    Comparable Sales Analysis
    Discussion of Comparable Sales
    Correlation of Comparable Sales
    Market Data Approach Value Estimate

Income Approach
    Subject Property's Monthly Rental
    Gross Rent Multipliers
        Analysis of Gross Rent Multipliers
        Correlation of Gross Rent Multiplier
        Calculation of Value Estimate
        Income Approach Value Estimate

Correlation of the Value Estimates

Fair Market Value

Certification of the Appraisal

ADDENDA

City Map (Indicating Subject Property)

Neighborhood Map Showing Land Sales
    and Comparable (Whole Property) Sales

Land Sales Data

Construction Data

Construction Cost Analysis (Square Foot Appraisal Form)

Comparable Sales Data

Include:
>Plot plans, maps, pictures, charts, statistical
and factual data pertinent to the value estimate
and necessary as supporting evidence which is
not included in the body of the report.

Appraiser's Qualifications

Summary of Important Facts and Conclusions

Purpose of Appraisal: (Form and opinion of fair market value)
Subject Property Location: (Address)
Land Data: Lot Size _____
              Zoning _____

Improvements (Describe very briefly. Include size, quality
of construction, condition, age, etc.)

Values Indicated by the:

Cost Approach
      Replacement Cost of Improvements $_____
      Total Accrued Depreciation $_____
      Indicated Value of Improvements $_____

Land Value $_____
      Total Indicated Value by
      the Cost Approach $_____

Market Data Approach
      Value Indicated by
      Market Data Approach $_____

Income Approach
      Gross Rent
      Multiplier $_____
      Estimated Monthly
      Rental of Subject
      Property $_____
      Value Indicated by the
      Income Approach $_____

Final Conclusion of Fair Market Value $_____
Date of Value Conclusion _____

STATEMENT OF LIMITING CONDITIONS

1. All facts and data set forth in this report are true and accurate to the best of your appraiser's knowledge and belief.
2. Your appraiser has made a personal inspection of the property appraised.
3. Your appraiser has no present or contemplated financial interest in the property appraised.
4. The fee for this appraisal report is not contingent upon the values reported.
5. No land survey has been made by your appraiser. Land dimensions given in this report are taken from available records and your appraiser assumes no responsibility for the accuracy of such land dimensions.
6. No investigation of legal fee or title to the property has been made and owner's claim to the property has been assumed to be valid. No consideration has been given to liens or encumbrances which may be against the property.

```
+-------------------------------------------------+
|          Photograph of Subject Property         |
|    (Front view; other photos may be included)   |
+-------------------------------------------------+
```

```
+-------------------------------------------------+
|                    Site Plan                    |
|      (Draw lot to scale, showing dimensions as  |
|   well as street, alley, distance to corner, etc.) |
+-------------------------------------------------+
```

```
+-------------------------------------------------+
|                Construction Plan                |
|        (Draw exterior plan of buildings and     |
|             improvements to scale)              |
+-------------------------------------------------+
```

```
+-------------------------------------------------+
|                   Floor Plan                    |
+-------------------------------------------------+
```

Date of Photographs _____

IDENTIFICATION OF THE PROPERTY

The property appraised in this report consists of the land and improvements of the single-family residence property located at _____.

PURPOSE OF THE APPRAISAL

This appraisal was prepared for the purposes of forming an opinion as to the fair market value of the subject residential property under conditions prevailing as of the date of this appraisal.

DEFINITION OF FAIR MARKET VALUE

The value estimated in this appraisal is the fair market value of the subject property. Fair market value for purposes of this appraisal is defined as follows:

> "The highest price estimated in terms of money which a property will bring if exposed for sale in the open market allowing a reasonable time to find a purchaser who buys with the knowledge of all the uses for which it is capable of being used, neither buyer nor seller being compelled to act."

The definition of fair market value is sometimes interpreted as:

The price at which a willing seller would sell and a willing buyer would buy, neither being under abnormal pressure to act.

APPROACHES CONSIDERED IN VALUING THE PROPERTY

The fair market value of the subject property was estimated after giving due consideration to the following approaches to value as developed in the appraisal:

COST APPROACH: Land value, exclusive of improvements, is added to the depreciated replacement cost of the residential construction to give an indication of the value of the subject property by the cost approach.

MARKET DATA APPROACH: Sales of similar residential properties in the neighborhood were analyzed and used to form an opinion as to the value of the subject property by the market data approach.

INCOME APPROACH: The subject residences estimated monthly economic rent is multiplied by a gross rent multiplier to give an indication of the value of the subject property by the income approach.

DATE OF VALUE ESTIMATE
The fair market value as set forth in this appraisal report is as of _____ and is based upon conditions prevailing as of that date.

PROPERTY RIGHTS APPRAISED
The property rights appraised in this report consist of the fee ownership in the land and improvements.

TRENDS AFFECTING THE VALUE
OF THE SUBJECT PROPERTY

Nation   (A brief narrative discussion indicating how the present and probable future actions of the Federal Government will likely affect the market value of the subject property.)

Region   (A brief narrative discussion indicating how the present and probable future actions of the State Government will likely affect the market value of the subject property.)

Metropolitan Area (A brief narrative discussion indicating how the present and probable future actions of the County and/or City Government will likely affect the market value of the subject property.)

Community   (A brief narrative discussion indicating how the present and probable future actions of the Community will likely affect the market value of the subject property.)

Neighborhood   (A complete narrative description of the neighborhood including boundaries, physical, economic, social and government characteristics. The discussion should include the present and probable future trends in the neighborhood which will likely affect the market value of the subject property.)

LAND OR SITE DATA
LEGAL DESCRIPTION:

The land appraised in this report is legally described as:

(Complete legal description including Lot, Tract, Book, Page, County, State.)

ZONING: (Discuss present and probable future zoning if a probability exists. Describe permitted uses.)

RESTRICTIONS: (Discuss public and private restrictions which presently exist on the property and the probability of future changes.)

EASEMENTS: (Discuss any easements affecting the site and their effect upon the value of the property.)

HIGHEST AND BEST USE: (Briefly discuss the present use and indicated trends toward other uses, if any). Make a definite statement as to the highest and best use of site (considering existing zoning) and give your reasons for your opinion.

REAL PROPERTY TAX DATA:
Assessed Values: The 20____ and 20____ assessed value of land and improvements is as follows:

Land	$_____
Improvements	$_____
Total	$_____

Tax Rate: The real property tax rate for this area is _____ per $100 of assessed valuation.

Current Real Property Taxes: The current real property taxes for the subject property are: $_____
　　Trend of Future Taxes: (Discuss the future trends of real property taxes and their likely effect on real estate values.)

PHYSICAL FACTORS AFFECTING THE SITE:

Frontage: The subject site has _____ feet frontage on _____ (Avenue).

Shape: The subject site is _____ shape with an average width of _____ feet and depth of _____ feet.

Area: The subject site comprises approximately _____ (square feet/acres).

Topography and Soil Conditions: (Briefly discuss the topography and contour of the site. Also discuss the type of soil and the possible and probable effect of erosion and drainage.)

Landscaping: (Discuss the landscaping which exists on the subject site.)

Available Utilities: The subject site has the following utilities available and connected (domestic water, electricity, sanitary sewer, natural gas, telephone).

RELATIONSHIP OF SITE TO SURROUNDING AREA:

Corner Influence: (if any)

Rear of Side Alley Influence: (if any)

Detrimental Influences: (Is site adjacent to commercial, industrial, multiple income, school, church, etc.? Discuss their effect upon the value of the subject site.)

Advantageous Influences: (Discuss desirable factors affecting the site such as view, proximity to park, etc.)

Street: (Discuss the width of the street, the type of street surface, curbs and sidewalks, if any, the type of lighting, and the location of the nearest fire hydrant. Also discuss the traffic pattern and its effect on the site.)

DESCRIPTION OF THE CONSTRUCTION

RESIDENCE: (Briefly describe the important features of the residence.)
Example: This is a one and part two story structure containing 1950 Square feet of livable floor area and 320 square feet of porch area. The residence has three bedrooms and two baths. It is a wood frame with stucco exterior, gabled type roof with wood shingles. The construction was completed in 1990. The structure is of good quality workmanship and in average condition.

GARAGE: (Briefly describe the important features of the garage.)
Example: This is a two-car (detached) garage containing 400 square feet of floor area. It is similar in construction and appearance to the subject residence.

YARD IMPROVEMENTS: (Briefly describe the important features of the yard improvements.)
Example: Yard improvements consist of concrete driveway and walkway, brick planter, concrete block and wood fencing, brick barbecue, lawn sprinklers, landscaping.

DISCUSSION OF CONSTRUCTION: Details of the construction, together with my estimate of the present replacement cost new, is set forth in the addenda. (NOTE: The above statement should appear in the report and a detailed description of the residence, garage and yard improvements should appear in the addenda. All cost information should also appear in the addenda.)

COST APPROACH: The value estimate developed by the cost approach considers the replacement cost of the construction, less depreciation from causes added to the value of the land. The land value is as if vacant and ready for development to its highest and best use.

LAND VALUE: The appraised value of the land is based upon:

1. Sales of similar sites in the area.
2. Interviews with active real estate brokers and knowledgeable property owners in the area.
3. Consultation with other informed sources in the area such as banks, lending agencies, etc.

LAND SALES ANALYSIS: Sales which are considered as an indication of the subject property land value are summarized on the following page. More complete information regarding each sale may be found in the addenda of this report.

(NOTE: The above statement should appear in the report, and a detailed description of each comparable land sale used should appear in the addenda of the report.)

Correlation of Land Sales: (Discuss in narrative form your estimate of market value of the subject land parcel and the reasons for arriving at the value.)

Land Value Estimate: Based on the foregoing factors and after consideration of the present and probable future highest and best use of the site, in my opinion, the fair market value of the subject land, exclusive of all improvements, is the sum of $_____.

CONSTRUCTION VALUE: An analysis of the structure was prepared. Detailed information pertaining to the construction, together with replacement costs may be found in the addenda of this report.

Replacement Cost: The replacement cost of all construction described in the addenda is as follows:

House	$_____
Garage	$_____
Yard Improvements	$_____
Total Replacement Cost	$_____

Depreciation: Depreciation from all causes is deducted from the total replacement cost to develop the depreciated replacement cost of the construction.

Depreciation factors considered are as follows (Discuss how the subject improvements are by each type of appreciation. Assign a dollar amount for each depreciation category. Values must be justified):

Physical Deterioration (Curable and Incurable): _____

Functional Obsolescence (Curable and Incurable): _____

Economic Obsolescence: _____

A summary of the depreciation factors, together with my estimate of the Depreciated Replacement Cost of the improvements is as follows:

Total Replacement Cost	$_____
Depreciation	
Physical Deterioration	$_____
Functional Obsolescence	$_____
Economic Obsolescence	$_____
Total Depreciation	$_____
Replacement Cost less	
Depreciation of Construction	$_____
Round Figure	$_____

Cost Approach Value Estimate: Based on the conclusions as set forth above the value estimate as indicated by the Cost Approach is as follows:

Land Value	$_____
Construction Value	$_____
Total Indicated Value by	
Cost Approach	$_____

MARKET DATA APPROACH

The value estimate developed by the market data approach considers comparing single-family residential properties which have sold and are of a comparable nature to this subject residence.

Your appraiser has gathered other information pertaining to single-family residential values from active real estate brokers in the vicinity of the subject property as well as knowledgeable property owners, officials in banks and other lending institutions active in the subject area.

Comparable Sales Analysis: Sales which are considered to be an indication of value of the subject property are summarized on the following page. More complete information regarding each sale may be found in the addenda of this report.

(NOTE: The above statements should appear in the report and a detailed description of each comparable whole property sale used should appear in the Addenda of the report. Please see the sample sheet in Addenda indicating the suggested information for each sale).

Summary of Comparable Whole Property Sales
(Percentage or dollar adjustments
are made for each varying characteristic.)

DISCUSSION OF COMPARABLE SALES:
(Discuss each comparable sale in relation to the subject property. It is necessary to justify the basis for arriving at the adjustments used in the analysis.)

A	B	C	D	E	F

NOTE:
The characteristics of each comparable sale is related to the subject property. Percentage or dollar adjustments are made to compensate for the variations. When making adjustments, be consistent in applying value differences.

CORRELATION OF COMPARABLE SALES: (Discuss in narrative form your estimate of the market value of the subject property by the market data approach. Give your reasons for arriving at the value.)

MARKET DATA APPROACH VALUE ESTIMATE: Based on the conclusions as set forth above, the value estimate as indicated by the Market Data Approach is in the sum of:

$_____

INCOME APPROACH
The value estimate developed by the Income Approach considers analyzing the subject residential property's economic monthly rental and relating it to a gross rent multiplier. The multiplier is derived from an analysis of several similar type single-family residential property sales where the monthly rental of each sale property is known.

SUBJECT PROPERTY'S MONTHLY RENTAL: If the subject property were offered for rent (unfurnished) on the open market for a reasonable length of time, your appraiser is of the opinion that an informed person would rent the premises for

$_____ Per Month (Economic Rent)

Rental Property	Monthly Rental	Size and Floor Plan	Advantageous or Detrimental Influences	Indicated Rent for Subject Property
I II III IV V	NOTE: Each rental property is adjusted to reflect the economic rent of the subject residence.			

The basis for my estimate of the subject property's economic rent is derived from an inspection and analysis of the following residences which are tenant-occupied and the rental is known.

Analysis of Gross Rent Multiplier

Address of Sale Property	Sale Price	Actual Rent Per Month (Unfurnished)	Gross Rent Multiplier
(1) (2) (3) (4) (5)		NOTE: The gross rent multiplier is obtained by dividing the actual monthly rental into the sale price of each property.	

GROSS RENT MULTIPLIER: An analysis of single-family residential transactions in the neighborhood of the subject property reveals that a number of properties which sold were rented at the time of sale. This information is used in analyzing the gross rent multiplier for the neighborhood, as follows:

Correlation of Gross Rent Multiplier: (Discuss in narrative form your estimate of the gross rent multiplier for the subject neighborhood. Give your reasons for arriving at the figure.)

Calculation of Value Estimate: The value estimate developed by the income approach is calculated as follows:

Subject property's monthly rental times the gross rent multiplier Indicated value of subject property by the income approach

Income Approach Value Estimate: Based on the conclusions as set forth above the value estimate as indicated by the
Income Approach is $_____

CORRELATION OF THE VALUE ESTIMATES

The value estimates developed by the appraisal procedures used are:

Cost Approach Value Estimate $_____

Market Data Approach Value Estimate $_____
Income Approach Value Estimate $_____

(Discuss in narrative form the merits and adversities of each approach. Explain any wide discrepancies which might exist between approaches. State your final estimate of market value and give reasons for your conclusion.)

FAIR MARKET VALUE

Based on the data and conclusions as set forth in this appraisal, in my opinion, the fair market value of the subject property, if offered for sale on the open market, allowing a reasonable time to find a purchaser, under the conditions prevailing as of the date of this appraisal is the sum of

_____ Thousand Dollars

$_____

CERTIFICATION OF THE APPRAISAL

I hereby certify that I have no interest, present or contemplated, in the subject property and that neither the employment to make this appraisal, nor the compensation, is contingent on the value of the property. I certify that I have personally inspected the property and that, according to my knowledge and belief, all statements and information in this report are true and correct, subject to the underlying assumptions and contingent conditions.

Based upon the information contained in this report and upon my general experience as an appraiser, it is my opinion that the Fair Market Value as defined herein of the subject residential property as of (Date of Value) is in the sum of:

_____ Dollars.

_____
(Signature of Appraiser)

ADDENDA

(Include one or more pages for each of the following:)

City Map (Indicate subject property)

Neighborhood Map showing land sales and comparable (whole property) sales in relation to subject property.

Land Sales Data

Construction Data

Square Foot Appraisal Form

Comparable Sales Data

Other items which might be included in the addenda, which are necessary to support the value estimate and are not included in the body of the report are:

> Plot Plans
> Maps
> Pictures - Subject Property and Comparable Sales
> Charts
> Statistical and Factual Data

Appraiser's Qualifications (a concise statement generally in outline form)

Land Sales Data

Sale Identification

Sale Price $ _____

Grantor _____

Address _____

Grantee _____

Address _____

Assessor's Identification:

    Book   Page   Parcel

_____ _____ _____

Address of Property _____

Legal Description _____

_____

_____

_____

_____

Land Size _____

Zoning _____

Improvements on Property at the

    Time of Sale _____

_____

Sale Confirmed by:

Name _____

Address _____

_____

Date of Confirmation _____

Remarks _____

_____

Recording Data

Date of Recording _____

Book _____   Page _____

Document No. _____

Date of Transaction _____

Revenue Stamps on Deed $___

Documentary Transfer Tax $___

Amount of Concurrent Deeds of
    Trust Recorded with this
    Document:

Amount   In Favor Of

_____   _____

Amount and Date of Deeds of
Trust Assumed by Grantee:

	Date	In
Amount	Recorded	Favor Of
___	___	___
___	___	___

Real Property Assessments

Year	Land	Improvements
___	___	___
___	___	___

Tax Rate

Year	Rate
___	___

[Note: This represents information for one comparable land sale. A separate page should be filled out for each comparable land sale.]

Construction Data

1. Basic Description:
   A. Type and Date of Construction
   B. Architectural Form
   C. Number of Rooms
2. Summary Square Foot Areas:
   A. Residence
      I. Ground Floor
      II. Second Floor
      III. Porches
      IV. Basement
   B. Garage
   C. Other Structures
3. General Condition and Estimate of Remaining Economic Life:
4. Exterior Description:
   A. Foundation and Substructure
   B. Exterior Treatment
   C. Roof Design and Cover
   D. Porches
5. Interior Description:
   (Room Descriptions)
   A. Space Allotment
   B. Floor, Walls and Ceiling Finish
   C. Built-ins and Fixtures
6. Mechanical Equipment
   A. Heating and Air Conditioning
   B. Electrical
   C. Plumbing
7. Yard Improvements:
   A. Fence
   B. Paving
   C. Landscaping
   D. Miscellaneous

Comparable Sales Data

Land Sales Data

Sale Identification

Sale Price $ _____

Grantor _____

Address _____

Grantee _____

Address _____

Assessor's Identification:

    Book   Page   Parcel

_____ _____ _____

Address of Property _____

Legal Description _____

_____

_____

_____

Land Size _____

Zoning _____

Improvements on Property at the
    Time of Sale _____

_____

Sale Confirmed by:

Name _____

Address _____

Date of Confirmation _____

Remarks _____

Recording Data

Date of Recording _____

Book _____ Page _____

Document No. _____

Date of Transaction _____

Revenue Stamps on Deed $_____

Documentary Transfer Tax $_____

Amount of Concurrent Deeds of
    Trust Recorded with this
    Document:

Amount	In Favor Of
_____	_____
	_____

Amount and Date of Deeds of
Trust Assumed by Grantee:

Amount	Date Recorded	In Favor Of
_____	_____	_____

Real Property Assessments

Year	Land	Improvements
_____	_____	_____
_____	_____	_____

Tax Rate

Year	Rate
_____	_____

[Note: This represents information for one comparable land sale. A separate page should be filled out for each comparable land sale.]

Appendix B
Outline of Factors Influencing the Value of Residential Property

I. **The Nation:** The national economy and the actions of the federal government can have a profound effect on every usable piece of real estate in the nation.
   1. Population Growth
      a) Present trend
      b) Anticipated trend
   2. Fiscal Policies
      a) Federal spending
      b) Attitude toward taxation
   3. Cost of Government
      a) Increasing
      b) Decreasing
   4. Inflationary or Recessionary Trend
      a) Shortage or surplus of labor and materials
      b) The effect on housing
   5. Federal Participation in Housing
      a) Subsidized housing programs
      b) Insured mortgages
      c) Redevelopment plans
      d) Money supply

II. **The Region:** Generally, a segment of the nation set apart from other areas by geographical boundaries that typically comprise a cluster of states, such as New England, the South, Southwest, Midwest, Atlantic Seaboard, Pacific Northwest.
1. Population Growth
   a) Present trend
   b) Anticipated trend
2. Economic Considerations
   a) Natural resources
   b) Labor supply
   c) Interest rates
   d) Tourist attractions (the beach, mountains, etc.)
3. Legislative Actions
   a) Existing laws
   b) Proposed legislation
   c) Attitude toward property owners
   d) Environmental restrictions
4. Climatic Conditions
   a) Effect on health and welfare
   b) Effect on the social and economic climate
5. Agricultural Production
   a) Growth and expansion
   b) Spin-off activity
6. Government Actions
   a) Subsidized industries and installation
      i. Aerospace and defense
      ii. Military bases
   b) Taxation policies

III. **The Metropolitan Area:** A large center of population including one or more central cities and the adjacent satellite communities.
1. Population Trends
   a) Increase
   b) Decrease
   c) Migration
2. Economic Activity
   a) Active vs. dormant industries

          b)   Recreational facilities
          c)   Labor market
             i.   Employment trend
             ii. Unemployment and prolonged strikes
             iii. Factors affecting these developments

a.) Influx or flight of industry
b.) Current labor-management relations
c.) History of previous job actions
d.) Natural disasters
      iv. Possibility of future occurrence

3. Construction Costs
    a)   Skilled labor supply
    b)   Adequacy of materials
4. Civic Government Policies
    a)   Tax increase
    b)   Assessments
       i.   Utilities
       ii. Maintenance
5. Major Improvement Programs
    a)   Redevelopment projects
    b)   Major construction projects
    c)   Highway and freeway development

IV. The Community: That part of the metropolitan area composed of a number of neighborhoods that have a tendency toward common interests and problems.

1. Geographical Pattern
    a)   Natural Terrain
       i.   Level areas; unimproved land
       ii. Mountainous regions
       iii. Natural barriers: hills, valleys, rivers, forests, lakes, ravines, and the like
       iv. Natural beauty
       v.   Hazards
2. Satellite Communities
    a)   Suburban areas
    b)   Residential districts
    c)   Regional shopping centers

    d) Industrial complexes
3. Civic Government Policies
    a) Tax increases
    b) Rent control
    c) Assessment
        i. Utilities
        ii. Maintenance

V. **Neighborhood:** A residential area with distinguishing characteristics comprised of people with similar interests. Numerous factors and trends affect the quality of the neighborhood.

1. Physical Characteristics
    a) Overall trend of the area
    b) Quality, convenience, availability of facilities
        i. Public schools
        ii. Public transportation
        iii. Shopping centers
        iv. Churches
        v. Cultural and recreational
    c)   Land and improvement characteristics
        i. Street patterns
        ii. Availability of utilities
        iii. Similar land uses; Size & shape of lots
        iv. Percentage of area developed
        v. Harmony of development
            Similar types and quality of improvements
            Monotonous housing tracts
            Cohesiveness of original designs
            (size, quality, price range)
    d) Manmade attributes
        i. Freeways
        ii. Boulevards
        iii. Railroad tracks
        iv. Industrial and commercial complexes
        v. Zoning designations
2. Economic Characteristics
    a) Family income traits
        i. Occupations

        ii.   Wage levels

        iii. Employment stability

        iv. Percentage of families on publi assistance

    b) Degree of home ownership

    c) Number of rentals

    d) Range of rental income

    e) Number of vacancies

3. Social Characteristics

    a) Density and composition of population

    b) Average family size and ages

    c) Prestige/Social status

    d) Attitudes of the inhabitants

        i.   Civic pride

        ii. Participation in community activities

        iii. Pride of ownership

    e) Existence and use of educational and cultural institutions

    f) School enrollments

    g) Absence or presence of vice

4. Real Estate Sales Activity

    a) Number and price of homes for sale

    b) Availability of office space

5. Sales Conditions

    a) Availability of financing

    b) Size of down payments made on purchases

    c) Willingness of lenders to participate in the area

    d) Number of foreclosures

6. Governmental Characteristics

    a) Taxation policies

        i.   Property taxes

        ii. Other taxes; city license fees

        iii. Delinquencies

    b) Municipal fees and assessments

    c) Zoning ordinances

    d) Building codes

    e) Health and fire regulations

Index

A

Adjusted Sale Price 58
Agriculture 106-107, 110
AIG (American Insurance
    Group) 34
Alameda Corridor 325-330
    update on 331
Annuities:
    versus real estate 33-34, 68
Apartment Buildings 10-11, 18,
    30, 65, 113, 131, 145, 178,
    257, 272, 274, 288, 304
Appraisal
    purpose of 349, 351
Arbitration 236, 314-315
Assessment 23, 121, 142-143,
    177, 217, 305, 368-370
Axiom 337

B

Bookkeeping 82, 287-288, 293,
    296
Boomtowns 3-4, 80, 97-98, 332,
    334
Brokers xii, 42-43, 58, 60, 70,
    142, 166, 167, 180, 193, 200-
    201, 223, 226, 229-230, 238,
    241-246-249, 251-252, 257,
    292, 338, 356, 358
    advantages of using 241-246
    disadvantages of using 247-
    250
Building Codes 28, 146, 313, 370
Buying Property *See Property,*
    buying